The Memory Hole: The U.S. History Curriculum Under Siege

Kansas is awesome!

The Memory Hole: The U.S. History Curriculum Under Siege

By
Fritz Fischer
University of Northern Colorado

INFORMATION AGE PUBLISHING, INC.
Charlotte, NC • www.infoagepub.com

Library of Congress Cataloging-in-Publication Data

The CIP data for this book can be found on the Library of Congress website (loc.gov).

Paperback: 978-1-62396-532-7
Hardcover: 978-1-62396-533-4
E-Book: 978-1-62396-534-1

Printed in the United States of America

CONTENTS

ACKNOWLEDGEMENTS

The most difficult section of a book to begin is the acknowledgements section, because there are so many people to thank, in no particular order. Many have helped me in thinking about this topic and writing this book. All can take credit for positive contributions. As to the blame for any errors, mistakes or misstatements, that is all mine.

I should begin by thanking all of those in the world of history education that have done so much over the years to help me focus my thoughts about historical thinking in the classroom. Teachers and researchers, they understand both how history is taught in a most engaging way and what history is most interesting and valuable for students to learn. Ed Ayers, Bill Virden, Bob Bain, Sarah Drake Brown, Daisy Martin, Matt Arleth, and Sam Wineberg, among others, have been most personally influential in this area. I most especially want to thank Bruce Lesh, with whom I have worked over a number of years in professional development workshops and whose classroom is the best exemplar I know of where historical thinking happens everyday in the classroom, and who agreed to read and critique a complete draft of the manuscript.

I want to thank my fellow board members of the National Council for History Education in helping me better understand the plight of history

The Memory Hole: The U.S. History Curriculum Under Siege, pages vii–x.
Copyright © 2014 by Information Age Publishing

in the schools. Besides for Ed Ayers and Bruce Lesh, whom I have already mentioned, I want to thank Linda Salvucci, Carol Berkin, Bill White, Mary Beth Immediata, Russ Heller, Dale Steiner, Pat Manning, Beth Scarbrough, Mimi Quintanilla, and the rest of the committed board members for dedicating themselves to the cause of history in the schools and helping me develop my ideas on the importance of history in the schools.

I want to thank the University of Northern Colorado for providing me with a sabbatical that allowed me to do most of my research, and my colleagues in the Department of History at the university for working with me on this project in department seminars. Some of my colleagues, including Aaron Haberman, T. J. Tomlin, Gail Rowe, and Ron Edgerton, read and critiqued drafts of specific chapters, and I am grateful for their expertise and advice. I am most grateful to Barry Rothaus, who read and critiqued the entire manuscript, and Joan Clinefelter, who agreed to take on the mind-numbing task of editing all of my notes and completed the task with the utmost good humor and professionalism.

Thanks to Information Age Publishing and George Johnson for agreeing to take on this project with me. This book falls into somewhat of a hybrid genre, and in today's world of publishing, not many publishers are willing to "go outside the box" and put their resources behind something different. I appreciate that they were willing to take the chance with me.

Finally, I would like to thank two groups of people who are central to both my life and my career. I have been teaching history at some level for thirty years now, and my students make it worthwhile and perpetually interesting. In many ways this book is dedicated to them, because I have learned over the years how powerful effective history teaching can be in helping advance thinking. I have learned most about teaching and thinking from those of my students who now teach history in the classrooms of Colorado and throughout the nation and am very proud of the fact that many are the most interesting, engaging, and effective history teachers I have ever observed.

Most of all, I would like to thank my family. Thanks to Shannon, Kylie, Eric, and Kevin, who have to endure endless discussions about history and history teaching at the dinner table as well as nearly endless rantings from dad about those who don't seem to understand what history teaching needs to be all about. My lovely, thoughtful, brilliant wife Lynn provides me with the motivation and initiative to work through the hard times and the good times. As the argument of this book attests, I value the idea of individual thinking as a cornerstone of education, but nothing is more important than the love and support of a family, and I feel eternally grateful to be part of such a loving one.

INTRODUCTION

Day by day and almost minute by minute the past was brought up to date. In this way every prediction made by the Party could be shown by documentary evidence to have been correct; nor was any item of news, or any expression of opinion, which conflicted with the needs of the moment, ever allowed to remain on record. All history was a palimpsest, scraped clean and reinscribed exactly as often as was necessary.

—George Orwell, *1984*, Book 1, Chapter 3

Winston Smith, the suffering hero of *1984*, explains the purpose of history according to "the Party" as he explains his role in Orwell's futuristic society. Smith's job is to examine writings from and about the past and, if those writings do not match the "needs of the moment," he was to toss the facts of the past down the "memory hole," effectively erasing them forever. Frighteningly enough, Americans in the twenty-first century live in a culture where reality is closer to approaching Orwell's vision than Americans would care to believe. The history being taught in America's schools is in danger of being so distorted that the true nature of history could be lost forever and the Orwellian nightmare might become our reality.

The Memory Hole: The U.S. History Curriculum Under Siege, pages ix–xix.
Copyright © 2014 by Information Age Publishing

Many powerful politicians and influential pundits believe that history is a simplistic, one-dimensional grab bag of facts and personalities that can be used as a political football by any group with political power. Whether it is Michele Bachmann on the presidential campaign trail or a seemingly unassuming dentist in control of the Texas State Board of Education, these ideologues believe, as Big Brother did, that history can and should be reinvented to serve the political needs of the moment. All history that challenges their interpretations should simply be erased, forever ignored as politically inconvenient.

Most frightening about these attempts to refashion the American past is the campaign to make these new stories into the "truth" about the past for schoolchildren. The re-inventors of history use a variety of means to change the curriculum of the nation's schools to fit their ideology. The American history that many want to be taught is not history at all, but an invented version of the past meant to support a political ideology. Ignoring facts, refashioning other facts, and pretending that there are no rules in the telling of history, these re-interpreters of the past place the minds of America's young people in danger.

Fortunately, there is a better way to do history, and there are clear responses to the invented history promoted by those who wish to erase history. America's founding fathers were not twenty-first century evangelical Christians, and the record and rules of history clearly show this. Ronald Reagan was neither "sleepwalking through history" nor an "eternal light for the world," as the facts and a focused historical mindset reveal.[1] History in the schools can move beyond partisan bickering towards exposure to a number of concepts valuable for the children of conservative and liberal alike.

Writing the stories of American history should not be a political exercise, and history cannot merely be the plaything of political analysts. U.S. history is a limitless landscape of fascinating stories, but there need to be guidelines on how they are told. An understanding of the past must be based on specific rules governing the use of evidence and the formation of argument. We must not reconstruct the past as we wish it to be; we are bound by evidence and an evaluation of its validity.

Ironically, at the very time many Americans have been sharpening their use of history as a political weapon, researchers in history education have been making more explicit the definition and purpose of what history should be in the schools. Students in history classrooms need to be reading and analyzing sources from the past and working to develop their own interpretations of what these sources tell us. History teachers should be helping their students examine the past in all of its complexity in order to teach judgment and analytical skills. Yet the teaching of this valuable process and the history it produces is in danger of being smothered by demands of the politically powerful to insert politically charged versions of the past into the classroom.

Before embarking on our journey through America's past, we need to set out the set of rules that govern the discipline and should govern the way in which history is taught in the nation's classroom. These rules will serve as the cornerstone of this book, guiding thoughts about how students need to try to understand the past. What are the rules of the discipline? What are the components of historical thinking? It is a way of questioning, examining, thinking about, and concluding about the past.

Over the past two decades, scholars throughout the United States have been creating a fundamental understanding of what it means to think historically. Some come from the field of cognition—understanding how the brain works.[2] Some have worked as teachers at the secondary level and now teach at the university level, while some are thoughtful and sophisticated current high school teachers.[3] All agree with the first rule of history: history is about questions, not about answers. Historian Jonathan Zimmerman sums up how historians feel about their discipline in this way:

> Surely one of the biggest myths of all is that history is simply about "facts." This year marks the 75th anniversary of [the late Cornell University historian Carl] Becker's famous speech [in which Becker said that history itself is interpretation], yet Americans appear no nearer to understanding that all pasts are "constructed," that all facts require interpretation and that all history is "revisionist" history.[4]

Historians ask questions and examine the "facts" about the past in order to find answers.

These answers, then, are of necessity complex, nuanced, and subtle, and this is a second critical rule of the discipline of history. The past is a very big place. Millions of people lived there, and their lives were just as complicated, messy, and confused as our lives today. In order to understand the past more completely, we must look at an issue from multiple perspectives and different points of view. Any search for simplistic, easy answers about the past will inevitably be incomplete and inaccurate. And to begin with an easy answer about the past, searching for evidence to sustain only that answer, is not "doing" history. It makes matters much more dangerous if one searches for that easy answer only to support a political view in the present.

A story from the past cannot fully justify a belief from the present, because the past was a completely different place than the present. The past is, as the saying goes, a foreign country.[5] This complexity takes may forms, and historians need to be attentive to all of them. Historians need to concentrate on chronology and cause and effect. Historians need to be attentive to the authorship of sources and the intent and motivation behind the creation of sources. Historians need to be skeptical enough about the past to look at all sides of the issue yet at the same time accepting enough of the past to attempt to recreate it.

Critical in the discipline of history is the use of evidence. Historians need to find support for their narratives and their arguments through the use of primary source evidence from the time they are studying. This evidence can take many forms, from letters, diaries, and journals to official government documents to newspaper accounts to photographs to artifacts such as clothing and furniture. No primary source tells the entire truth, although all primary sources tell a part of the truth about the past. Interestingly, very few of the people examined in this book reject the special importance of engaging primary sources in the telling of history.

The history they are eliminating is rarely the *idea* of using primary sources. Rather, it is the *way* in which these sources are often used that becomes the problem. As we shall see, many of those who wish to reinvent the past do so by selectively choosing which primary sources to use to tell the story of the past and which to toss aside. They cherry-pick quotes and events from the past to support their own particular view, a view stemming not from an argument about the past but from a mindset of the present. They search and search for just the right quotation to support their current view, ignoring any evidence that might make the past messier, more complex, and less connected to the present.

Of course, historians can't use *all* of the evidence from the past in order to tell their stories. One cannot use all of the quotes from all of the actors in a given event. Historians attempt to fashion a readable and understandable story succinct enough to be accessible to the reader. Historians must also work to make sense of the past by crafting arguments about that past. Such arguments will always include a point of view, or even a specific bias. The best, most elegant arguments about the past include as much evidence as possible and as much complexity as possible while still making a clear, coherent, interesting argument. Is such an argument the complete "truth" about the past? No. Yet historians need to strive as much as possible towards this ideal, because it is in the very act of examining the past in all its complexity and attempting to understand that complexity where students of history can learn the skills of judgment that make the study of history worthwhile. Of all disciplines, only history is endlessly complex and diverse while still being accessible, providing opportunity for students to learn how to think in profound and sophisticated ways.

Another important aspect of the discipline of history often neglected by those who want to reinvent it is in the use of secondary sources. History is about asking questions about the past and the struggle to answer them. Yet it is not a lonely pursuit. Others have asked these questions and have provided answers. Still other historians disagree with these answers and debate about them. They also ask new questions, or ask the old questions in new ways. This is what Zimmerman was referring to when he stated that all history is revisionist. History is always changing, and, importantly, the new questions that are asked often *do* have much to do with contemporary social, political, and cultural issues. They must, because otherwise, very few people would care about the past. True, the past is a foreign country, but it must in some way connect to the contemporary world. For example, there is little question that the burst in scholarship beginning in the 1960s and 1970s about the lives of African Americans was directly connected to the civil rights movement of the 1950s and 1960s. Historians and history students rightly asked new questions about the past because of present circumstances.

A problem arises when those who write about the past start with new answers about the past based on contemporary beliefs rather than merely asking new questions based on these beliefs. An anonymous blogger on a website sponsored by the conservative Intercollegiate Studies Institute argued very eloquently against this sort of history:

> One of the dangers of politicized history is that it uses the criteria of contemporary politics to answer this question and, perhaps more significantly, to interpret the evidence. The result is that, instead of American history *tout court*, we end up with so-called liberal American history and conservative American history, as exemplified by such titles as *The People's History of the United States* and *A Patriot's History of the United States*. But the suggestion that there is a conservative history of the United States that all conservatives must embrace is to betray the purpose of historical study, because it implies that the facts of the past must be sifted according to the terms of today's political debates. It rejects the idea that historical evidence must be weighed on its own terms.[6]

Some left-wing historians have done this as part of their crusade for social justice in the twenty-first century. Similarly, right-wing historians have sought to do the same in connection to the history of the founding fathers. The problem is not that new questions are being asked about the religion of the founding fathers; the difficulty is that new answers are being presented that do not fit all of the complicated evidence on this issue, and these new answers are being forced into the nation's classrooms.

The first chapter of this book engages this very issue, the issue of the religion of the founding fathers. Over the past generation, right-wing politicians and pundits have had much to say about the history of the founding era of the United States (encompassing approximately the years 1760–1800). In fact, much of the worldview of the "Tea Party" political movements beginning in 2009 seems to derive directly from a particular interpretation of this late eighteenth century era.[7] Chapter One provides an in-depth examination of the twenty-first century conservative beliefs about history, specifically examining their unwavering commitment to a story about the evangelical Christianity of the founding fathers. This story alters much of the actual history of the founding era and is, in fact, much more dangerous than mere "historical fundamentalism." Both the facts and the context of this era clearly contradict this newly invented story, yet that has not slowed the attempts to put this new story into the nation's schools.

Right-wing politicians and inventors of a new American history have a much broader agenda than to change how the history of the founding era is taught. Chapter Two will examine attempts to retell the economic history of the United States in the 1875–1940 period. This is an attempt to retell the history of American capitalism; in fact, they wish to eliminate the word capitalism itself from the discussion because, in their view, liberal historians have muddied a brilliant and near perfect system with unfair negative connotations. Instead, conservative politicians and "free market historians" want to retell the story of American economic history as the history of the free enterprise system, an always sunny and positive story. The "free market historians" raise up the "unfairly tarnished" robber barons to the status of "captains of industry" and instead paint the Progressives, and especially Theodore Roosevelt and Woodrow Wilson, as enemies of the good. The real villain in the story is Franklin D. Roosevelt, and they toss any sort of nuanced understanding of the New Deal into the Orwellian memory hole, replacing it with a story that paints a uniformly negative and depressing picture of Roosevelt's economic program, the purpose being to lay the groundwork for a contemporary political agenda. Just as with the history of the founding fathers, this new history of the American economy is now staple fare for many American schoolchildren, whether or not it represents the actual messy and complicated economic history of the United States.

The third chapter also looks at a broad and important topic in U.S. history, American involvement with the rest of the world. Right-wing anti-historians insist on disassociating the ideas of empire with American history, instead asserting the uniqueness and exceptional nature of the American experience. In fact, the term "American exceptionalism" has experienced a major resurgence in the twenty-first century, despite the fact that historians rejected the idea in the middle of the twentieth century. The idea that the United States is and always has been a chosen nation stems in part from the topics of the first two chapters, the argument being that America's unique greatness stems in part from its evangelical Christian beginnings and also from its special and successful brand of free market economics. The belief that the United States is not an empire nor has ever been an empire and has always been a force for only good also contributes to its role as an exceptional nation. Insisting on a timeless and universal goodness in America's role in the world flies in the face of historical fact.

Chapter Four investigates the return of a story from U.S. history that new evidence had pushed historians and history teachers away from. This is the historical narrative of the 1950s, an era promoted at the time and seen in some cultural memorials as a golden age in American history, a time of prosperity, social peace, and cultural calm. In this story, the only blight on the landscape of the 1950s was the specter of the communist menace, but Americans were protected by the vigilance of Joseph McCarthy, J. Edgar Hoover, and others dedicated anti-communists. This one-dimensional narrative provided an easy target for attack for historians for the next fifty years, who consistently added complexity and disorder to the narrative. They argued effectively that the 1950s was certainly not a golden era for many Americans, from African Americans to women to gay Americans. Perhaps most obviously, the bullying tactics and overreach of McCarthy exemplified a culture of conformity and paranoia run amok, and McCarthy became a far different historical character in the historical record.

However, enthusiasts for a retelling of the history of the 1950s want once again to tell the story of the decade and, most specifically, the story of McCarthy as a story of a near perfect time for an America protected from evil influences by the likes of McCarthy. Another resurgent hero of the 1950s is Phyllis Schlafly, a leading anti-feminist who first gained her leadership position in this decade. On the other hand, those who wish to retell the history of the era want to eliminate a hero of the early civil rights movement, Thurgood Marshall, from the historical narrative. Right-wing politicians and anti-historians believe it is critically important to retell this story in order to promote their twenty-first century worldview, refashioning the 1950s as a bygone prelude to a more perfect contemporary world.

It is not only those motivated by right-wing ideologies that seek to erase history and teach a new, incomplete story of the past in the schools. Although it is true that such right-wing ideologues are more interested in demanding the teaching of *only* their version of the past, it is also true that left-wing ideologues have fallen into the same trap of ignoring the rules of the discipline in order to advance a particular ideological agenda. The fifth chapter will examine the attempts from the left to tell only their version of the past. These quasi-historians oversimplify the past and cherry-pick sources in the same way the right-wing ideologues do, telling stories of villains and heroes quite at odds with the stories of their right-wing counterparts.

In some cases, politicians have also become involved in these issues and have sought to change the school curriculum to reflect these oversimplified, incomplete stories of good versus evil. In a depressing twist, it is the very existence of this left-wing history that has motivated many calls for right-wing history, and vice versa, leading to a potentially endless cycle of historical retelling that does not serve students well. Again, historical "revisionism" is not the villain, as it always remains important to ask new questions about the past, many of which might be broadly based on contemporary issues. My argument is against those who seek to use the teaching of history as a political weapon, in the process ignoring the true discipline of history and its usefulness for teaching students the value of thinking through complex and confusing issues.

Nowhere is the discipline of history more under attack than in the attempt to tell the story of the presidency of Ronald Reagan. The final chapter will examine this contentious issue, an issue that will elaborate on all of the central themes of the book. Issues of the role of religion, the free market economy, American exceptionalism, the Cold War, American cultural values, and the place of race, class, and gender in American history all play a role in the historical discussions of Ronald Reagan and his place in American history. In almost every case, the story of Reagan is overly simplistic, narrow, incomplete, and unworthy of the name of "history." It has been more than a generation since Reagan retired to his Santa Barbara ranch, yet since he and his ideas still play such a role in American politics, telling his history still serves as a political football to be tossed from the left to the right. Right-wing ideologues work diligently to tell the Reagan story as one of unabashed success, while many on the left seek to tell the story as one of unabated horror. Both groups, especially those on the right, have worked very hard to insert their version of Reagan into the school curriculum and the national student consciousness.

This book does not examine the entire K–12 U.S. history curriculum. Rather, it examines a certain collection of eras and ideas that recent politicians and ideologues have sought to re-invent over the past two decades. I do not examine some topics that have been consistent areas of disagreement in the U.S. history curriculum, such as the Civil War. Rather, I explicitly examine topics that have become political targets in our contemporary era of polarization and partisanship. This tug-of-war has dragged the past into the toxic debates of the present, thus both trivializing our understanding of the past and diminishing the importance of history in the schools. My goal is to move history above the fray by focusing the discipline on a set of rules in its practice rather than particular interpretations of its content. Only then will students be able to experience the rich and valuable understanding that can come from a thoughtful examination of the past.

The beleaguered hero of this book is the discipline of history. The study of history needs to follow specific rules of evidence. Historians and history classes need to utilize a variety of "History's Habits of Mind" requiring complex, sophisticated, and subtle thinking about the past.[8] The attack is coming from the left and the right, ideologues attempting to imprint their own idiosyncratic view of the past on the national student consciousness. History should not follow the old saw as being only told by the winners, even though some might believe that it is naïve to assume that history can ever be anything else. It is true that history is not a science, because historical hypotheses can neither be proven nor replicated. Yet there are rules that both historians and history students in the classroom need to follow. If the rules of the discipline and the habits of mind of a historian are ignored, our nation faces the danger of losing its history down the memory hole, and without that history, the past is ripe for manipulation by those who would seek to destroy the ability to think.

CHAPTER 1

THE FOUNDING FATHERS, EVANGELICAL CHRISTIANITY AND TEACHING HISTORY

George Washington praying at Valley Forge. With the possible exception of Emanuel Leutze's *George Washington Crossing the Delaware*, no image has become so iconic of Washington, his character, persona, and meaning for the nation. This particular image was created by Henry Brueckner in 1866 and is currently housed at the Library of Congress.

The Memory Hole: The U.S. History Curriculum Under Siege, pages 1–24.
Copyright © 2014 by Information Age Publishing

The most famous depiction of this scene is much more spectacular than this, a beautiful and arresting color painting of Washington's act, complete with icy cold horse's breath and Washington in impecable, colorful General's uniform. Many school children learn that the *Crossing of the Delaware* was painted long after the event actually occurred and teaches us much more about mid-nineteenth century American patriotism than about Washington. Many do not know, however, that this famous depiction, *The Prayer at Valley Forge*, is of far more recent vintage and was actually painted by Arnold Friberg in 1976. Just as Leutze's painting, Friberg's tells us more about late twentieth century American culture than it teaches us about the life and attitudes of America's first president.

The problem is that many political and cultural leaders in the twenty-first century want Americans to believe that Friberg's painting tells the "truth" about the depicted historical event in order to advance a twenty-first century political agenda, whether or not such "truth" is historically accurate. The painting is used in dozens of teaching lessons, provides the symbolic centerpiece of countless discussions of Washington, and even plays a starring role in former Secretary of Education William Bennett's morality tales for American schoolchildren. There is no question that Washington could have prayed in such a manner at Valley Forge. Yet in making this relatively modern image into an iconic Washington image, the rules of historical evidence have been ignored, and the context of the historical time has been eliminated.

The misuse of this image is part of a concerted effort to stress the evangelical Christianity of the American founding fathers and teach this to the nation's schoolchildren. Leaders of the movement, such as W. Cleon Skousen, David Barton, and Glenn Beck, as well as organizations from WallBuilders to the 9-12 Tea Party, seek to, as WallBuilders proclaims, present "America's forgotten history and heroes with an emphasis on our moral, religious, and constitutional heritage."[1] The premise of the movement is to emphasize Christian morality in the founding era, rather than to work to understand the historical complexity of that era. To accomplish this, this movement obscures some historical evidence and overemphasizes other evidence while ignoring the historical context of the times. As one opening example, the reason I could not open this chapter with Friberg's painting is that Friberg's copyright requires that any use of his art conform to only Friberg's vision of the past. So the use must "align with and uphold Judeo Christian values and beliefs" and must not be "disparaging to Mr. Friberg."[2] Since I argue that the incident probably never took place, and it displays a type of Christianity antithetical to the Christianity of the founding fathers, the image could not be displayed in this book.

The religious beliefs of George Washington and the other founders were diverse, complex, and deeply embedded in their times. However, it is clear their beliefs neither match nor even resemble the beliefs of twenty-first century evangelical, fundamentalist Christians. Some, most notably Thomas Jefferson and to some degree Benjamin Franklin, can properly be categorized as "deists." John Adams was an observant Unitarian, while other signatories to the Constitution were staunch Calvinists. The fact that they held a wide variety of beliefs points to the most critical idea regarding religion they all shared. Knowing that they all held divergent beliefs, and living in the context of over a century of religious violence and tyranny, all wanted to separate their private religious devotions from the laws and policy of the new government. The revolution they fostered was designed to ensure untrammeled liberty, including liberty from a potential governmental tyrant imposing religious dogma.

How does George Washington and his prayer at Valley Forge fit into this discussion? Historians require evidence to interpret the past. The only evidence that such a prayer ever occurred is a single oral deposition given by a man named Isaac Potts to Reverend Nathaniel Randolph Snowden, a Presbyterian minister, nearly 40 years after Washington and his forces camped at Valley Forge. Potts related the story this way to Snowden:

> I tied my horse to a sapling and went quietly into the woods and to my astonishment I saw the great George Washington on his knees alone, with his sword on one side and his cocked hat on the other. He was at Prayer to the God of the Armies, beseeching to interpose with his Divine aid, as it was ye Crisis, & the cause of the country, of humanity, and of the world. Such a prayer I never heard from the lips of man....[3]

Potts said he then rode home and related the incident to his wife Sarah.

This story became the basis for a story that appeared in one of Parson Weems' famous tales on Washington, appearing in the text with the cherry tree story. Artist Paul Weber painted a version of this scene that was first exhibited in 1854, but the specific basis for Friberg's painting came in 1866, when Henry Brueckner painted the scene that begins this chapter. However, most historians believe that the story is "utterly without foundation in fact."[4] We do not know whether Potts actually lived at Valley Forge in the eighteenth century, as records do not confirm his presence there until after 1800. Also, he was not married until the nineteenth century, so he could not have told the story to his wife Sarah. Finally, the fact that the story was retold with no corroboration, more than a generation after, in the midst of a time of fervent religious revival, and in such a neat and tidy fashion should give pause to the historian attempting to piece together evidence. In short, as John Fea, a leading scholar on the relationship of Christianity and the founding era observes, "these discrepancies have led historians to discredit it [the story]."[5]

Yet, here is the rub. Rather than questioning the incident, which historians do, many anti-historians are intent to take this example as truth because it reinforces a Washington they wish to have existed. As one blogger on a website entitled "American Christian Heritage" argues, "The evidence of Washington's faith is sufficiently established to satisfy a layman, if not an historian."[6] In other words, the rules of historical evidence and an understanding of historical context are unimportant. Fea warns against this type of argument, believing that we need "to see the danger of cherry-picking from the past as a means of promoting a political or cultural agenda in the present."[7] In choosing only the quotations and incidents from the past that support a current view, those who want to see a particular Christian past toss out the real, messy, complex, and contradictory past.

This argument does not deny that Washington prayed at Valley Forge, nor that a person named Isaac Potts might have witnessed him doing it. The issue is that as historical arguments go, this one is relatively flimsy and, weak as it is, has become a central lesson for our nation's children. More important than the depiction of the specific incident, the way the incident and the image are used provides a key insight into the importance of this image.

Ironically, the image could be used as a centerpiece of a very effective classroom history lesson, even with a very young age group, as a fascinating historical lesson developed with the Library of Congress attests. In that lesson, the children are asked to look at the image and develop their own hypothesis about what the image portrays. One student decided that it showed "People firring and George Washington siting on the ground because he doesn't wote to be hert." A thoughtful and interesting reading of the evidence, which, though incorrect, does suggest that the student is using his or her imagination in order to understand a vision of the past. Another student came closer to the purpose of the image in saying that it depicts "Geoge Woshington is praying in the piccher he is in the forest."[8] As a historian, *both* answers reflect historical thinking and are in that sense "right." Yet for those pushing their Christian brand of history, only the second answer could be correct. The image itself has become historical evidence for those who argue that a particular brand of Christianity was central to the founding fathers' belief system and philosophy.

The reason for this argument is not the discovery of a new cache of historical evidence or even a rethinking of the context of the times. As we will see in other chapters, historical understanding of a time period can and should evolve. But it should only change based on new evidence or a new perspective about the actual evidence from the past. In this case, a group of Christian conservatives want to retell history because they believe strongly that only those with a strong core of fundamentalist, evangelical Christian beliefs should be elected to serve in government. As Katherine Harris, Florida Secretary of State from 1998–2002 (and the official responsible for counting ballots in Florida's contested presidential election in 2000) and Congressional member from 2002–2006, put it in 2005, "If you're not electing Christians, then in essence you are going to legislate sin." She went on by directly connecting her argument about Christianity in the twenty-first century with an interpretation of history that she believes to be critical to her argument. "Separation of church and state is 'a lie we have been told,'" Harris said in the interview, saying separating religion and politics is "wrong because God is the one who chooses our rulers."[9] Harris and other Christian conservatives believe the only way to legitimize their core beliefs about the connection between Christianity and politics is to assert the truth of their brand of history.

So in the world of these Christian conservatives, what does the history of the religion of the founding fathers look like? Mark A. Chancey, a professor of religious studies at Southern Methodist University, provides the most complete explanation in an article he composed in 2007:

> In this narrative, the Founding Fathers were predominantly theologically conservative Protestants whose views roughly correspond to those of the contemporary Christian Right; they intended the United States to be a distinctively Christian nation; the Bible was the most significant and direct inspiration for the Declaration of Independence and Constitution; until recently, Protestant Christianity dominated the nation's educational system; the country has departed from the Founding Fathers' intentions and has entered a period of chaos and decline; the cessation of Bible reading in public schools is both a symptom and a cause of this decline; the nation should reclaim its Christian heritage and administer its government according to Christian biblical principles.[10]

The key point is that all of these arguments within this narrative are assumed to be true. They cannot be questioned; they cannot be denied. Of course, this violates another fundamental aspect of the discipline of history. History must be about questions, not necessarily about answers. We must follow the evidence to the most accurate argument about the past we can craft, rather than beginning with the answer and accepting only the evidence that supports that answer.

In the case of George Washington, the issue is not whether the event actually occurred, but instead how the event in the image represents Washington's core beliefs. Making the image central to a depiction of Washington makes religion, in this case a very specific kind of evangelical Christian religion, central to the character and philosophy of George Washington. As historian Ron Chernow argues in the most recent definitive biography of Washington, "The image seemed designed to meld religion and politics by converting the uniformed Washington into a humble supplicant of the Lord…The reason to doubt the story's veracity is not Washington's lack of faith but the public nature of his devotions. He never would have prayed so ostentatiously outdoors, where soldiers could have stumbled upon him."[11] This is why the context is so very critical. Washington was extraordinarily circumspect, especially about his religion, and was the opposite of a twenty-first century evangelical in his devotions. Above all, Washington was, as historian Gordon Wood insists, "a child of the eighteenth century Enlightenment." He made himself a man of virtue, a man who could "control both his passion and his destiny" and he was "thoroughly caught up...in the rational rolling back of parochialism, fanatacism and barbarism." This is why he shied away from public prayer and why the scene in Valley Forge does not truly reflect his character. On the other hand, Washington *did* stage the play *Cato* for his troops at Valley Forge, a play meant to teach "what it meant to be a stoical classical hero."[12]

John Fea might dispute, at least in part, the arguments of Chernow and Wood about Washington's Christianity. Fea's Washington might have prayed in the open at Valley Forge. Fea agrees that Washington was "very private about his religion" and notes that in virtually none of Washington's extant writings does he speak openly of his religion, Jesus Christ, or specific theological points. Washington consistently left church before the administration of communion, was "notorious for not kneeling to pray in public worship," and never once publicly made the case for the inclusion of explicit Christian devotions in public life.[13] In short, Washington was not a model twenty-first century evangelical Christian. However, Fea argues persuasively that Washington believed in and often wrote about God's "Providence" in connection with the new United States and its role as a "chosen" nation. Fea provides convincing evidence that Washington was also "biblically literate." In the end, the question of Washington's Christianity is a complex one, with no simple answer or explanation, and that is the point. In a book of primary sources on the topic of religion in revolutionary America, historians Matthew Harrris and Thomas Kidd reinforce this complexity: "As you read the documents in this book, you will find that religion played a very important—and very complex—role in the era of the American Founding. Anyone trying to project current political disputes onto the revolutionary past quickly stumbles."[14]

The Prayer at Valley Forge is just one example of the deliberate misunderstanding of Washington in an effort to advance a contemporary political agenda. An even more dangerous invention is the quote appearing on more than 500 websites that has Washington saying "It is impossible to rightly govern the world without religion and the Bible." Many seem to want Washington to have said it, so he must have said it. The leading proponent of this idea has been David Barton, the founder of the WallBuilders organization mentioned earlier. His take on the statement is the following: "There is overwhelming evidence to support this thought as belonging to Washington. However, since the quote has not been documented to date, it appears unlikely to be found."[15] Barton believes Washington must have believed it, so we need to teach that he said it.

As the nation's first leader and first president, George Washington is in many ways the paramount symbol of the early United States, and so has received much attention from those who want to reinvent history in the nation's classrooms. As it happens, the story of the entire founding era is under assault. It is here that the campaign to toss history down the memory hole has become most strident and most dangerous.

We need to take a bit of an aside from our discussion of this time period in order to properly introduce some of the central characters in the story of America's disappearing history. I have briefly mentioned David Barton and the organization he founded, called WallBuilders. Barton is the most influential leader of the movement to change the history learned in schools, as he argues: "WallBuilders' goal is to exert a direct and positive influence in government, education, and the family by (1) educating the nation concerning the Godly foundation of our country; (2) providing information to federal, state, and local officials as they develop public policies which reflect Biblical values."[16] In other words, Barton's version of history is to begin with the assumption of the "Godly foundation" and then make sure that this assumption is accepted by schools, political leaders, and families throughout the nation, regardless of whether such a "godly foundation" provides an accurate portrayal of the American past. Barton has written many pamphlets, booklets, and essays presenting his version of the history of America's founding, and he serves as a close political and historical confidant of Rick Perry, Texas Governor and 2012 presidential primary candidate.

Perhaps even more influential in the evangelical Christian attack on historical scholarship and understanding are the writings of W. Cleon Skousen. Skousen, who passed away in 2006, was a long-time leader of the John Birch Society and a prolific author on the topics of the evils of communism and the fundamentalist Christian roots of the American Constitution, most famously in his book *The 5000 Year Leap.*[17] Skousen traces the Anglo-Saxons back to the Black Sea area and then to Israel, asserting that Anglo-Saxon (and hence American) culture derived beliefs in individual liberty, representative government, and even the idea of checks and balances from the tribes of Israel and then later the early Christian apostles.

This belief is not new—it echoes the unsubstantiated claims by some anti-Semitic supporters of eugenic "science" in the early twentieth century. As we will see in a later chapter, Skousen's first entry into the world of historical invention came with books he wrote attacking communism and attacking those in America whom he believed to be too cozy with communists. In his search to defend the United States against godless communism, he dedicated the later years of his life in proving the Christian roots of American politics and culture, which led him to the writing of *The 5000 Year Leap* and his status of one of the intellectual forefathers of the movement to reinvent the history of the American founding era. Skousen's writings, along with Barton's arguments, serve as the underpinnings of the movement's drive to create a new understanding of the Declaration of Independence and the Constitution and put this new understanding into America's schools. Glenn Beck, popular TV host for Fox news from 2009–2011, proudly proclaims Skousen to be his mentor on issues of religion and history and happily peddled a new edition of *The 5000 Year Leap* on his television show in 2009, leading to a 15 week run on the top of the national best seller list for Skousen's generation old book.[17]

What does this new story look like? The story begins at the very beginning, the founding of the first English colonies. As one scholar puts it, "Christian Americanists like to point to the religiosity of early colonists, and they accurately note the explicitly Christian content of many colonial governing documents from the 1600s and early 1700s."[18] The vast majority of primary sources and the weight of scholarly opinion would accept the contention that a new kind of Protestant Christian sensibility was central to the founding and early governance of many of the English colonies in the seventeenth century. From the Pilgrim and Puritan experiments in New England to the Quaker and German Protestant emigration to the middle colonies, religion proved to be central to the English North American colonial enterprise. As best selling historian John Barry points out, "it is no myth that the Puritans who founded Massachusetts came to build a Christian country...they believed themselves and this nation to be chosen and blessed by God."[19]

However, the entire context of the early colonial era reveals a very contentious and complex world, where religious disagreement, dissent, and controversy provide an equally significant legacy. Perhaps the best example is provided by the life and career of Roger Williams. Williams was himself a Puritan pastor but believed strongly that the church should separate itself from the state because the state would inevitably corrupt the church. In the mid seventeenth century, Williams wrote a number of the earliest and most persuasive arguments in support of the need for separation of civil and religious ideas. For example, in a letter written in 1655 known today as the "Ship of State Letter," Williams thoughtfully compared the state to a ship at sea and pointed out the need for the captain's powers to be paramount in the running of the ship, while the individuals should all continue to have complete "Liberty of Conscience," regardless of whether they were "Papists or Protestants, Jews or Turks."[20] Williams was banished from the "city on the hill" in Massachusetts for beliefs such as these, but his ideas nevertheless represent an important strain of American thought that should not be ignored in the schools. As John Barry argues, "And it is also not a myth but reality that another informing principle runs like a great river through American history and culture…the state must not enforce those of the Ten Commandments which defined the relationship between humanity and God."[21]

Even if we ignore this context and accept the early Christian influence on the founding of the English colonies, the real problem with the story actually comes as the narrative progresses. The story continues on much shakier ground, to "draw a straight line from these early, explicitly religious documents that emanate from particular communities and colonies all the way to the Declaration of Independence and the Constitution."[22] This narrative skips at least a century, ignoring a series of critical events and changes in the colonies, from a series of brutal colonial wars to the beginnings of a market economy (to say nothing of the English Civil War and Glorious Revolution). Most important and shocking, the argument about the biblical Christian origins of the United States completely ignores the years of the Enlightenment and the impact of these new philosophies on the leadership of the colonies. It is the context that is missing, as well as an understanding of the complexity of narrative.

Barton, as other "Christian Americanists," carries on the narrative by asserting, with no evidence, that "many [founding fathers] were outspoken evangelicals." He points out that "over half" of those who signed the Declaration of Independence "received degrees from schools that today would be considered seminaries or Bible Schools."[23] The first assertion he makes with no evidence; the second he combines the context of the present ("today would be considered") with that of the past. Yes, the statement is true insofar as these schools (presumably, he is referring mostly to Harvard, Yale, and Princeton) were at the time explicitly connected to a church. Yet the founding fathers who attended these schools were not training as seminarians, nor were they learning twenty-first century evangelical Christianity, nor did they have any choice in the matter: *all* universities of the time were in some way tied to a church.

Barton's focus on the founding era in *America's Godly Heritage* consists of a mere 20 pages. He provides a scattering of quotes to defend his argument, selectively picking from the mountain of writings from the founding era. *America's Godly Heritage* includes only one quotation from George Washington and, naturally, ignores such figures as the rabidly anti-clerical Thomas Paine altogether. It is also very significant to note that Barton does not quote a single secondary source in this pamphlet. This fact in itself violates the principles of the discipline of history because of necessity historians learn from one another, build on one another, and take advantage of the understanding of historical context provided by historians who have written previously on the subject.[24]

According to those who attack history, the rules about how to study history are incorrect and need to be rethought. In the most radical expression of this idea, Rev. Steven Wilkins of the New Life church argues that rather than attempting to ask open-ended questions, "Christians are to view all things from God's perspective. We are to think like God thinks." This means that "the rule of God over history is absolute," and that "history is inescapably covenantal."[25] The only purpose in examining the past is to find God's plan. According to Skousen, the founders came upon their plan for government by "studying the record of the ancient Israelites," a plan which put God's plan into action.[26] He asserts this with no evidence whatsoever, hoping that his readers can make the leap from Bible to founding documents on faith in his word. Skousen then outlines 28 principles the founders followed in creating their plan, and each of these principles flow from the idea that "without religion the government of a free people can not be maintained." Opposite the page where Skousen introduces this principle, he placed a picture of Washington praying at Valley Forge.[27]

For Skousen, Barton, and Beck, the most significant point about the founding era is that the founders intended the country to be based on evangelical Christian religion. But what about the well-known and oft-cited constitutional requirement of the separation of church and state? As Jon Fea puts it, "these writers assume that if the founders were Christians, then they must have opposed the separation of church and state and favored the establishment of Christianity as the official religion."[28] David Barton begins his pamphlet *Separation of Church and State: What the Founders Meant* by relating an anecdote about a conversation with a U.S. congressman after Barton gave the congressman a copy of the Constitution and proved that the phrase "separation of church and state" is not in the document. Of course, Barton is correct, shocking the congressman, who says "I can't believe this! In law school they always taught us that's what the First Amendment said."[29] Clearly, the congressman is not remembering his law school lessons correctly (or, for that matter, the lessons he was probably taught in fifth grade!), because they assuredly taught him not that the First Amendment said this, but that the First Amendment *means* this.[30] And this is where Barton, Glenn Beck, and political figures from Michelle Bachmann to Rick Perry find the problem. They take issue with any interpretation of the First Amendment that might limit the power of religious organizations. And so they set out their point by reinventing a new history to prove their contention.

How does Barton do this? First, of course, he must grapple with Thomas Jefferson, because the phrase "separation of church and state" comes from a letter that Jefferson wrote to the "Danbury Baptists" in 1802. In this letter, Jefferson references the First Amendment and then argues that the amendment builds "a wall of separation between church and state." The first issue that Barton and others complain about is the very use of this letter and its ideas in relation to the Constitution. They claim that it is inappropriate for the Supreme Court to ever cite this phrase, as they have, because it is not actually in the Constitution. Of course, the Supreme Court often cites a variety of ideas from the founding era not found in the actual text of the Constitution, including *The Federalist Papers*, so such a complaint holds little legal merit. More important for our focus is that historians need to examine the facts of how the phrase has actually impacted history rather than dismissing the phrase because we might not like it.

Beyond this, though, Barton and others find it necessary to attempt to build a case that ignores the idea of a separation of church and state and the way it has been interpreted for the past century. Barton quotes three members of the founding generation, Fisher Ames, Benjamin Rush and Noah Webster, in order to demonstrate that "The Founders understood the numerous societal benefits produced by Biblical precepts and values...."[31] To Barton this proves that the founders believed the Bible and prayer should be a central part of government-sponsored schooling. Yet if the founders wanted the Bible to be central to schools, why didn't anyone at the time even suggest such a policy or promote such a law? Jefferson was very clear that he believed government should be inolved in creating public schools, and the Northwest Ordinance of 1785 did establish a system for paying for such schools, but nowhere is the centrality of the Bible mentioned.

In the end, the ideas of Barton, Skousen, Beck, and others about Jefferson's Chistianity not only lie very far outside accepted historical scholarship, but most are demonstrably incorrect. Barton does intellectual cartwheels, for example, to argue that Thomas Jefferson really did not mean to separate church and state. Jefferson's own words are inconvenient on this score, but Barton tries to explain this away by parsing Jefferson's words, arguing that Jefferson's call for a "wall of separation" meant only that the state should stay away from the church, but not that religion should be separate from the state. In the end, according to Barton, Jefferson's beliefs really are consistent with twenty-first century fundamentalist Christianity.

Yet Jefferson was perhaps the ultimate religious iconoclast, even going so far as cutting and pasting his Bible in order to create a Bible that eliminated all references to miracles and God's direct hand in human affairs. Jefferson referred to the deity of Christ and the resurrection as "*deleria* of crazed imaginations."[32] Jefferson was religious, but in his own way; as Jefferson scholar Eugene Sheridan put it:

> For Jefferson, human reason, not supernatural revelation or ecclesiastical authority was the sole arbiter of religious truth. Thus, through rational investigation he came to believe in a supreme being who created the universe and continued to sustain it by means of fixed, mathematically precise natural laws.[33]

Jefferson put his ultimate faith in reason and the secular ideals of the enlightenment.

In a letter written in 1820, Jefferson wrote "that Jesus did not mean to impose himself on mankind as the son of God, physically speaking, I have been convinced by the writings of men more learned than myself."[34] Jefferson returns consistently to the ideals of enlightenment philosophy when discussing his personal struggles over his own religious beliefs. In part because of these personal struggles, he was also very clear on the need for religious beliefs to remain a private matter.

Most instructive in this area is the "Virginia Statute of Religious Freedom," a law that Jefferson considered one of his greatest achievements. As the law was debated, some in the Virginia legislature proposed adding "Jesus Christ" to the law's preamble, "but, as Jefferson later noted, 'the insertion was rejected by a great majority, in proof that they meant to comprehend within the mantle of its protection the Jew and the Gentile, the Christian and the Mahometan, the Hindu and infidel of every denomination.'"[35] In the final version of the law, Jefferson made very clear his absolute dedication to a "wall" between the ideas of religion and government, even going so far as to state, directly in the statute, "That our civil rights have no dependence on our religious opinions any more than our opinions in physics or geometry."

Many other founding fathers shared Jefferson's religious skepticism to one degree or another. In his *Autobiography*, Benjamin Franklin famously relates an incident where he discusses feeling swindled in the midst of a Great Awakening sermon. Franklin saw Jesus as an important moral teacher, yet he and most of the founders drew the bulk of their thought from British enlightenment "Whig" philosophy rather than from the Bible. Naturally, we can point to a select few of the founders, such as John Witherspoon, Patrick Henry, and John Jay who "affirmed the cardinal tenets of orthodox Christianity."[36] Yet the great majority of the founders' political beliefs and the founding documents they created clearly derive most fundamentally from a secular, enlightenment philosophy of the rights of man, as a raft of political and religious scholars have argued for generations.

From the perspective of the fundamental rules of the discipline of history, which are neither politically liberal nor politically conservative, Barton, Skousen and others pushing this new understanding of the founders commit a number of sins beyond ignoring the context of the times. Perhaps most interestingly, some of Barton's harshest critics are scholars at religious institutions. Derek H. Davis, director of church-state studies at Baylor University, a Baptist institution in Waco, Texas, argues that "the end product" of Barton's study "is a lot of distortions, half-truths and twisted history."[37] Richard T. Hughes, professor of religion at Messiah College in Pennsylvania, argues "When these 'Christian America' guys say the Founders were

Christian, they're absolutely right; many of them were Christians. When they point to the respect for Christianity that the Founders had, they're right.... But virtually none of the Founders wanted to impose Christianity by the state. I read some of this stuff these people put out, and I just scratch my head. They must be kidding."[38]

This all might look like an esoteric battle about words and ideas from long ago. However, many powerful and influential political leaders have taken the ideas of Barton, Skousen, and others and made them a central part of their political ideology. Michele Bachmann, Congresswoman from Minnesota, Tea Party leader, and 2011–2012 presidential candidate provides perhaps the strongest example. At the "Rediscover God in America" conference in the spring of 2011, Bachmann called David Barton "a gift to our nation" and proudly trumpeted her goal to take every one of Barton's special religion and history field trips in Washington, D.C.[39] Even beyond these field trips, Bachmann has sought to market Barton and his ideas directly to her colleagues in the U.S. House of Representatives: "There are strong, believing members of Congress who get it about our nation's heritage and we love and appreciate David Barton." [40]

Other prominent conservatives have practically stepped on one another to be first in line to praise Barton and his ideas. Newt Gingrich, another candidate in the 2012 presidential primaries, attached himself firmly to David Barton: "I can assure you that if we do decide to run next year, we're promptly going to call you and say 'we need your help, and we need your advice, and we need your counsel.' It's more than a voting matter. If we decide to run, David, we're going to need you."[41] Mike Huckabee, former governor of Arkansas, 2008 candidate for president, and important contributor to Fox News, declared only half jokingly that all Americans should be "forced at gunpoint" to learn the point of view of Barton and WallBuilders on the religion of the founders and declared that Barton is "maybe the greatest living historian on the spiritual nature of America's early days."[42]

The fact that many conservative politicians are so complimentary of Barton provides a hint at one true motivation behind his work, because Barton is first and foremost a political activist. He served as vice chairman of the Texas Republican Party from 1997 to 2006. In 2004, the Republican National Committee tapped him to energize "Christians for George W. Bush." In much of what he writes, he makes direct connections between the ideas of the past and controversies of the present. He proudly told the *New York Times* in 2011 "I keep being amazed at how much the founders wrote about issues that we're dealing with today...Can you believe it, James Madison opposed a bailout and stimulus plan in 1792!", pointing out a Congressional debate over subsidies for the codfish industry.[43] He has publicly argued that the federal government should regulate homosexuality and stated "God's the one who drew up the lines for the nations, so to say open borders is to say, 'God, you goofed it all up and when you had borders, you shouldn't have done it'" in an effort to limit immigration.[44] He claims to be at the immediate beck and call of Republican presidential candidates and has appeared at a number of events and fundraisers for Bachmann, Texas Governor Rick Perry, and for Mike Huckabee. For Barton, the past is merely a weapon to wield to enforce his view of the present.

Why should others worry about those who see history as a political plaything rather than as an investigation into understanding a complicated past? Because these zealots have sought and continue to seek to take their version of the past and make it the version of the past learned by the nation's children. They seek to eliminate any other version of the past. Rather than accepting that the past is a contentious place, they insist on teaching America's children about a simple, static past that existed solely to create the present as they wish it. They do this through a variety of means, from attempting to enact federal laws to working to change the public school standards in states throughout the country to building special programs that teach only their version of history to creating false and historically inaccurate curriculum materials.

In 2007, Michele Bachman, Ron Paul, and Paul Ryan joined ninety other House co-sponsors in promoting House Bill 888, a bill to sponsor the creation of "Religious History Week" in the nation's schools. The bill listed seventy five points of religiosity from American history, the vast majority taken from the founding era and the vast majority of those coming straight from the writings of Barton and Skousen.[45] Historical researcher Chris Rodda examined each of the points of religiosity in depth and found every single one to be based on incomplete quotations, contextual misundertstanding, or outright fabrication of the past. For example, Rodda carefully examined the claim that Congress appropriated money for the "importation" of Bibles in 1777. In fact, Rodda shows, this was only a committee motion and was never passed by the full Congress and, in the end, "A second motion was then made to pass an actual resolution to import the Bibles, but this was postponed and never brought up again. No Bibles were imported."[46] Another claim in the bill repeats a claim found in many Christian textbooks that the Congress of 1782 appropriated money for the printing of a congressionally endorsed Bible. In fact, Congress did not appropriate money for this particular Bible, but upon a petition of the private printer of the Bible, Robert Aitken, Congress "recommended" the Bible in question as an example of one printed with "care and accuracy" in order to illustrate it as "an instance of the progress of arts in this country."[47] In other words, Congress wanted to advance the nation's printing industry, and of course the most commonly printed book was the Bible.

House Bill 888 even misquotes Justice William Paterson, a signer of the Constitution, saying that he said "Religion and order...are necessary to good government, good order and good laws" when Paterson never uttered the phrase, which was instead a quote from a partisan newspaper reporter in 1800.[48] The entire bill, in other words, was based on faulty history. Yet a significant minority of the U.S. House of Representatives sought to impose a "Religious History Week" on American schoolchildren based on this false history.

The most influential campaigns to change the way the founding era is taught have taken place at the state level. It is no coincidence, in fact, that Michele Bachmann first gained political prominence in her home state of Minnesota during a battle over the adoption of teaching standards for the state's history classes in the 2003–2005 period. At the time, Bachmann was defended by a group of Minnesotans calling themselves "EdWatch," who insisted that the standards "reflected an anti-Christian bias" and were written by "the leftist University of Minnesota Professor crowd."[49] EdWatch praised Bachmann because she "led the charge in Minnesota against the radical changes in our schools."[50] EdWatch and Bachmann brought David Barton to Minnesota to testify about the standards and to bolster their argument that the new history standards needed to include their version of the religion of the founders.

EdWatch did not stop with the attempt to influence the legislature and change the required curriculum in Minnesota. They wrote their own curriculum on the topic. This curriculum required students to memorize the Declaration of Independence and then to learn 12 "truths" about the Declaration and its meaning, by "listing" and then "understanding" these truths as defined by EdWatch. EdWatch found many of these principles from the work of Skousen and presents them in the unit plan as "the American Creed." These principles include, for example, the following assertion: "That is, the colonists state their conviction that there is a God in the Heavens who governs the affairs of men. The signers of the Declaration were convinced that their cause was just and that the just God, earlier in the Declaration referred to as the 'Supreme Judge of the world,' would be on their side." This is an interpretation of the Declaration of Independence, not the truth about the Declaration. The lesson does include a series of questions, but the questions are about the application of the principles of the Declaration as defined by EdWatch. So, for example, students are asked to conclude how this "American Creed" applies to "levels of taxation" and the recent "*Kelo* decision of the supreme court."[51] These "questions" force the students towards a predetermined answer, as the inclusion of *Kelo* suggests.

In *Kelo v. City of New London* (2005), the U.S. Supreme Court allowed the city of New London, Connecticut to take land from a private landowner and give it to another private landowner in order to facilitate a public development. *Kelo* became a *cause célèbre* for conservatives, who believe it was wrongly decided because it allows for what they consider to be unconstitutional government attacks on private property. Such a lesson is bad history teaching because it does not ask the students to examine evidence to come to a conclusion about the past. Instead, it provides the student with a pre-determined interpretation of the past, an interpretation that flows from a present day political belief rather than a reasoned understanding of the past.

A critic might say that EdWatch" and these educational "modules" represent the lunatic fringe and really never had the power or support to raise the specter of tossing history down the memory hole. After all, another one of the units called for the teaching of "Dinosaurs in Ancient Art" in order to support the ideas of creationism, and the editor of the curricula is Allen Quist, who trumpets his book attacking state standards by saying that state standards defend the ideas of pantheism. Yet the fact that Bachmann used these ideas as her springboard to national politics should cause pause. It is precisely these ideas that drew attention to Bachmann and made her a prominent figure in the American political and cultural landscape. It seems clear that a significant number of Americans are willing to toss away the rules of the discipline of history so that their own present-derived version of the past should be taught in schools.

Although the changes that Bachmann and Barton wanted instituted in Minnesota never came to pass, they had better luck a few years later in 2010 in Texas. Every decade, the Texas State Board of Education is tasked with writing the guidelines for curriculum and instruction in the state. These guidelines also serve as the guidelines for any materials to be bought in conjunction with this curriculum, including the purchase of textbooks. Texas is one of the few states where the state department of education has control over the curriculum of the entire state, and this, paired with the fact that Texas is such a large state, means that the decisions made by the State Board of Education have potentially oversized implications for not only the state but the nation as a whole. In the past, the large numbers of textbooks ordered by Texas to conform to their curriculum has had an important influence on the national textbook market.

The process created by the Texas State Board of Education did not appear to be at first glance particularly controversial or uniquely different from the process other states use to create standards and curriculum.[52] However, the Texas State Board of Education ensured that there would be two crucial differences in their process. First, the State Board got to choose the "experts" to review the state standards. Second, the State Board reserved for itself the power to actually change the standards, rather than merely voting to approve or not approve the standards as in other states.

The Texas State Board made its process different because it was their stated goal to have complete control over the Texas school curriculum. The members ran for election for the school board for the very purpose of inserting their view of history (and science) into Texas classrooms. They believed that Texas history classrooms were being taken over by the "liberal educational elite," and they wanted to not only slow this process, but reverse it by bringing twenty-first century conservatism into the history classroom. As leading conservative activist Phyllis Schlafly put it, "the liberals want to teach what's wrong with America instead of what's right and successful."[53] The Texas standards were meant to fix that. As board member and Chair Don McLeroy put it, "the greatest problem facing America today is that we have forgotten what it means to be an American."[54] And that meant, according to Mark Chancey, a religious studies professor at Southern Methodist University in Dallas, "For McLeroy, apparently what it means to be an American is to be a Christian—more specifically, a Christian like him."[55] McLeroy proudly proclaims himself to be a "Christian fundamentalist" and outlines his philosophy this way: "Christianity has had a deep impact on our system. The men who wrote the Constitution were Christians who knew the Bible. Our idea of individual rights comes from the Bible. The Western development of the free-market system owes a lot to biblical principles."[56] His goal was to make sure that the Texas standards reflected these beliefs.

One of the main methods of accomplishing this was to hire the "right" sort of experts for the review of the standards. The standards law required the hiring of five experts to vet the standards. In the end, only two of the chosen experts had the traditionally required education and publication record to be considered an expert in the study of history. The most important factor in choosing the "experts" was standing in the world of Christian conservatives. One of the experts chosen was Peter Marshall, the leader of the Peter Marshall Ministries and a leading author of a series of Christian textbooks for homeschoolers. Peter Marshall Ministries is dedicated to "helping restore America to its Bible-based foundations through preaching, teaching and writing on America's Christian heritage."[57] Marshall argued in his first response to the Texas standards that the key point that students must understand is the "Biblical influence on American Government."[58] Eight of the nine pages of Marshall's review focus on the need to change the standards in regards to the religion of America's founding era.

Most significantly, the star expert turned out to be none other than David Barton. For the topic of the history of the founding era, Barton immediately attacked the draft of the new standards written by the committee of teachers. He argued that the standards require that the following set of ideas be memorized as the basis of the Declaration of Independence:

1. There is a fixed moral law derived from God and nature.
2. There is a Creator.
3. The Creator gives to man certain unalienable rights.

4.   Government exists primarily to protect God-given rights to every individual.
5.   Below God-given rights and moral law, government is directed by the consent of the governed.[59]

One could derive these precepts from a reading of the Declaration. Barton's interpretation is a plausible one. However, it is not the *only* plausible one, deserving required memorization. The great majority of historians would argue, in fact, that it is not even the *most* plausible one. Gordon Wood would argue that "republican virtue" was the fundamentally most important concept to understand regarding the Declaration. Other historians have argued that the list of grievances put special focus on the King's restriction of economic freedom, and so the ideas of economic liberalism are paramount.

The central meaning of the Declaration must be viewed in the context of the times, including the reason for writing the document in the first place. The document is a political document, focused mostly on a list of abuses of the King, and the philosophical basis for the document comes much more from Enlightenment political thinking of the seventeenth and eighteenth century than from the religious background dictated by Barton.[60] And it is the "dictating" that is the crucial point. Barton argues "These fundamental five precepts of American government must be thoroughly understood."[61] In other words, students *must* understand *Barton's interpretation* as the basis for the Declaration of Independence. No questioning, no inquiry, no alternative understanding.

After the first draft of Texas' new standards were written, Barton wrote a lengthy second review in which he continued his campaign to promote his inaccurate version of the founding era. For example, he recommended that the standards include a reference to "Washington's emergence as a nationally recognized figure following the providential preservation of his life during the Battle of the Monongahela," a reference to an early battle in the French and Indian War when Washington survived despite four bullet holes in his coat and two horses shot from underneath him.[62] A wonderful and exciting story to be sure. However, the key point here is Barton's desire to teach in history class that this event was "providential."

This concept that American history is the fulfillment of God's plan cannot be verified through the process of historical study. No actual historian can include the concept of "providence" as a required concept to be learned in school. A class might discuss whether or not Washington himself believed it to have been a "providential" moment, and indeed the evidence suggests that he did. But historians cannot accept this as required standards to be learned by all fifth graders in the state of Texas.

The actual standards as finally approved did not include this reference to the providential nature of Washington's life. In part because of the national firestorm about the standards, a few of the most obviously faulty of Barton's arguments did not make the final cut. However, more than a few did, as we will see in other chapters of this book. In the case of the religion of the founding era, one particular standard did make the cut: "describe how religion and virtue contributed to the growth of representative government in the American colonies." On the face of it, this standard can connect with the arguments of the most well respected colonial historians. There is no question that religion played a significant role in the founding of the English colonies of North America and that these colonies developed systems of representative government. The belief that religion was the basis of this representative government, however, is not supported by the evidence or the context of the times. And the standard, like many others, asks students to "describe" this "fact," as if there is no contention about it. A better standard might be that students should be able to "evaluate the evidence to determine to what extent religion contributed to the growth of representative government."

The idea of "virtue" in this context in similarly problematic. First, the concept was not centrally important during what Barton calls the colonial era, for it was not a central point of discussion among seventeenth century colonists. On the other hand, it was a central idea in the world of the eighteenth century revolutionaries. One of the most significant arguments of Gordon Wood, a leading historian of the revolutionary era, is that "virtue" played a significant role in the minds of the revolutionary colonists. Wood has written many books that dig very deeply into this idea of virtue and what it meant to Americans at the time, and his argument is so convincing that it spawned an entire field of writing about this time period known as the "republican consensus." He observes that in their obsession with the idea of virtue, the American colonists were discussing "republican virtue," an idea that drew from sources as varied as the Italian Renaissance, seventeenth and eighteenth century British Whig politicians, and French enlightenment philosophers.[63] Wood defines this idea of virtue as a "willingness of the people to sacrifice their selfish interests for the sake of the general good" in the form of "the state or the community."[64] Religion had its place in the creation of this virtue, but it was by no means the single source of this virtue. Actually, Jefferson believed that virtue and religious morality were completely separate concepts. As he put it, "In their [religious sects] particular dogmas all differ, no two professing the same. These respect vestments, ceremonies, physical opinions and metaphysical speculations are totally unconnected with morality and unimportant to the legitimate objects of society."[65] But for Barton and others, virtue is a Christian religious concept, so he sought to pair religion with virtue to bring his ideas about religious virtue into the Texas classroom.

The writing of standards, such as we have seen in Minnesota and Texas, is not the only arena where Christian fundamentalists seek to reinvent the meaning of history as it connects to the American founding era. Standards writing is a long, arduous process in each state that requires a process of compromise that has frustrated those who would eliminate the teaching of history they don't like and replace it with a history they have invented. So in recent years, Christian conservatives have sought new, unique and imaginative ways of inserting their invented history into the nation's public classrooms. In Texas, this happened almost a decade before the 2010 standards controversy. In 2003, under the leadership of Superintendant Rod Paige, later Secretary of Education for George W. Bush, the Houston Independent School district commissioned the writing of supplementary social studies curriculum for the district's high school students. They teamed up with the right-wing American Heritage Education Foundation to write "America's Heritage: an Adventure in Liberty," a document including background information and lesson plans on a number of fundamental topics in U.S. history. The very first lesson, "From Oppression to Liberty," repeats, in many places, word for word the work of W. Cleon Skousen, including Skousen's dubious and unsubstantiated claims of a connection between the views of the founders and the "ancient" beliefs of the "Anglo-Saxons." The entire first half of the one hundred and fifty page curriculum document is based on the writings of Skousen, in some cases quoting his work verbatim three times on each page.

The best example of an attempt to re-teach an understanding of the religion of the founding fathers in schools is a campaign that began late in the first decade of the twenty-first century to try to focus National Constitution Day on the idea of the biblical basis of the U.S. Constitution. Constitution Day was the brainchild of Senator Robert Byrd of West Virginia. Byrd was a stickler on the constitutional prerogatives of the Senate, clashing with presidents of both parties on issues as diverse as war-making powers and the congressional power of the purse. He famously carried around a copy of the Constitution and often read from it in Senate speeches. Byrd added a rider to a 2004 appropriations bill requiring all schools, from pre-schools to universities, that received any kind of federal money to teach about the Constitution every year on September 17. The bill as it was intended and as it reads is non-partisan, a tool to ensure that the Constitution is at least discussed in an educational landscape that seems ever more hostile to the teaching of the past.

Recently, various groups have latched onto this legal requirement in an attempt to enshrine *their* version of constitutional history as the true and accepted Constitution Day story. These groups are affiliated with the loose conglomeration of right-wing activist groups known as the Tea Party movement. These groups seek to dispense constitutional history materials to schools throughout the country. This grassroots effort has parents soliciting their local school districts on behalf of materials that teach the evangelical Christian basis of the Constitution. Some schools, desperate to fill a void created by a lack of Constitution Day materials or programs and lacking any funds to purchase these materials and afraid of upsetting any constituents by refusing to fill the void, accept the materials and the programs offered. For example, in September, 2011, the Redondo Beach, California school board approved the showing of a movie entitled "A More Perfect Union," a religiously inspired "documentary" about the Constitution, fourteen copies of which were provided to them free of charge by the South Bay Tea Party.[66]

What are these materials, exactly, that these Tea Party groups provide to schools to teach students about the Constitution? The movie in Redondo Beach is promoted by an organization called the National Center for Constitutional Studies, a very legitimate and scholarly sounding name for an organization. Yet the organization is focused primarily not on analyzing the history and background of the Constitution, but on some of the following ideas:

> According to an article published in the *Review of Religious Research,* the center's targets included "the Occupational Safety and Health Administration, the Environmental Protection Agency, the Federal Communication Commission's fairness doctrine in editorial broadcasting, the federal government's change of the gold standard in currency, all subsidies to farmers, all federal aid to education, all federal social welfare, foreign aid, social security, elimination of public school prayer and Bible reading, and (that familiar right-wing nemesis) the United Nations."[67]

This organization was the brainchild of W. Cleon Skousen, and the major "textbook" peddled by NCCS is Skousen's *The 5,000 Year Leap,* which as we have seen argues that there was a direct jump from the era of lawmaking described in the Old and

New Testaments to the era of lawmaking in the United States in the late eighteenth century. The fundamental lesson of the NCCS was nicely summarized by legal scholar Garret Epps in a lengthy analysis of NCCS materials in the *Atlantic Monthly:* "That's because we have to learn the basic truth about the Constitution: God wrote it."[68]

The National Tea Party movement worked to institutionalize and spread these ideas with their "Adopt a School" campaign beginning during the summer of 2011. According to the Tea Party Patriots' website, adopting a school was easy: "Simply identify a school or schools, in which you are willing to contact to discuss with them the need to fulfill the 2004 law requiring public schools have a constitutional education program each September

17th. Once contact is made you are willing to donate constitutional materials as needed."[69] The materials are, of course, materials created by Skousen, Barton, and other like minded re-interpreters of the past. Many local Tea Partiers took the suggestions to heart and ran with the idea. For example, Tea Partiers in Gilbert, Arizona created an official looking website at *www. constitutionweek.com* where interested teachers and students have the teachings of Skousen at their fingertips with easy to follow links. The Gilbert, Arizona chapter sponsored a Constitution Fair and a "Making of America Seminar" for those interested in a deeper understanding of Skousen's principles.

The attempt to influence standards and the attempt to reinvent Constitution Day are, at least in part, attempts to influence the nation's public schools. Yet a large number of self-described evangelical Christians have given up on the public school system altogether. They have decided that for a variety of reasons, from teaching evolution to what they see as a generally morally bankrupt atmosphere, the public school curriculum is not right for their children. One significant reason for their decision appears to be the belief that the history taught in the public schools reflects the "liberal slant" of academia and the educational world at large. As Larry Schweikart, author of *A Patriot's History of the United States*, puts it,

> All our founders believed…that a multiculturalist view of the world would destroy the nation. They came close to even using those terms. They also all believed that some form of Christianity should be a part of every curriculum. Since I think it is impossible to turn back the clock on the poor public education system today—even up to the college level—I think a massive disempowerment of the public school system through private schools and home schools is the only hope left.[70]

They want their children to learn what they believe "true" history to be. The answers are what is important, not the questions, as long as the answers conform to their twenty-first century Christian belief-system.

The homeschooling movement has become very significant and can now boast of at least one and a half million students nationwide, although most analysts agree this number is low because many states do not require parents to register homeschooled children, and many homeschooled parents refuse to answer government surveys. This is more students, for example, than are educated in states the size of Georgia or New Jersey. Most analysts also agree that the largest percentage of these students study an avowedly "Christian homeschool" curriculum. With large numbers comes potential big business, and many have sought to serve this Christian homeschooling movement with curricular materials and books. Most famously, Bob Jones University and A Beka Publishing have created materials to teach what they claim to be the true understanding of America's founding to Christian homeschoolers. John Fea synthesized the central tenets of these materials and, not surprisingly, found a series of ideas that look very much like the ideas of David Barton. For example, the key concept is that "God is sovereign over history" and that historians can "accurately discern" His special plan for the exceptional United States. This is the "providential" history idea that Barton inserted into the Texas standards. As a matter of fact, one of the texts is even titled *America's Providential History*, which not coincidentally features Friberg's *The Prayer at Valley Forge* on its cover.[71] Another title from this genre is *The Light and the Glory: Discovering God's Plan for America from Christopher Columbus to George Washington*, and one of the authors of this book is Peter Marshall, one of the hired "experts" from the Texas standards debate. A Beka books argue that the founders were men of "deep Christian faith" as that is defined in the twenty-first century, and of course George Washington's faith is most important of all.

The idea of "revisionist" history is ruthlessly attacked in these materials, with the implication being that there is only one history to learn and that history can never change. One Christian homeschooling website put the argument this way:

> What is History and how do we go about teaching history? History is "His Story"—God's plans and purposes for this world, the study of the actions of men, the decisions they have made and the consequences of those decisions.[72]

God has created a single history, and we just need to understand its truth. The contrast is obvious with the rules of the discipline of history, which require that our interpretation of the past changes with the incorporation of new evidence and the addition of new perspectives on the past.[73] The important fact about these books is not that people make these arguments about history, nor that they are being used in direct connection with religious education at a Sunday school. These materials are being used as homeschool curriculum materials, meaning that they take the place of the materials and lessons that follow the rules of the discipline of history.

The argument is not about which history to teach or whose history to teach. This is not the time-worn battle between the "winners" and the "losers" with history always being told by the winners. The history told by Barton and his followers is not actually history at all. It is a version of the past designed solely to bolster a worldview of the present. For the tens of thousands (at least) of children influenced by new history standards, attending homeschool, reading explicitly Christian curriculum materials, and learning this version of the past online, real history has been shunted aside. The rules of evidence are stretched, context is eliminated, and complexity is ignored. In the case of the founders of the late eighteenth century and their religion, the culprit is the twenty-first century Christian evangelical movement. We will see other villains attempting to reinvent the history of the nineteenth century, not from the standpoint of religion, but from the perspective of economics.

CHAPTER 2

ROBBER BARONS AND RAW DEALS IN THE CLASSROOM

Wayzata, Minnesota, the prototypical small Midwestern town. Situated almost on the shores of Lake Minnetonka, Wayzata sponsors an annual all-American small-town festival featuring the expected softball games and

The Memory Hole: The U.S. History Curriculum Under Siege, pages 25–46.
Copyright © 2014 by Information Age Publishing

speeches and even some quirky events such as a wiener dog race and a Westie parade. Most fascinating to the historian is that the festival is named for James J. Hill, founder of the Great Northern Railroad and late nineteenth century developer of the American northwest. After all, the reason the town sits near, and not on, the shore of the lake is that Hill's railroad follows the shores of the lake. Hill qualifies as the classic "robber baron," and his legacy for the town and the area is mixed at best, so naming a patriotic celebration for him seems an odd choice. Yet, according to one increasingly popular text, Hill should instead be immortalized as the quintessential American hero because he made "a difference in the way the world worked."[1]

Hill's reputation and legacy have undergone a twenty-first century renaissance. In the 2012 election, Republican presidential candidates were ready with their James J. Hill story. Ron Paul earned notoriety and online plaudits from the Tea Party in favorably citing Hill's story in response to comments on economic organization by Massachusetts Senatorial candidate Elizabeth Warren. Warren argued that the free market was not truly free, due to the need for support from "social capital" (everything from roads to bridges to police protection to education) supplied by the government. Paul proudly and quickly cited Hill as an example of an entrepreneur who was able to truly succeed without any government support. Eventual Republican vice presidential candidate Paul Ryan has often favorably cited Ayn Rand's fictional version of James J. Hill as he stumps for his economic ideas.

In the past two decades, politicians and ideological leaders of the right have scoured the history books in search of narratives in support of their twenty-first century views on free market economics. The story of James J. Hill seems to fit the bill. Oddly enough, Grover Cleveland has also become a near-hero in this new American myth, a *near* hero only because he was inconveniently a Democrat instead of a Republican. Ironically, one of the villains in this new American history is Republican Theodore Roosevelt, along with any other politician categorized as "progressive." The arch-villain is Franklin Roosevelt, and the most important new story to tell about the past is about the utter failure of the New Deal. These new stories all fit into the grander, larger story of the continuous success and ultimate triumph of the American "free enterprise system." These new stories are necessary to support a new understanding of the American economy in the twenty-first century.

There are a number of ways in which this new narrative of history is problematic. First, as we shall see, this new story deliberately omits facts and events that muddy the newly burnished image of American capitalism. The new set of narratives read as clear, focused morality tales, consciously ignoring historical facts that confuse the issue. Of course, this type of history breaks the rules of the discipline, a discipline that should focus on attempting to uncover the truth, no matter how messy or complex. Admittedly, historians from the left and right have been failing to mask their ideology since the invention of the professional discipline of history, and the belief that history can recover the unvarnished truth is a chimera. Yet there is more going on here. In the case of the invention of this new history of American free enterprise, the story is being told by those who are first political operatives and only secondly historians. They make no pretenses—their goal is a presentist ideological goal, not a detached scholarly goal. And they seek to accomplish their goal by breaking another fundamental rule of the discipline of history. They completely ignore an entire genre of historical research and writing, a genre that seeks to understand and incorporate the stories of the powerless in larger history, in order to accomplish their goal. The evidence suggests that these ideologues have purposefully ignored more than three decades of historical scholarship because it does not comport with their view of the world.

The issue becomes even more problematic because these writers hope to make their new story into *the* story of American history, and this is the story they desire should be taught in the schools. Just as in the case of retelling the story of the founding fathers in schools as a religious story, these writers seek to re-imagine the curriculum of the nation's schools in the area of the economy. For these activists, the purpose of teaching about the history of the economy is to teach about the positive aspects of American capitalism in the past. Actually, in Texas, they reject the use of the term "capitalism" because "one of the right-wing fanatics said that capitalism had a bad connotation—that people referred to us as a 'capitalist pig.'"[2] Texas seeks to eliminate any possible negative connotations that connect to the idea of capitalism. In fact, Texas has renamed its required high school economics class "Economics with an Emphasis on the Free Enterprise System and its Benefits." In one fell swoop, the Texas school board eliminated the complex and checkered past of capitalism. As school board member Lawrence Allen puts it,

> I think there are a number of citizens today who say, well, I don't have a job, I don't have any money, so I don't know how wonderful the free enterprise system has been. I think that capitalism and these systems have made some of our citizens very fat and a large number of them very thin, and so I don't favor that at all.[3]

The goal, then, is not to teach judgment, not to allow students to examine the pros and cons of the system. Instead, they attempt to throw out any possible negative discussion about the U.S. economic system, past or present. The assumption to be taught in schools is that the free market system works, and it always has, for all American citizens.

So from where exactly does the scholarship emerge to support this new brand of history ideologues and politicians want taught in America's schools? Just as in the case of re-teaching the history of the founding era, where the intellectual hero of the new school of history is David Barton, the re-teaching of American economic history has an intellectual guru—two, in fact. Unlike Barton, Burton W. Folsom, Jr. and Larry Schweikert earned doctorates in history and have taught history at the university level for many years. Like Barton, though, and unlike the overwhelming majority of historians, the research of Folsom and Schwiekert is overtly political, and their research and writing aim to accomplish political, rather than scholarly, ends. The main political end is to retell the history of capitalism in a way much more supportive of the free market system, both in the past and in the present.

Burton Folsom's original foray into the history of American capitalism is *The Myth of the Robber Barons: A New Look at the Rise of Big Business in America.* He begins his study by looking at the earliest big business in America, Commodore Cornelius Vanderbilt's steamship line, and traces his story through the remainder of the nineteenth and into the early twentieth century. The first real hero of his book is none other than James J. Hill, and it is to Folsom that we owe the recent fascination with Hill as a hero. Folsom attacks the historians who have denigrated the entrepreneurs of the great American railroad boom for their "greed and corruption." He further disparages these historians because they missed the story of Hill, who built the Great Northern Railroad "with no federal aid whatsoever."[4] The remainder of his study of Hill shows him as the true "market entrepreneur," whereas other railroad builders, such as Mark Hopkins and Leland Stanford, were "political entrepreneurs" who took advantage of and misused federal government subsidies to build their railroads. Folsom argues that these subsidies made these railroads fundamentally inefficient, eventually forcing them into bankruptcy and government handouts. This led to disastrous government corruption, exemplified in everything from the Credit Mobilier scandal during the Grant administration to the Teapot Dome scandal under Harding. The problem, according to Folsom, was neither the size of the enterprises nor the lack of regulation nor the greed of the capitalists. The problem was government involvement. On the other hand, since Hill built his empire without federal government support, he was able to sustain success. And, in Folsom's words, this leads to Hill's ultimate enshrinement as an America hero:

> He had built the best railroad in America and had used it to beat subsidized rivals time and again. He helped open the Northwest to settlement and the Orient to American trade. He had made a difference in the way the world worked. To some viewers, he was the real hero in the drama of the American transcontinental railroads.[5]

Folsom continues his argument with studies of Charles Schwab, John D. Rockefeller, and Andrew Mellon. None of the other stories are as uplifting as Hill's. Schwab dies wasted and in debt, in part because he retired from his entrepreneurial life and so lost his entrepreneurial vigor. Rockefeller fares better, because he could combine the imagination of his entrepreneurial vision with the precision of a bookkeeper and avoided the extravagant and un-Christian living of Schwab. In general, the real hero of Folsom's story is the free market and the world of conservative business of the nineteenth century. It is no surprise, then, that the publisher of his book is not an academic publisher, nor is it even a trade press, interested in selling a large number of books in the open market. *The Myth of the Robber Barons* was instead published by the Young America's Foundation (YAF), an organization "dedicated to promoting the principles of free enterprise, individual liberty, and a strong national defense among American students." The YAF proudly boasts that "the conservative movement starts here," making it clear that the organization and its publications are intended to promote political ideals.

The YAF would be very proud of how it has helped Folsom spread his ideas. The *Myth of the Robber Barons* is in its sixth edition, and the story of James J. Hill has clearly gone viral, as we saw earlier in the words and beliefs of Ron Paul. Conservative and Tea Party Internet sites are littered with blogs and essays quoting Folsom at length. James J. Hill, along with Rockefeller, is often cited as a model of the free market in action. And, of course, the object here has little to do with gaining a new understanding of history. The purpose instead is to find evidence in support of a new understanding of the present, in order to achieve political ends. Folsom himself encourages and participates in this, beginning with his blog site, burtfolsom.com, "where history, money and politics collide." In this blog, Folsom highlights with stunning consistency and predictability the ever present failures of Barack Obama and twenty-first century progressivism based on his arguments about the American past.

From the perspective of historians, history teachers, and the discipline of history, though, Folsom's arguments and "scholarship" fall short. First, his arguments are too simple, as they ignore the complexity and deep context strong history requires. In an effort to tell his morality tale, Folsom's stories whitewash the past. In a review of Folsom's work for the *Business History Review*, Mansel Blackford of Ohio State declares that "neither scholars nor students will benefit from this study" and correctly observes that "Folsom's division of entrepreneurs into just two categories is simplistic in the extreme: the complexity of the American business scene does not come through in this book."[6] The large number of activists who appear take Folsom's work as the historical truth are being shortchanged.

Hill's relationship with government and with "the people" was also far more complex than explained by Folsom. First, the railroad he purchased to serve as the basis of his Great Northern, the St. Paul & Pacific Railroad, *was* built with a number of state and federal subsidies.[7] Second, a careful look at some of his specific practices suggests that Hill *did* make use of public largesse to grow his empire. One interesting example brings us back to Wayzata, Minnesota. According to local historians, Hill played hardball with the town, ignoring pleas to clean up a railyard and relocate outdoor toilets at a station, and, rather than fixing the problems, relocated a station farther from town, thus stalling the town's economic growth in the late 1880s. He fought with other local towns over his right to buy land at what he considered a fair price and about where to locate his tracks. Locals even made up a little poem in honor of Hill:

> Twixt Hill and hell there's just one letter;
> Were Hill in Hell, we'd feel much better.[8]

Clearly Hill participated in practices that angered many in his own time. In Seattle, for example, Hill was not above offering a local judge an annual railroad pass in order to obtain favorable right of way treatments versus the Northern Pacific railroad.[9] In St. Paul, he had no compunction in demanding free real estate from the city for his railroad.[10] Hill also spent time in Washington lobbying for government subsidies to send goods overseas to Asia.[11] Folsom makes it seem that only elite historians have painted Hill, Rockefeller, and others as robber barons, for their own strange and elitist purposes. Yet we find that they were by no means viewed universally as heroes, and their actions were not viewed as doing universal good.

This lack of complexity and deep understanding lead to a much more serious problem with Folsom's "scholarship." Ignoring a detailed and nuanced understanding of the impact on the greater society of the time, Folsom's work ignores an entire branch of the discipline of history. He ignores the great mass of people living in the nineteenth century, and he appears to do so consciously and purposefully. The most obvious example is lack of any discussion of Labor history in his work. *The Myth of the Robber Barons* focuses on the late nineteenth century and does not include a single mention of unions, strikes, wages, working hours, or the welfare of the workers who helped build the empires of James J. Hill, John D. Rockefeller, and Commodore Vanderbilt. One might say it is unfair to criticize Folsom on this point because his chosen subject is businessmen, not laborers. Yet when he makes the concluding statement that his study means "we have to sacrifice the textbook morality play of 'greedy businessmen' fleecing the public," it is incumbent upon him to examine not only the businessmen, but the "public" as well.[12]

Folsom's chapter on the Scranton family and Scranton, Pennsylvania, actually his strongest as it is based upon some interesting original research, consistently argues that the entrepreneurship of the Scrantons made Scranton a better place to live, and "thousands of Americans had new opportunities in life."[13] To his credit, he provides a limited discussion of social mobility. But he provides no examination of the actual life of these people: their living conditions, their education, their social interactions. He fails in his job as historian, because he fails to examine and even attempt to utilize all of the tools and information at his disposal. He oversimplifies to reach his predetermined grand conclusions about the positive impact of his heroic entrepreneurs.

Conservative political activists use Folsom's stories to support their interpretation of the twenty-first century economy. *Wall Street Journal* columnist Daniel Henninger bases an editorial on robber barons on Folsom's ideas, an editorial that is worth quoting at length:

> Let's bring back the robber barons.

> "Robber baron" became a term of derision to generations of American students after many earnest teachers made them read Matthew Josephson's long tome of the same name about the men whose enterprise drove the American industrial age from 1861 to 1901.

> Josephson's cast of pillaging villains was comprehensive: Rockefeller, Carnegie, Vanderbilt, Morgan, Astor, Jay Gould, James J. Hill. His table of contents alone shaped impressions of those times: "Carnegie as 'business pirate.'" "Henry Frick, baron of coke." "Terrorism in Oil." "The sack of California."

> I say, bring 'em back, and the sooner the better.[14]

He goes on by taking Folsom's words and ideas to craft a justification for why robber barons should return. Since they were good for the economy and good for the country, we should encourage a return of their type and, significantly, the types of laws and government where their type could flourish. History needs to be used to encourage policy, rather than studied in an effort to struggle with the complexity, contradictions, and uniqueness of the past.

Folsom's hero is really the "free enterprise system." For Folsom and other writers in this genre, the free enterprise system, or free market system, represents a fundamental idea in American culture history. As a centerpiece of an American culture that is unique and providentially chosen to reign supreme in the world, this system should not be attacked or criticized. Instead, it must be consistently defended and supported, regardless of any unwelcome facts that might get in the way. Thus, there is no point in dredging up aspects of social history that might dampen the otherwise enthusiastic and positive business history of Folsom and others.

This leads to the very unique, odd (for a historian), and relatively new fetish for studying and defending an otherwise forgotten president...Grover Cleveland. Known in popular culture and in history classrooms merely as the answer to a trivia question (who is the only President to serve two nonconsecutive terms?), Cleveland has reached hero status in the blogosphere. Ranked first or second on the top ten presidents list of many libertarians, Cleveland also earns praise from leaders of educational organizations such as the Free Enterprise Institute.[15] Presidential candidate Ron Paul even introduced Cleveland as his favorite president to Jay Leno's "Tonight Show" audience: "To me he has always been a great president," noting that Cleveland was "one of the last presidents who had some concern about limited government."[16] Cleveland earns praise for such action as the rejection of a request for relief from Texas farmers and the use of his veto powers so often that many of his current fans have given him the sobriquet "Dr. No." Further, Cleveland was a "prophetic" president who held a "constitutional view of relief" for the poor.[17]

This narrative again ignores a huge body of evidence suggesting Cleveland did not act because he was in the thrall of American business power. He did call out federal troops to quash the Pullman strike, for example. The heroic story also ignores the fact that the United States suffered one of the most severe depressions in its history while Cleveland was at the helm. Average Americans suffered unmitigated hardships during this depression, and a wide array of historians have written about the persistent conflicts and deprivations of the era.[18] Those who deify Cleveland ignore this social history because it does not fit their vision of the perfect economic system, and, as we shall see, this is the story they believe needs to be taught in America's classrooms.

Folsom and the other free enterprise historians would be happy to replace Theodore Roosevelt's face on Mt. Rushmore with that of Grover Cleveland. While Cleveland earns praise for his sterling free market record, Roosevelt earns opprobrium for being a Progressive. The first problem here is the conflation of the late nineteenth/early twentieth century term "Progressive" with the early twenty-first century idea of progressive. Actually, this equating of these two very dissimilar ideas provides a prime example of the failure to be true to the dictates of the discipline of history. Twenty-first century progressives are actually very uncomfortable with many of the ideas held by turn of the twentieth century "Progressives," especially on issues of race and other social issues. Yet, to Folsom and others, who want to tell U.S. history as a simple morality tale, "Progressives" are and always have been on the wrong side of the past because they attacked the fundamentally good principles of the free market.

Both grass roots Tea Partiers and "talking head" Fox News analysts pull no punches in their attacks on Theodore Roosevelt. The Kona, Hawaii Tea Party website declares that "An era of 'neo-socialism' began in 1901 with President Theodore Roosevelt's failure to understand capitalism and the industrial nature of modern America. Teddy's business-bashing and anti-trust laws paradoxically forced businesses into a structure that made them larger and more powerful."[19] No longer is Teddy the thoughtful conservative progressive, leaving an enlightened legacy for future Republican leaders to follow. Any tampering with the market is branded as socialism, despite the fact that Roosevelt was roundly attacked by Eugene Debs and the actual socialists of the time. Chris Stirewelt, a political editor on Fox News, agrees with this line of argument, explaining that

> What Teddy Roosevelt was calling for was a sort of a socialistic nationalism, in which the government would take things away from people who got things that he didn't think they should have [and] give it to the working man. They talk about "the square deal," "fairness," all of these new mandates for government—something the Republican Party has walked away from in very decided fashion certainly since the Reagan era in terms of what the role and purpose of government is.[20]

In other words, the present can now redefine the past. Stirewelt explicitly takes Roosevelt out of the context of his times, redefining him in the context of the twenty-first century. He tosses the real Teddy Roosevelt down the memory hole, ignoring Roosevelt's attempts to make the free market work in a complex world, to say nothing of Roosevelt's vehement dislike of socialism.

Ironically, the reinvention of Roosevelt came to the fore in conservative circles after a speech by President Barack Obama in Osawatamie, Kansas, site of a famous speech Theodore Roosevelt made in 1910. Obama sought to outline his economic agenda by purposefully connecting himself to a famous Republican president or, as Stirewelt put it, "This is Obama embracing a Republican icon of a bygone era." Obama's strategy confused Fox host Megyn Kelly, who asked, "Why would President Obama want to do anything that would associate himself with that word 'socialist' which has been used against him by so many of the Republican presidential candidates, among others?"[21] The confusion of terms, ignorance of context, and disregard of the complex meanings of the past are so legion here that they led analyst John Nichols to dub it "bizarro history."[22] If this only represented an outlying "bizarre" viewpoint, the significance would be small and perhaps easily ignored. Yet those stating the case are influential analysts with the ear of large numbers of Americans, and, as we shall see, these ideas have begun to alter the teaching of this era of American history.

Before we examine the impact of this newly invented free market history on America's schools, we need to take a brief journey into the tale of the biggest villain in American history, according to the purveyors of this free market history. Theodore Roosevelt is a minor actor in this drama in comparison to the role played by his distant cousin, Franklin Delano Roosevelt. For these free market historians, it is critical to reinterpret the legacy of FDR and the New Deal. Because these analysts believe New Deal programs still in existence such as Social Security and the FDIC are harmful to the current economy, it is critical they disparage the original New Deal. Their purpose in studying and analyzing the New Deal is not historical, but contemporary and political.

The free market historian taking the lead in this attack is, once again, Barton Folsom, who published *New Deal or Raw Deal: How FDR's Economic Legacy has Damaged America* in 2008. Even the title suggests that this is not a work of history designed to follow the rules of the historical discipline by studying the work in historical context. Instead, the book is designed to choose aspects of the New Deal that damaged America. Historians need to look at an event or a political program of the New Deal in toto, learning about the program and then developing an argument about the value of the program in its time. Folsom starts with an argument based on his current political beliefs and then searches for supporting evidence from the past, while tossing away any contradictory evidence.

New Deal or Raw Deal emphasizes every possible weakness and failing of Roosevelt. He failed in business in the 1920s, "pursuing futile schemes" towards a "string of business failures," acted "deceitfully on issues large and small," "never felt bound by the truth when pursuing his ends," and even managed to be the lightest tipper in his social class.[23] Folsom's goal is much larger than merely attacking Roosevelt's personal foibles, however. Folsom seeks to paint FDR as the president who sought to destroy capitalism. In this story, FDR's goal was to "scare rich Americans into sending the government more of their money" because "Capitalism had failed, and this opened the door for...government ownership and government direction of the economy."[24]

The end goal of Folsom's argument is to attack the basis of Barack Obama's new "new deal," as the book's introduction penned by *Wall Street Journal* writer Stephen Moore clearly points out. Folsom ignores any possible positive qualities in FDR and any possible positive aspects of the New Deal. While he devotes a twenty-five page chapter to the Democratic machine's use of patronage in the elections of 1934 and 1936, he discusses the gigantic public works projects of the New Deal in a single paragraph and FDR's banking laws in two sentences.[25] Historians are trained to attempt to make a balanced examination of the evidence before them, but Folsom does not pass this test. It is of course true that Folsom is not the first to commit this historical sin; the problem is that many want to take his story as *the* story of the New Deal and put it into America's classrooms.

From the standpoint of the discipline of history, the problem with Folsom's book on the New Deal is not that it challenges what he believes to be the accepted wisdom about the New Deal. Historians challenge each other all of the time...ironically, that is what "revisionists" do. "Revisionist history" is actually a redundant phrase, because historians revise and refine arguments about the past all of the time. Folsom's book fails instead because it views the New Deal with a myopic lens focused more on present-day political feuds than on attempting to more clearly see the past. The New Deal is only a "raw deal" if examined in a simplistic fashion, beginning with the goal of arguing that it failed.

As a contrast to Folsom's book, let us examine the work currently accepted by historians as the leading study about Franklin Roosevelt and the New Deal, David M. Kennedy's Pulitzer Prize and Frances Parkman Prize winning book *Freedom From Fear: The American People in Depression and War, 1929–1945.* Kennedy's role as a historian is neither to attack or defend the New Deal, but to understand it. He freely points out that the New Deal committed "economic crimes," did not lead to immediate economic recovery, and created often inherently contradictory policies.[26] Yet, unlike Folsom, he does not stop there, because that is not the full story. He examines the New Deal in all its complexity in an attempt to develop an argument about what actual historical impact the New Deal had. Kennedy's argument is that the pattern of the New Deal "can be summarized in a single word: security." [27] As a good historian should do, he then marshals evidence in support of this thesis. He points out convincingly "the New Deal's premier objective, at least until 1938...was not economic recovery but structural reform."[28] To evaluate, damn and excoriate Roosevelt for the New Deal because it failed to bring economic reform, as Folsom does, is to miss most of the point of the program. As Kennedy says, "Humankind, of course, does not live by bread alone. Any assessment of the New Deal would be incomplete if it rested with an appraisal of New Deal economic policies and failed to acknowledge the remarkable array of social innovations nourished by Roosevelt's expansive temperament."[29] The writing of history needs to take into account as much as possible of the meaning of the past in an effort to tease out its subtleties and complexities. The work of Folsom and others fails this test of history, for they seek to toss out these subtleties and complexities in an effort to distort the past for their own political purposes.

Other avowedly conservative historians have jumped on the anti-FDR bandwagon in an attempt to forward their free market principles. Larry Schweikart, coauthor of *A Patriot's History of the United States,* a textbook designed explicitly to counteract a perceived liberal bias in history textbooks, provides an excellent example of this. Schweikart is also the author of *48*

Liberal Lies about American History, another book that presents its anti-historical argument about the past right in the title and a book revered by the Tea Party movement. In his glowing review of Folsom's book, Schweikart concludes by saying that "There is no question, when you finish, that Roosevelt stuck most Americans with a 'raw deal' to ensure he remained in the White House for more than a decade."[30] Schweikart's goal is purely political. As he stated when asked about his policy goals for the Tea Party movement in an interview with *All Right Magazine,* "My own guess is that the U.S. has such untapped power and reserve that if the right man or woman would come along and galvanize (most of) us, we could undo the 60 years' worth of New Deal garbage in three or four years."[31] The New Deal, then, is not so much a subject of historical inquiry as it is a symbol for twenty-first century political attack. Above all, it is important for Schweikart, Folsom, and others to protect the sanctity of the unfettered free market and write history that attacks any action that attacked this free market.

Of course, this history plays very well with right-wing, conservative politicians. These politicians and free market historians then feed off each other, quote each other, and use each other as experts in providing evidence for their views. The newly invented interpretation of the New Deal even made an appearance in the 2012 presidential debates, when Texas Governor Rick Perry declared "If what you're trying to say is that back in the '30s and '40s that the federal government made all the right decisions, I disagree with you."[32] Analyst Bill Schneider explained that Perry doesn't have a problem just with Social Security. He has a problem with Franklin D. Roosevelt and the whole New Deal. This is more than supported by an examination of Perry's book, *Fed Up!.* Perry declares that "the whole thing was a fraud and simply does not stand up to history." He follows this declaration with two paragraphs of analysis and one quotation from Henry Morgenthau, FDR's Secretary of the Treasury, and then rests his case: "And there you have it: the vaunted New Deal did not bring the country out of the Great Depression, but the bigger problem now is that its numerous programs never died, and like a bad disease, they have spread.[33] This is the worst possible example on how to "do" history: cherry-picking a single quote out of context, claiming that it proves that a previously accepted interpretation is "bad," and then using it to defend a current policy stance.

Minnesota Congresswoman Michelle Bachmann had her own, very unique, take on the story told by the "free market historians." On April 28, 2009, on the floor of the House of Representatives, Bachmann defended the actions of Calvin Coolidge, claiming that his free market, *laissez faire* principles contributed to the economic boom of the roaring twenties. More important, she argued that FDR and his New Deal caused the "recession" he inherited to blow up into a ten year Great Depression. Her example of a misguided New Deal policy was the "Hoot Smalley" tariff. Presumably, she was really referring to the Smoot-Hawley tariff bill enacted by a Republican congress and signed into law by FDR's predecessor, Herbert Hoover. Bachmann was widely and understandably mocked for her series of historical flubs, but the silly errors masked the fact that the history she garbled was in fact the worst kind of overly simplistic, one-dimensional historical explanation. Economists and historians do list this tariff as one contributing factor to causing the Great Depression. Yet the free market historians put a very large emphasis on it and argue that if only this tariff was eliminated, the Great Depression would not have happened. Bachmann accepted this argument without revision, except of course for the perhaps accidental revision that the tariff was part of the New Deal.

Former Alaska Governor and 2008 Republican vice presidential candidate Sarah Palin also takes the free market historians' viewpoint as truth, using this argument as the basis for many of her political arguments. In her book *Going Rogue, an American Life,* she writes "Massive government spending programs and protectionist economic policies actually helped turn a recession into the Great Depression."[34] This, of course, condenses the arguments of Folsom and Schweikart in a neat package.

Progressive author Paul Street articulately sums up Palin's historical views and the historical views of the "free market historians" in this way:

> The rhetoric is colored by fake-populist nostalgia for a mythical simpler national time. Like many white nationalists with a Tea Party flavor, Palin pines for a lost 19th Century age of entrepreneurial capitalism, when owners managed their own businesses and knew their own workers and customers and when firms operated free of giant corporations and "big government." That's when America was supposedly one big happy family, joined together beyond coercion and oppression by the glorious, supposedly free market.[35]

Or, as Robert Reich, Secretary of Labor in the Clinton administration, put it "They'd like to return to the 1920s— before Social Security, unemployment insurance, labor laws, the minimum wage, Medicare and Medicaid, worker safety laws, the Environmental Protection Act, the Glass-Steagall Act, the Securities and Exchange Act, and the Voting Rights Act."[36] To put it another way, they would like to eliminate the history they do not like and replace it with a history that conforms more closely to their view of the world.

Is the only problem with this simplistic and invented view of the past of the free market that it offends the sensibilities of historians? After all, historians are not that significant, and the country could easily choose to ignore the view of the "free market historians" and their political adherents. Unfortunately, the problem is not so easily dismissed. This newly invented view of America's economic past is beginning to be taught as the *only* understanding of the American economic past. This view appears in widely read textbooks, takes center stage in standards, is being marketed aggressively by non-profit educational groups, and is accepted as curricular dogma in home-schools across the nation. Many American youth learn this incomplete and historically flawed story as the *only* story of the American economic past, taking the word of the economic anti-historians as gospel and, in so doing, ignoring the complex and contentious realities of the past.

As in the case of inserting religion into the story of the founding fathers, one of the main angles of attack for the "free market historians" is to make their version of history the version of history that appears in the state standards for K–12 education in each state. Depending on the state, this often means that any required textbooks be written in accordance with the standards. Even more important, curricula and assessments throughout the state need to be adjusted in order to follow the dictates of standards, so any change in standards has significant impact.

One of the first states to experience a political movement to change its history standards to better conform to the ideas of the "free market historians" was Minnesota, just after the turn of the millennium. The crusade to change the Minnesota "profiles of learning" was led by then State Senator Michele Bachmann, who won election to her seat in part due to the support of the Maple River Education Coalition, later named EdWatch. Board Member Michael Chapman lauded changes made in the state profile in learning trumpeted by Bachmann, declaring the standards improved because "students will also learn that the United States is primarily a free market economy…and that protecting property rights is a primary role of government."[37] In other words, students would learn that the free market is good and always has been good, and government should only protect business and never regulate it.

The successor to EdWatch, Education Liberty Watch, remained hard at work in 2011 in an effort to influence the standards in Minnesota. In an evaluation of the Minnesota standards, EdLibertyWatch.org found much to disagree with, especially in the way the standards treated the free market:

> The phrases "free markets" or "free market enterprise" found in the current standards have been removed in the draft. Capitalism is mentioned only once in the draft, and then in a very negative light ("Examine the role authority and governance played in the progressive era in relation to addressing problems of industrial capitalism, urbanization and political corruption."). Apparently, the committee wants to make sure that the standards reflect the stunningly rapid destruction of free market capitalism that is taking place via the Obama administration and being attempted by the Dayton administration in Minnesota.[38]

Here, again, we see the reason for the desired change in standards. It has nothing to do with new historical sources coming to light, nor even with the new interpretations (shallow as they are) of the "free market historians."

No, the reason to focus on free market history is to provide another reason to attack "progressives" and "liberals"—a political reason, having nothing to do with the discipline of history. These ideas have also migrated south of Minnesota to Nebraska, where state board of education member John Sieler argues "We need to say [in the new Nebraska History Standards] free market enterprise is good. Socialism is bad. To me, it's black and white."[39]

Agitators for the teaching of free market history followed the blueprint of Education Liberty Watch in Texas with more success. In Texas, those who sought to insert this incomplete brand of history in the classrooms managed to obtain a majority on the Texas State Board of Education, the agency responsible for writing the curriculum and textbook standards for all of the schools in the nation's second largest state. The chair of the Texas State Board of Education in 2010 was Don McLeroy, a Republican political operative and a firm adherent to goals of the Tea Party. His stated goal in writing the standards, as we have seen with the curriculum on the religion of the founding fathers, was to insert his understanding of history, replacing what he saw as a faulty liberal version of history. Nowhere is this more apparent than in the area of the newly invented free market history discussed in this chapter. McLeroy declared that "The free enterprise system is the dominant economic theme of our new history standards…Our new history standards teach the benefits of free enterprise; they highlight the failures of planned economies."[40] McLeroy did not even attempt to mask his intent. Strong history should be the process of teaching students to weigh evidence on all sides of an issue, working towards a complex, nuanced understanding of the past based on a study of all of the available evidence. Not in the classrooms envisioned by McLeroy and the Texas School Board. And McLeroy is also clear about why students need to learn this: "The free enterprise system makes better people. The free enterprise system rewards hard work, diligence and competence; it punishes laziness, cheating and free loading."[41] His goal was not to follow the rules of historical understanding; his goal was to indoctrinate students in order to fix a system he saw as broken.

David Barton, who plays such a prominent role in the reinvention of the history of the founding fathers, also contributed his ideas on the history of the free enterprise system as the "expert reviewer" for the Texas standards. He declared that the Texas education standards *must* include assertions about the centrality of "freedom from government, regulation, interference and subsidy" in a free enterprise system. This is one of the elements that must be "presented, identified, learned, discussed, and understood by students if they are indeed to function in a free enterprise society."[42] Barton worries about this because "We are now at a point in our history where we can no longer assume that the previously universally understood ethical basis of the Free Enterprise System will still be observed, understood, or embraced."[43] Of course, he supplies no evidence about the time period when everyone understood this system's universal ethical basis. Was it the late nineteenth century? Certainly that would have been news to Mother Jones, Eugene Debs, and even Mark Twain, each of whom went to great efforts to mock what they believed to be the fundamental inequalities and immorality of the system. No matter for Barton, who concludes his review of the Texas standards by insisting that in the Texas history standards, not only should the word capitalism be banished, but the term free enterprise system only be discussed as the "ethical free enterprise system."[44]

Barton believes that changing the way economic history is taught has been ordained by God. According to Barton, "God believes that government needs to stay out of it and let individuals do it and government needs to reward those that make a profit."[45] This attitude led to the creation of a new course for the Texas curriculum called "Economics with an Emphasis on the Free Enterprise System and its Benefits." This new course is designed to be "the culmination of the economic content and concepts studies from Kindergarten through the required secondary courses." The problematic nature of the course title so obviously violates the basic principles of the historical discipline as to be hardly worth analysis. Oddly, the course description discusses that students are supposed to "evaluate the costs and benefits of economic issues," although it is difficult to tell whether this is actually possible when students are required to required to "explain the benefits of the free enterprise system." The act of "explaining" means that students will be required to parrot a list of benefits provided them by their teacher or their school district or, perhaps, by a website that might list such benefits.

Examining the details of the required course content reveals even deeper ideological tenets. For example, students need to understand the right to "own, use or dispense of private property." They then need to identify restrictions that the government places on the use of property, with the obvious conclusion being that such restrictions infringe on the absolute right identified. Students are not asked to examine the historical changes in the definition of private property or the struggles over the concepts of private property and the public domain. Further, the standards demand that students "analyze the decline in value of the U.S. dollar, including the abandonment of the gold standard." This is perhaps the most insidious requirement of all, because the only place a teacher will find information on this is in the writings of the free market anti-historians. In all other writings about the value of the dollar, analysts stress the fluctuations of the value and the fact that the value is only relative. Only when the free market anti-historians are consulted do we see an argument about the consistent devaluation of the dollar. Again, we see an attempt to erase the discipline of history, to be replaced by indoctrination in an incomplete, flawed, and ahistorical set of beliefs about the past.[46]

The ideas of these free market "historians" have also penetrated deeply into the textbooks favored by home-schoolers and conservative charter schools. The education page of the Heritage Foundation, for instance, provides the playbook to be followed by conservative textbook writers and publishers. In this view, the Progressives believed that "America needed to abandon the old ideas of the Founding in favor of a new expansive conception of the role of government." FDR and the New Deal took this new conception to the extreme, departing from the understanding and beliefs of America's founders in three significant ways, culminating in Roosevelt's desire to "undermine the Founders' understanding of rights and freedom."[47] *America's Providential History*, mentioned in Chapter One as a popular Christian home-school book for the middle grades, takes as gospel these conclusions. The book declares that "welfare states are not biblical and do not work. America in recent decades has shown this to be true."[48] The book "proves" this point through the citation of a smattering of debatable statistics gleaned from the works of the free market "historians." Belliles and McDowell continue in this vein, attacking the Fed for causing inflation by printing "money with no precious metal backing," a central argument for the free market anti-historians.[49] The Fed and its policies cause forms of "tyrannical taxation." These "facts" are stated as truths for student to learn, the equivalent of the existence of other historical facts and events. *America's Providential History* almost completely ignores Social Security and the New Deal, introducing them in part of only one paragraph in a book on almost 300 pages, and then introducing them only as part of the "propagation of socialism," along with the introduction of the income tax, which is attacked as "another corrupting event" in the nation's history.[50] This textbook clearly intends to indoctrinate, rather than present evidence for students to examine, evaluate and analyze.

Other, more widely used, textbooks also accept and promote the ideas of the free market anti-historians. As we saw in Chapter One, the most widely used series of textbooks in the home-school market is the A Beka book series. Perhaps the most complete high school history text in this series is *United States History in Christian Perspective: Heritage of Freedom* by Michael R. Lowman, George Thompson, and Kurt Grussendorf. For their chapter on the late nineteenth century, the authors reject traditional titles such as "Age of Industry" or, of course " Age of the Robber Barons," instead choosing the title "The Great Age of Enterprise." By itself, such a choice is perfectly reasonable, and historians and textbook authors always make choices that reflect their personal beliefs about a particular event or era. Yet Lowman, Thompson, and Grussendorf move several stages further away from accepted historical practice in their specific discussion of free enterprise and of the events of the era. They declare at the very beginning of the chapter that the system of free enterprise "is the only economic system consistent with personal freedom and responsibility" and that whenever the people turn that responsibility over to the government by "demanding government services and regulations, the nation loses its freedom."[51]

From the very start, then, the authors expect students to believe that one particular interpretation of this system is correct, and any other ideas about the system of free enterprise are suspect and, literally, un-American. This dictate is re-emphasized in the chapter review section, meant to prepare students for assessments, when the student is asked "under what type of economic system are individuals free to follow their economic pursuits as they see fit."[52] The chapter also includes a full-page highlighted subsection touting the "moral values of capitalism."[53]The section of the chapter concludes with another half page discussion of the "benefits of capitalism."[54] The labor strife, protests against capitalist excess, and the populist attack against what many at the time argued was an unfair system are either ignored or quickly glossed over in this paean to free enterprise capitalism. There is no attempt whatsoever to ask students to examine the complexities of the era or to evaluate evidence that might help students reach their own conclusions.

Heritage of Freedom saves its harshest attacks for Franklin Roosevelt and the New Deal. It introduces the section with the expected attack on the Federal Reserve for causing the Great Depression. Then it diminishes the depth and breadth of the Depression in a section entitled "Socialist Propaganda," which belittles John Steinbeck for "trying to magnify the crisis in order to move the United States towards socialism."[54] Continuing by pointing out that the Depression was worse in "Communist Russia," the textbook authors skim over the economic realities and move toward a discussion of American culture at the time. So in this narrative, the Depression really was not so bad. Of course, this flies in the face of the historical evidence, both statistical and experiential. It erases the experiences of the people of the time in an attempt to set up an argument about the New Deal.

And what is that argument? That the New Deal was unnecessary because the Depression was not so bad and, following the arguments of the free market anti-historians, that it did not solve the problem and attacked American freedom and liberty in the process. Under Roosevelt, the nation took a "large step away from a constitutional republic based upon law toward a socialist democracy based upon total 'equality' for the masses."[55] *Heritage of Freedom* wraps up the chapter on the New Deal with a recap of "New Deal failures," admitting no New Deal successes and allowing for no student evaluation of the relative merits of the program. There is nothing in the chapter that even remotely reflects the thinking and subtle arguments of David Kennedy or other renowned historians writing about the era. These historians are ignored because of their "liberal bias," despite the fact that they followed the rules of the historical profession in their use of evidence and in their complex, multifaceted arguments about the past. *Heritage of Freedom* toys dangerously with the past in an effort to promote a vision of the present and future, ignoring and twisting history for its own purpose.

Right-wing think tanks and educational institutions have moved beyond state standards and textbooks in order to indoctrinate American students with the arguments of the free market "historians." For example, the Young America's Foundation is dedicated to reinventing the history of the American free market and spreading these ideas to American youth. As they put it on their website,

> As the principal outreach organization of the Conservative Movement, the Foundation introduces thousands of American youth to these principles. We accomplish our mission by providing essential conferences, seminars, educational materials, internships, and speakers to young people across the country.[56]

One of their featured historians is Burton Folsom, whom they pay to present his ideas on free market "history" to the students in their programs. Recall that Folsom's book, *The Myth of the Robber Barons*, was published by the Young America's Foundation.[57] As just one example of the work he does for the Foundation, Folsom presented on the "true entrepreneurial beginnings" of American Capitalism at the Twelfth National High School Leadership Conference sponsored by YAF. The goal of the presentation and the conference was to present a "crash course in conservative thought" for the students in attendance. The purpose, in other words, was political, partisan, and not in any way academic. Folsom is not a historian in these talks; instead, he refers to the past in a way that supports his political views and the political views of his benefactors. In *1984*, at least Big Brother and the party made the pretense of attempting to reconstruct real history and teaching it to the masses.

The Young America's Foundation is not the only avowedly conservative organization seeking to teach American students the "truth" about the history of American capitalism. For example, the Foundation for Economic Education (FEE) offers high school economics seminars that promise to "make sense of it all" when it comes to the confusing world of economics and economic history.[58] Of course, "making sense of it all" means focusing on the ideas of the "free market historians," including defense of the "free enterprise system" of the late nineteenth century and attacks on the New Deal. The FEE website highlights an essay by FEE president Lawrence W. Reed entitled "Great Myths of the Great Depression," and one of their leading faculty members is Burton Folsom. In the spring of 2012, FEE offered a free "Spring Break with FEE" seminar in Atlanta for the first 80 students who signed up, featuring Folsom and Reed as speakers. The ultimate purpose for FEE is to dismantle the current "socialized education system" and replace it with "education for liberty." As we have seen, this new education system would be one that replaces the discipline of history with a politically tainted vision of the past.

There is a clear and obvious connection between the ideas of educational outreach organizations such as YAF and FEE and the educational ideas of the Tea Party movement. One educational goal of the Tea Party is to teach that

> America is #1. Other systems of government are not. Therefore, our children should be taught that our system is the best, and also that other systems—like socialism or communism, are not the best and, in fact, are objectively bad (on economic and humanitarian grounds).[59]

All educational policy, therefore, needs to follow from what the Tea Party believes is this inarguable truth. No facts, events, or ideas need get in the way. The curriculum needs to start with this answer, not with questions, whereas true history needs to start with the questions and not any answer. For economics and economic history, this means "we must teach Capitalism, the proven best economic system in the history of the world."

Such ideas seem to provide a caricature of the Tea Party movement, but they are central to the Tea Party belief system on education. The Internet is rife with sites, many which claim to be written by teachers, that parrot the ideas of Folsom, Schwiekert, and the Tea Party Patriots. For example, one blog from "a conservative teacher" blames the Great Depression on government policies, especially those of the Federal Reserve, at which point "FDR took these mistakes and expanded on them and enlarged them, and the result was that a real recovery never took place."[60] This is a superb synthesis of the Folsom/Schwiekert/free market anti-historian argument about the era, and as we have seen, the story is incomplete at best and a purposeful fiction at the worst. Most important, it is not history. It is a version of the past replete with mistakes, errors, and oversimplifications, designed not to help students think but to forward a political cause. And it is clearly influential in our nation's classrooms and in the minds of thousands of students throughout the nation.

We see perhaps the most frightening aspect of this move to teach free market "history" in the actual lessons taught in the "free market classrooms." One place to look for these classrooms is in the Patriot Camps, the summer classrooms sponsored by the Tea Party movement and meant to provide Tea-Party-acceptable education in a whole range of areas. A group called "Utah's Republic" sponsored one such camp in the summer of 2011. This camp was sponsored and facilitated by Oak Norton, a Utah political and educational activist. Norton, active in causes such as school board elections throughout the first decade of the twenty-first century, apparently decided to take upon himself civic education for local students, and then post the results online in YouTube videos. Not surprisingly, the ideological basis of much of Norton's work comes from the work of W. Cleon Skousen, whom we met in Chapter One. The most instructive of the lessons that took place at his 2011 Patriot Camp was his lesson on "Republic vs. Democracy." The lesson is most instructive because he centers the lesson on the economic basis of the difference between a republic (which he vehemently insists is the system designed by the founders for the United States) and a democracy (which he insists with equal vehemence does not describe the American system or a system Americans would ever want). Of course, in a technical political sense, he is right. And to ask students to ponder the differences between the two and discuss the relative merits between the two would be an excellent exercise. The problem is that he oversimplifies both systems and is proud of the fact that students literally view "democracy" as a bad word at the end of the lesson.

Further, he confuses economic issues with the political differences, and the reason he does this is instructive in that it flows from the philosophical basis for the ideas of the free market "historians." In his lesson, Norton gives students candy when they perform certain tasks (singing a song, doing pushups, etc.) and then shows them how unfair it is to take away their hard-earned booty when he acts as the government, arbitrarily taking a candy tax. According to Norton, this is an example of democracy in action, because the rest of the class voted for it. Only in a republic is it possible for laws to protect from such a "taking." In this lesson, and those that follow, *any* government interference is shown to be evil and antithetical to American values. This is the same basic idea that motivates the free market "historians." *Any* government interference in economic affairs is anti-American and so must be depicted as ineffective and antithetical to American liberty. The purpose, then, of history and civics in the schools is to show the failure and inappropriateness of government interference, both today and in history.

And so we now come full circle back to our friend James P. Hill. Hill is a hero because, in the story told by Folsom and others, he disdained any government support and so represents the ultimate example of a liberty- and freedom-loving American. We have already seen how this version of the Hill story is overly simplistic, incomplete, and in many ways inaccurate. No matter, as far as the students in the Houston school district are concerned. For Hill takes a prominent place in the supplemental curriculum created for the Houston schools by the American Heritage Educational Foundation, the same curriculum that centers its lessons on the religion and the founding fathers on the ideas of Skousen and Barton. In this curriculum, the "character education focus" for the month of April is on "Entrepreneurs in History," and James Hill is a centerpiece. And, of course, all of the information comes from the work of Burton Folsom. The biography provided to the students is completely positive, and no mention is made of any of the laborers who worked for Hill. The term "robber baron" never appears in any of the materials about these "captains of industry" (this term is used). The lesson for Hill and the other industrial leaders asks students to "illustrate the impact of providing freedom of expression to entrepreneurs, allowing them to gain or lose economically based on the response of the market."[61] In other words, students are asked to retell Hill's story as it is provided to them, with no opportunity for questioning, research, or discussion of potentially contradictory evidence. Hill's story allows the Houston school district to toss the discipline of history and the complex nature of Hill's actual life down the memory hole, robbing those students of the chance to think for themselves that the teaching of history should provide.

CHAPTER 3

THE MISUSE OF AMERICAN EXCEPTIONALISM

1776		1789		1863		1941		1964		2001	
	1763		1814		1848		1901		1964		2003

This is a number puzzle that I present to many of my university level U.S. history students and to history teachers attending professional development presentations. As students and teachers of history, the participants always recognize the most basic idea about the number puzzle: the numbers are all years, representing a particular spot on a timeline of the past. This might not seem to be much of an insight, but it is important, because the fact that these are dates is part of our understanding of the discipline of history and of historical thinking. Dates are one of the most fundamental rules about the past. They cannot be changed on a whim; they do not bend to the dictates of one or another political ideology. Such seemingly obvious ideas about how we think historically are often ignored and overlooked, leading in part to the ability of some to reinvent American history for their own partisan purposes.

The Memory Hole: The U.S. History Curriculum Under Siege, pages 47–63.
Copyright © 2014 by Information Age Publishing
47

The next significant insight about this puzzle is that each year represents a significant date in American history. Participants usually reach this insight almost as quickly as they identify the numbers as dates, mostly because the very first date, 1776, seems to be ingrained into the American conscious-ness. In fact, most of the dates in the top row stand out as important dates in American history. At this point, many reach the next insight, a critical one representing a relatively mature stage in historical thinking. The years in each horizontal row seem to be connected in some way; they seem to tell a story, or present an argument. History is not merely a jumble of dates and events without connection. Historians and history students learn that dates connect with one another and can be arranged to tell a particular story about the past.

What is the story of American history told in these numbers? That is easy, participants believe, at least for the first row of numbers. The first row, they argue, *is* American history, the unique and special story of liberty and equality. 1776 represents the signing of the Declaration of Independence, and 1789 the ratification of the Constitution. 1863 is somewhat more dif-ficult, although most recognize it as being part of the Civil War Era. A little prodding and a little thought from those more steeped in U.S. history re-veal this as the year of the Emancipation Proclamation. 1941 is the year of the infamous attack on Pearl Harbor and the U.S. entry into World War II. They are often stumped by 1964, until some make the connection to the civil rights movement and the Civil Rights Act of 1964. Finally, 2001 is now firmly entrenched in memory and history as the date of the terrorist attacks on the United States and the U.S. response in Afghanistan. How do these dates connect into a story? They present the story of the creation and de-fense of American freedom. All of these dates are stepping stones towards the fulfillment of the American destiny.

Many believe that this row of dates represents the *only* story of America. These dates and ideas seem familiar to all. It is the exceptional story of America. America's story is the story of the founding fathers bringing the enlightenment ideas of liberty, freedom, and justice into active reality. It is the story of Abraham Lincoln and a generation of Americans willing to sacrifice to bring the blessings of this freedom to African Americans, and the story of those willing to sacrifice, protest, and die for these freedoms in the twentieth and twenty-first centuries. America's story is unique, special, uplifting, hopeful, representing steady progress.

What, then, does the bottom row of numbers depict? This often mysti-fies participants, because their training in history suggests that this must be a historical story as well. Yet if the top row presents the exceptional story of America, what can the bottom row represent? A couple of dates seem familiar, especially the first date, 1763, which might stand out as the end of the French and Indian War, the war for empire that consolidated power for the British in North America and made George Washington an accepted colonial leader. Some might venture a guess that 1814 must have something to do with the War of 1812, and in that they would be correct, because in this case it signifies the Battle of Horseshoe Bend, the key battle to end the power of Native American nations and ensure the westward course of empire for the United States. And now the pattern starts to emerge, for 1848 was the year of the signing of the Treaty of Guadalupe Hidalgo and the year of the gold strike in California. These two events together ensured that the United States would spread from coast to coast and stop at nothing to grab its "manifest destiny."

The story in the second row, then, seems to connect to American expansion, sometimes at the expense of "other" peoples. We see a new phase in this story with 1901, as that represents the defeat of the Filipino "insurrectionists" and the growth of American power across the Pacific. Then, oddly, 1964 pops up again, in this case representing something quite apart from the Civil Rights Movement. Instead, it is the year of the Tonkin Gulf Resolution, the central symbol of American involvement in Vietnam. Finally comes 2003 and the American invasion of Iraq, an attempt to spread American political ideas and the American economic system into the Middle East. Is this also the story of America? Of course it is; every one of these events occurred, and every one is part of the story of America. Yet this story is not the traditional story of American exceptionalism, because in this story, the United States acts as an empire, part of a system of competing world empires. In this story, liberty and equality do not play the starring role, and the United States is not as special or unique.

I am indebted to historians Fred Anderson and Andrew Cayton, who present this idea in a different form in the introduction of their book, *The Dominion of War: Empire and Liberty in North America: 1500–2000.* They examine the structure and organization of the national mall in Washington DC, arguing that the "monuments on the mall speak unmistakably to Americans about the relationships between and the relative importance of, five wars" in American history.[1] They point out that the Korean and Vietnam War memorials stand below and to the side of the Mall, whereas the Washington, Lincoln, and World War II memorials take center stage in the layout of the nation's most important memorial park. Further, other wars, including the War of 1812, the Mexican-American War and the Filipino-American War merit no monuments at all. This projects messages about the importance and meanings of these wars, and "all these messages are rooted in a commonly accepted 'grand narrative' of American history, a story so familiar that the meanings of the memorials can be deciphered by almost any citizen who has had the benefit of a public school education."[2] This narrative centers on Americans' "solemn obligation to defend their own—and others'—liberty."[3] So on the Mall, just as in the number puzzle, the stories of

America coexist and live side by side in an awkward, uncomfortable, complex, and messy way.

Unfortunately, it is this messiness and this complex story that many political leaders and educational activists would like to eliminate from our understanding of the past and our nation's classrooms. These people want only the first story told, only the story of an exceptional America of liberty, justice, and freedom. They want to throw the other story, the story of American empire, down the memory hole, a story to be permanently ignored because it complicates their view of America's role in the world in the twenty-first century. Yet the key historical concept is that *both* stories are the story of America. Both include important and valuable insights about our past, and ignoring either story is not historically complete. Students will be robbed of part of their heritage, and of a nuanced and complex encounter with their own country's past.

Many twenty-first century political conservatives believe that accepting only the first story, the *exceptional* story of American liberty, is the only possible way to understand American history. They argue that only this exceptional story explains the America they believe in and work for, and so only the exceptional story can be true. Richard Lowry and Ramesh Ponnuru, editors of the conservative *National Review*, provide an eloquent statement of this belief in a 2010 online article:

> What do we, as American conservatives, want to *conserve?* The answer is simple: the pillars of American exceptionalism. Our country has always been exceptional. It is freer, more individualistic, more democratic, and more open and dynamic than any other nation on earth. These qualities are the bequest of our Founding and of our cultural heritage. They have always marked America as special, with a unique role and mission in the world: as a model of ordered liberty and self-government and as an exemplar of freedom and a vindicator of it, through persuasion when possible and force of arms when absolutely necessary.[4]

The other story, the story of the Unites States acting as a great empire in competition with the other great empires of the world, cannot explain American history, because teaching exceptionalist history demands that only one story be told.

Several key points define the re-inventors' version of "American exceptionalism." First, the wording of the term itself: the United States is and always has been a unique, distinctive nation. It does not act, nor has it ever acted, like other nations in the world. An "exceptional" United States cannot be an imperialist nation, nor could it ever have acted in an imperialistic way. Empire has been the goal of other nations in history, but since the United States is an exceptional nation, it is not possible, nor has it ever been possible, for the United States to act in an imperialistic way. As conservative author Charles Krauthammer puts it, "In terms of how we conduct ourselves abroad, we are also unique in many ways in that we never sought hegemony...we're a commercial republic and we do not hunger for empire."[5]

Krauthammer ignores facts of history, such as the hegemony the United States did impose on places such as Hawaii and Puerto Rico. He ignores the fact that American leaders of the past were very comfortable in comparing themselves to other empires. In discussing his vision of how to govern the newly conquered Philippines, Senator Henry Cabot Lodge said it would be governed by "a class of men precisely like those employed by England in India."[6] One of Lodge's colleagues and friends (and also good friend to Theodore Roosevelt), author and naval officer Alfred T. Mahan, very forthrightly admitted, "I am an Imperialist."[7]

British historian Geoffrey Hodgson points out a variety of obvious facts that contradict the exceptionalist thesis. For example, he shows clearly that the economic expansion of the West was "largely fueled by European investment and European markets as well as by European immigration."[8] Later, after World War II, as the United States established military outposts throughout the world, "it was often hard to distinguish them from traditional colonies," as the Americans "behaved toward sovereign governments rather like "the British did towards their colonies in the 19th century."[9] Yet for many who wish to begin with the idea of American exceptionalism, the facts do not matter, because American exceptionalism needs to be accepted truth, and if the facts seem to contradict this, then the facts need to be eliminated or reinterpreted.

One way of reinterpreting these facts is, of course, to eliminate terms that historians use to describe the actions of other countries, such as the term "imperialism." This mindset appears in the reactions of political leaders who believe in American exceptionalism and then are asked about American imperialism. For example, when asked to what extent the U.S. invasion of Iraq was an act of imperialism, Secretary of Defense Donald Rumsfeld responded in this way: "We don't seek empire...We're not imperialistic. We never have been. I can't imagine why you'd even ask the question."[10] Some cynical critics might attack Rumsfeld for being obtuse at best or phony at worst, but that is not the case. In this worldview, a worldview that does not allow for a more complex, nuanced understanding of the term empire, the United States has been exceptional and has never been an empire. President George W. Bush agreed with his subordinate, declaring indignantly in a 1999 campaign speech "America has never been an empire."[11]

What other qualities, beyond lack of an imperial history, have made the United States exceptional in this view? Not coincidentally, two of the significant qualities are the protestant Christian beliefs of the founding fathers, which led them to create a religiously inspired republic, and a free market entrepreneurial history. In other words, exactly the same invented pseudo-history we encountered in the first two chapters. Dennis Prager, conservative radio talk host, argues: "What is American exceptionalism? The belief that America often knows better than the world what is right and wrong... And from where does this belief in American exceptionalism derive? Mostly from the religious beliefs that underlie American values."[12] The editors of *National Review Online* eloquently connect exceptionalism to America's free market past:

> This framework of freedom made possible the flourishing of the greatest commercial republic in history... In the latitude provided by this relatively light-handed government, a commerce-loving, striving, and endlessly inventive people hustled its way to become the greatest economic power the world has ever known.[13]

The idea of American exceptionalism is certainly not new; in fact, historians have been debating the issue for over fifty years. "There's a vast literature on whether and to what degree U.S. society actually is exceptional," as British essayist Mike Marquesee puts it.[14] Authors and historians as prominent as Richard Hofstadter, Seymour Martin Lipset, and David Potter examined the subject from dozens of angles. Historians and pundits seem to relish the opportunity to mine for the first mention of the term, and there is a somewhat quirky and fascinating debate about whether nineteenth century French traveling philosopher Alexis de Tocqueville or Soviet dictator Joseph Stalin first coined the term in the sense that it is understood today.

Many scholars since have questioned to what extent the United States was unique and exceptional at a variety of points in its history. As historian Michael Soto pointed out in 2010, however, claiming a connection to this long history of scholarship about what might comprise the "American character" is merely a smokescreen for a more politically motivated curriculum. The understanding of exceptionalism is, according to Soto, a product of "shoddy scholarship." In fact, the scholarship is intentionally shoddy and represents a deliberate misunderstanding of the debate about American exceptionalism.[15] As Pulitzer Prize nominated historian Greg Grandin put it, in the hands of conservative pundits, "American Exceptionalism boils down to little more than a synonym for the tautology 'we are powerful because we are God-blessed; we are God-blessed because we are powerful.'"[16] Even conservative pundits such as former Reagan advisor David Stockman recognize that the idea of "American exceptionalism" has become much different from the ideas originally discussed by Tocqueville:

> The word is neo-con speak, code for an aggressive foreign policy. It's for more Bush, with even more aggressive intent. It's about beating the war drums in Iran, It's about keeping the military establishment—which is vastly greater than we need—fully in place. That's what exceptionalism is all about.[17]

Ironically enough, then, the very exceptionalism that insists that the United States has never been an empire seems to support the arguments of those who want the United States to be imperialistic in the twenty-first century. The purpose of championing American exceptionalism has become "corrupted over the past thirty years or so by hubris and self-interest," as historian and cultural critic Godfrey Hodgson notes.[18]

Students should examine the significance of the idea of exceptionalism in American history, and there are many examples of thoughtful methods for integrating the idea into the classroom. Kevin Levin, an instructor of American history at the Gann Academy near Boston, articulates this idea most effectively:

> Honestly, I don't care at all what my students believe about the broad sweep of American history. I am as indifferent to a student who believes that the United States is the greatest nation in the history of the world as I am with a student who believes the exact opposite. What I care about is whether they can articulate reasons for their preferred view. I care about whether they can utilize the tools of a historian that I do my best to teach year after year.[19]

In this example, Mr. Levin models how to "do" history, beginning with an interesting question about a contentious topic and allowing his students to hunt for the answer. Questioning the value of the idea is an important pursuit; it becomes a problem when education "reformers" demand that the idea is taught as an undeniable truth.

For those worried about the elimination of history from the curriculum, the concern brought up by the idea of "American exceptionalism" is twofold. First, should the idea of American exceptionalism be accepted as *the* central idea of U.S. history, with all historical ideas flowing from this original idea? And, second, when exceptionalism is accepted as a central tenet of U.S. history, does that mean alternative ideas must be scraped away from the American narrative and ignored by future students of history?

These ideas of American exceptionalism are inextricably connected to the role of the United States in the world and world affairs. This is one reason why those dedicated to promoting the idea are so upset about the teaching of imperialism in the schools. If the United States is and always has been exceptional, the argument seems to go, then the United States is not and never could have been imperialistic, because imperialism has been a goal of other world powers and cannot be an idea unique to the United States. This worries some left-leaning political analysts, because they believe it provides precisely the correct excuse for the United States to act in an imperialistic fashion. Glen Greenwald puts it this way:

> The fact remains that declaring yourself special, superior and/or exceptional—and believing that to be true, and, especially, acting on that belief—has serious consequences. It can (and usually does) mean that the same stan-

dards of judgment aren't applied to your acts as are applied to everyone else's (when you do X, it's justified, but when they do, it isn't). It means that you're entitled (or obligated) to do things that nobody else is entitled or obligated to do.... It means that no matter how many bad things you do in the world, it doesn't ever reflect on who you are, because you're inherently exceptional and thus driven by good motives.[20]

This, of course, is one of the dangers of insisting on the history of American exceptionalism and the elimination of teaching about the history of American imperialism. Eliminating this particular part of American history provides the stereotypical opportunity for history to "repeat itself" because of ignorance of potential mistakes from the past.

One American political leader and educational "reformer" who wishes to make an understanding of "American exceptionalism" central to the study of U.S. history is Newt Gingrich. In the later years of his career, including his run for the presidency in 2012, Gingrich has based his entire political philosophy on his definition of "American exceptionalism." He titled his 2012 campaign broadside *A Nation Like No Other: Why American Exceptionalism Matters.* In this book, he declares "America is simply the most extraordinary nation in the history. This is not a statement of nationalist hubris. It is an historic fact."[21] This illustrates one of the fundamental problems with the anti-historian view of history and is, of course, surprising, because Gingrich earned a doctorate in history. In Gingrich's view, exceptionalism is a fact to be accepted and memorized, not challenged or debated. But by definition, this statement is an argument, because we have already seen other historians disagree with it.

Gingrich's definition is heavily rooted in the arguments of David Barton about the Christian motivations of America's founders. Gingrich teaches a course on American exceptionalism at Liberty University, where the core curriculum is his book and a set of DVDs produced and narrated by David Barton. According to the course syllabus, "American Exceptionalism is an elective course designed to introduce and affirm the importance and unique role that America has and will play in modern history."[22] The problematic verb in this statement is "affirm," because affirmation is diametrically opposed to the historical habit of questioning. The first learning objective for the course is to "defend the notion of American exceptionalism from a Biblical and historical perspective," meaning that the idea is neither examined nor questioned during the course. Instead, the course begins with the idea we encountered in Chapter One about the centrality of Christianity to the founders and takes this idea many steps further by insisting Americans have always acted in a uniquely moral fashion.

In the spring of 2012, the call to refer to the history of America as exceptional reached the level of a crusade for many on the right. "In an interview in August with *Politico*, former Arkansas governor Mike Huckabee went so far as to declare of Obama: 'His worldview is dramatically different than any president, Republican or Democrat, we've had.... To deny American exceptionalism is in essence to deny the heart and soul of this nation.'"[23] In the heat of the 2012 presidential campaign, Rick Santorum, the former senator from Pennsylvania, told a group of College Republicans at American University: "Don't kid yourself with the lie. America is exceptional, and Americans are concerned that there are a group of people in Washington who don't believe that any more."[24] Three different featured speakers at the C-PAC conference, the self-declared leading convention for the conservative movement, included the idea of American exceptionalism in the title of their remarks.

William Ames, a conservative education activist in Texas who volunteered to be part of the movement to rewrite the Texas standards in 2010, started from his belief that the image of the United States was under relentless attack in the schools. Ames felt compelled to participate in the rewriting of the standards because of the "attempt to paint United States history in as negative light as possible thru dwelling on the negative, even coloring overall positive events in terms of any negative effects. The result, if left unchecked, will be to eliminate our real history."[25] Ames provides variety of examples of his viewpoint, such as the following:

> Excessive negativity centers on the annexation/acquisitions of Hawaii, Puerto Rico, Guam, and the Philippines in 1898. The current standards define these as "U.S. expansionism," leading to a historical focus, as believed by Theodore Roosevelt, on growth, progress, commerce, and mutually beneficial self-interests shared with the territories. Today, both the U.S. and the territories are better off as a result. A majority on my writing team disputed this, however, changing "U.S. expansionism" to "U.S. imperialism," and these educators made it abundantly clear that this issue was not about shared opportunity, but rather about American oppression of indigenous natives.[26]

Ames believes that even mentioning the possibility of "U.S. imperialism" had as its only purpose negative depiction of the United States. Even though many of Roosevelt's contemporaries, and indeed Roosevelt himself, discussed the issue in terms of the relative merit of American empire, Ames believes the term and any possible negative connotations of these American actions should be off limits for students. He rejects the use of the term "imperialism," insisting that any "oppression" of the "natives" should be ignored because he believes the people living in these areas are "better off as a result."

Instead, Ames has a proscription for the teaching of history that would preserve "American exceptionalism" and eliminate negative attacks on the history of the United States. In the second part of his series of articles about history teaching in Texas, Ames explicitly calls for "a focus on American exceptionalism, that is, the United States occupies a special niche among nations."[27] In order to do this, he calls for "factual, unbiased, balanced social studies standards that include events and individuals that are both significant and represent traditional, American Judeo-Christian values." These standards should "teach our youth to be proud Americans, and that America is a great country that has an overall positive history." Left unexplained is what happens when the "factual and unbiased" history might counter the idea of a "positive history."

In the case of imperialism, the answer is to either ignore or change the meaning of events in such a way that they fit the "overall positive history" that needs to be taught. Of course, this is exactly how Winston Smith spent his time in *1984*: whitewashing the past to fit the needs of the present. Ames does not merely suggest the elimination of the term imperialism from the curriculum; he demands it. In testimony to the Richardson, Texas school board in 2013, he complained that he went into one classroom and noticed a placard labeled, "1890–1920: American Imperialism." This was unacceptable because it utilizes the "negative, leftist term 'imperialism,'" meaning that "students who enter the classroom every day, after 15 years of existence of the 'expansionist' standard, are still being indoctrinated that America is imperialistic...." Ames then warns the school board, "It seems that we need to discuss who you work for... you DO work for the citizens and taxpayers of the community, and we are here tonight to help you understand we are not pleased...." Ames is insisting his anti-historical point of view become the required point of view of all employees, teachers, and students in the district, regardless of the historical truth.[28]

Beyond the type of bullying exemplified by Ames, those who want to put American exceptionalism into the school curriculum and eliminate discussion of U.S. imperialism have followed a variety of strategies to accomplish their goal to change the U.S. history curriculum in the schools. They lament the diminution of the concept in the curriculum and blame it on an attempt to indoctrinate students in left-wing ideology, as curriculum crusader Kyle Olson argues:

> unfortunately, the concept of American Exceptionalism is no longer being taught in many of our schools. Instead, the mainstays of the progressive movement—union leaders, globalists, environmentalists and multiculturalists—are bringing their agenda into our classrooms in an attempt to plant the seeds of socialism in the minds of our young people.[29]

Olson continues in this vein, declaring that the "blame America" crowd believes that "America would have no borders" and "our financial and natural resources would be redistributed throughout the world."[30] Olson sees a vast left-wing conspiracy to eliminate American exceptionalism. In Olson's thought, teachers *must* teach this concept, whether or not it fits the facts, because if teachers do not teach American exceptionalism, they must be teaching that America should be part of a communist, one-world government.

Those leading the charge to eliminate the possibility that the idea of imperialism was ever part of American history included the members of the Texas State Board of Education (SBOE) in 2010. Don McLeroy, chair of the SBOE in 2010, explicitly focused on changing the Texas state standards by again eliminating the word "imperialism" and replacing it with the word "expansionism" in the study of nineteenth century U.S. history. McLeroy and others on the board insisted that the U.S. annexation of Hawaii, Puerto Rico, and the Philippines, for example, was fundamentally different from the European expansion of the same period, and so the word "imperialism" should not be used.

After the negative national notoriety Texas received during the debate over adopting the standards, the state legislature replaced McLeroy with Barbara Cargill. Yet Cargill, another right-wing educational ideologue, believes just as strongly as McLeroy in eliminating any trace of the word imperialism from the U.S. history standards. During a discussion of the standards on September 17, 2009, Cargill discussed her disappointment that "there appears to be some negatives" about U.S. history still in the standards. Her stated goal was to "guide the work groups" to "take out the negatives that seem to be appearing in the rough draft." Most especially, she argued for the need to eliminate the word imperialism in connection to United States history. It appears she had no regards about whether the word accurately described the history. She felt it was important to eliminate it because it portrayed the United States in a negative light.

Anti-historians in Tennessee pushed Tennessee legislators to take a different tack in their attempt to codify the ideas of American exceptionalism in their classrooms. Tennessee Tea Party leaders petitioned the legislature in January, 2011, lobbying for a law that would have stated "No portrayal of minority experience in the history which actually occurred shall obscure the experience or contributions of the Founding Fathers, or the majority of citizens, including those who reached positions of leadership." These groups explicitly lobbied for a law to "compel" the teaching of "proper" U.S. History. The proposed wording of the law, of course, not only *asks* that teachers and students ignore historical facts, but *demands* that they ignore the historical facts. Fayette County attorney Hal Rounds, the group's lead spokesman, said the group was motivated by "an awful lot of made-up criticism about, for instance, the founders intruding on the Indians or having slaves or being hypocrites in one way or another."[31] For some reason, Mr. Rounds believes that the fact that Washington, Jefferson, Madison, and others owned slaves is not a fact, or at the very least not a fact worth teaching in a history class. For Rounds, the only important part of the story of America's past is that Americans, and especially American leaders, of the past were exceptionally moral, just, and freedom loving, regardless of whether they owned slaves or sought to eliminate Native Americans.

Political leaders in other states are less brazen in their attempts to whitewash American history but nevertheless insist that American exceptionalism be the centerpiece of the history curriculum. In Nebraska in 2012, State Board of Education member John Sieler articulated his idea simply and candidly: "We need to teach that we are the good guys. That doesn't mean we have to hide some of the things that we are not proud of as a nation. We've made some mistakes but we are on the right course. We're not out to conquer countries and enslave people."[32] Dinesh D'Souza, conservative author and one-time president of King's College, agrees with this viewpoint: "We should be jubilant. American foreign policy has made the world much better... Thank God for America."[33] In the present tense, historians have no basis to argue with this thesis about the United States as good guys. But the facts about the past don't always tell the same story; Americans did enslave people and did conquer countries, and American foreign policy has not always made the world a better place.

A group in Florida called the Florida Textbook Action Network, led by activist Sherri Krass, works to attempt to accomplish the same sorts of goals as the Texas school board through grassroots action. Under the moniker "Restoring Truth to History Class," Krass is working to organize activists to eliminate ideas that do not conform to her definition of American exceptionalism. She focuses on keeping exceptionalism in the classroom, and imperialism out, by reviewing improperly written textbooks.

The most unique example of connecting a political agenda to the teaching of the past is a series of videos written and produced by former Arkansas governor and 2008 presidential candidate Mike Huckabee. Huckabee cofounded a company called "Learn Our History" that creates videos about various events and periods in U.S. history. The website for the company proudly proclaims that the goal of the videos is to "recognize and celebrate faith, religion and the role of God in America's founding and making our country the greatest place on Earth." We again see that the roots of American exceptionalism for Huckabee derive from the incomplete historical understanding of the religion of the founders. Beyond this, Huckabee's key argument is the American exceptionalist idea of the "greatest place on earth." Such a declaration is an ahistorical argument in ignoring the complexity and facts of U.S. history.

In an editorial on the Investors.com website, Huckabee declares:

> Unlike the current presentation of our history as one of racism, sexism and imperialism, we seek to help our children and teachers understand who and what have made America the greatest country in the world.[34]

Imperialism is again erased from the American story, along with sexism and racism. Huckabee takes great pains, though, to insist that the history in his videos is the "true" history. He even goes so far as to include the following question in the site's frequently asked questions section: "What does it mean that Learn Our History is 'unbiased'?" The immediate answer is that "Learn Our History's products have been developed to correct the 'blame America first' attitude prevalent in today's teaching."[35] It is unclear how this eliminates bias, however, because Huckabee himself presents an unvarnished bias here, correcting what he believes to be a false liberal history by replacing it with the "correct" attitude towards America's past. And because the series is presented in a cartoon form, and the time travelers in the cartoon are theoretically observing the actual historical events, these videos do more than merely "promote" a particular viewpoint. As law professor R. B. Bernstein notes, "their actual effect, if they work at all, would be to *indoctrinate* children with a particular ideological flavor of American history."[36]

Mike Huckabee is not the only political figure to try to change the American history taught to children in this way. Callista Gingrich, third wife of Newt Gingrich, wrote a short series of children's books as part of what she calls her "campaign to educate kids about American history." Her goal, as she said in an interview with conservative talk-show host Sean Hannity, was "to be an introduction of our pivotal moments of history for young children ages four to eight. So they can appreciate the beauty of this nation and understand why we're so special." In case any of his audience was unclear about what this meant, Hannity rephrased the answer by saying that this is necessary because "some kids grow up and they have these professors that indoctrinate them," which leads to the unfortunate result: "they don't believe in American exceptionalism."[37] Callista Gingrich, like her husband Newt, writes and publishes books with the express purpose of advancing a specific version of the American past. As a children's book starring a cute and energetic elephant, the book itself is not a clear and present danger. Yet it is another example of a concerted effort to promote a specific American story that is purposefully devoid of the complexity and confusion that characterize any nation's past, including the American past.

A major target for the advocates of American exceptionalism is any curriculum that appears to be connected to teaching an understanding of other nations or that appears to put other nations on an equal footing with the United States. Janice Rogers Brown, a U.S. Appellate Court Justice and former California Supreme Court Justice, wrote eloquently about her firm belief in American exceptionalism in an article entitled "The Fortress Stone of American Exceptionalism" for the conservative Fund for American Studies. One of her arguments in this article is: "A brief reference to our nation's favorite superhero illustrates the point. If I asked any audience of people my age: 'What does Superman fight for?' the answer would come back almost reflexively, 'truth, justice and the American way!'"[38] According to Brown, unfortunately young people respond to that question with blank stares because Superman is now an "international hero," and the "American way" appears to be under attack in the international arena. To be clear, Brown does add complexity to her argument by raising a variety of problems associated with the historical record in the United States, not the least of which is racism and slavery. Her overall point, though, is still that the United States has always been the greatest nation on earth and that conclusion needs to be taught in the schools. Students need to learn the American way, and they need to know that way has always been the best. In the legal arena, that means rejecting legal precedents, doctrines, and thought from other nations, while in the educational arena it means being at least suspicious and being prepared to be hostile towards any "foreign" methods of teaching about history.

Many conservative educational advocates insist such a "foreign" method is the International Bacalaureate (IB) program. The IB program was originally created worldwide in 1968 to be an internationally accepted high standards high school age diploma program, where any student could attend any IB school in the world and receive the same high quality education. The standards, curriculum, and even the testing for the program are international in scope and acceptance. The program has become increasingly popular in the United States since the 1990s, and there are now more than 3,000 IB schools in over 140 countries throughout the world.[39] Originally loosely affiliated with the United Nations, the program is headquartered in Geneva, and therein lies the problem.

Beginning in the early twenty-first century, a movement began "in America to shut such programs down because their international orientation is considered socialist, anti-American, and anti-Christian."[40] Despite the fact that the program is nearly always voluntary in the schools in which it is offered, a few schools began to drop the program in the 2000s. A school in Pittsburgh dropped the program after parents complained that IB "rejects the Judeo-Christian values held by the majority of families in our district and instead promotes the atheist, Secular Humanist principles of multiculturalism, one-world government and moral relativism." Here we encounter at least two of the areas in U.S. history that so bother conservative educational activists: secular humanism and "one world government." The fear is that the children will learn that the U.S. should not stand up for its rights in the international arena, eschewing a muscular, independent, and exceptional policy towards the rest of the world, instead following the ideas of the UN.

EdWatch in Minnesota—the same EdWatch that supported the early campaigns of Michele Bachmann to teach the religion of the founding fathers and championed the teaching of free market capitalism in Minnesota schools—opposes the IB program on ideological grounds because it teaches "a sense of global citizenship which is contrary to what it is to be an American citizen."[41] A parent in Idaho led a protest against IB in the Couer d'Alene schools because "they want to change the way your child thinks, not feed your child's mind with information, and information about our history, heritage and why we believe what we believe."[42] This is quite an interesting statement, actually, because it reveals a misunderstanding of what the discipline of history needs to be. History needs to create new ways of thinking. History should not merely be fed to students, and students should not be ordered to believe in any certain way. This parent, apparently, believes that students should be ordered to think in a certain way, following the precepts of American exceptionalism.

EdWatch criticized the International Baccalaureate Organization (IBO) because the IBO promotes its curriculum as the "best possible curriculum," focusing on "beliefs and values it says are universal." EdWatch mocked this belief because IBO promotes its beliefs and values as "superior to the limited beliefs and values of the United States." The anti-IB manifesto from EdWatch continues by insisting that the IB "creed" is in direct opposition to the "American creed." In the view of EdWatch, then, the IBO refuses to adhere to the idea of American exceptionalism, and so International Baccaluareate must be rejected as a curriculum.[43]

Those opposed to the IB program have been successful in eliminating the program from a number of school districts across the country. In April of 2013 in Monticello, New York, a group calling itself "the truth about IB" helped eliminate the program because "IB is 'internationally-minded' indoctrination that distracts your children from their ABCs. IB attempts to instill what it claims are 'universal values' which may not be your family's values at all."[44] City Councilwoman Carolyn McClarty in Munroe Falls, Ohio is working to stop the IB program because it advances something she calls "Agenda 21," which promotes making "the Liberal-Progressive goal for one world education a potential reality" and is "sustainability indoctrination."[45] House Bill 1403 in New Hampshire in 2012 sought to prevent school districts from using education programs that "subject to the governance of a foreign body or organization," including IB, but the New Hampshire senate unanimously killed the bill.[46] In Utah, the anti-IB crusade reached the state senate, where Senator Margaret Dayton convinced the Senate Education Committee to reject funding for IB programs because "I'm opposed to the anti-American philosophy that's somehow woven into all the classes as they promote the U.N. agenda."[47] The list of politicians and anti-historians seeking to erase the IB program from the nation's schools is seemingly endless.

Other critics seek to eliminate the Model UN program from schools for similar reasons. Columnist and blogger Daniel Greenfield argues that schools should reject Model UN programs for putting Harry Truman on a mock trial, "Islamic indoctrination," and supporting global multilateralism.

Greenfield criticizes the program because "the Model UN program teaches American students that global government is better than national government."[48] In this view, American exceptionalism is ignored in favor of acceptance of some kind of international worldview, and American students should not be exposed to such a worldview.

Furthermore, the IB anti-historians seek to eliminate the IB program because they believe it portrays the United States as historically imperialist. For example, EdWatch argues, "The United States is treated as an 'imperialist' country by IB, of course, and is compared to Japan during World War II."[49] Again, EdWatch misses the point. The curriculum outlines the historical fact that the Japanese believed the United States to be imperialistic at the time. As we have seen, an important historical thinking skill is historical empathy. Students need to be encouraged to understand the mindsets of those in the past, even if those in the past might have had an incorrect interpretation.

One controversy in Texas in 2013 brings us back full circle to the opening concept in this chapter about the different meta-narratives of American history. Conservative activists in Texas, led by those we have met before such as Bill Ames, Barbara Cargill, and Rick Perry, uncovered what they believed to be the "smoking gun" of radical educational philosophy. They learned that many Texas schools, especially those in rural, poor school districts, utilized a Texas company called CSCOPE to create lesson plans and other curricular materials. One problem with this company was the strange cloak of secrecy that seemed to cover their actions. More alarming to the conservative activists, however, was the content of some of the lesson plans produced by CSCOPE, specifically one lesson plan about terrorism and the Boston Tea Party. Of course, the Boston Tea Party has significant symbolic resonance for conservative political activists, as they have taken the event as the symbol for their twenty-first century political resurgence. The Boston Tea Party is firmly entrenched as a centerpiece of the exceptionalist narrative of American history, the narrative of freedom, liberty, and equality introduced at the beginning of the chapter.

The problem with the CSCOPE lesson plan is that it attempted to challenge the meaning of the Boston Tea Party. As part of a lesson intended to promote thinking about the definition of terrorism, one of the CSCOPE lessons asked students to consider whether an event where a group of people disguising themselves and then illegally boarding ships and dumping the ship's cargo into the sea was a "terrorist act." The obvious reference to the Boston Tea Party caused a furor among conservative educational activists. Texas State Senator Larry Taylor said "he was especially disturbed by lessons that tried to equate the Boston Tea party to the 9-11 terrorists." Kyle Olson, whom we met earlier as a leading national conservative anti-historian, complained, "You know America's changing when leftists have even infiltrated Texas schools." Most tellingly, Senator Larry Taylor said, "They actually referred to it as a terrorist act... Throwing tea into the harbor is nowhere near a terrorist act. To have our kids even thinking that...."[50] His last phrase is the most telling: Kids "can't even think that." They can't think that because it challenges the fixed narrative of American history that conservative historians demand be taught in the schools.

CSCOPE was defended by rural school districts as an efficient way to provide their teachers with teaching ideas and lessons. "'It's built by teachers, designed by teachers and that's what's powerful about CSCOPE,' said Wade Lebay, director of state CSCOPE at the Region 13 Education Service Center in Austin." Dina Webb, director of curriculum in Lackland, Texas, agreed: "'For us, CSCOPE is a lifesaver.'"

Yet Lebay, Webb, and other educators had no chance in this fight. In the narrowly focused, simplistic rendering of the American story, terrorists are only bad guys. They appear at the end of the first timeline presented at the opening of the chapter as those who attack the American way. One can never, ever connect the good guys and the bad guys. In fact, this particular lesson is indeed problematic, as it violates the rules of the discipline of history because it oversimplifies and ignores historical context, but we will examine the failing of radical left-wing history in Chapter Five.

For now, however, we see the danger of the focused attack by conservative anti-historians on anything but America's "exceptional" history. The Texas Education Patriots, Kyle Olson, and conservative state senators won their battle, not only removing the offending lesson about the Tea Party but completely eliminating the CSCOPE curriculum company. Texas teachers no longer have access to these lessons. Where will they turn for help in shaping their curriculum? It is too early to tell, but it is very possible they will turn to curriculum prepared by the anti-historians of the right, curriculum that will shield them from attacks of the right. Shield them it may, but it will also deprive students of an ability to think for themselves and tease out for themselves the complexity of American history. Eliminating CSCOPE is only the most recent example of erasing any ideas or concepts disliked by right-wing anti-historians, opening the way for them to prevent a chance for students to "even think that."

CHAPTER 4

TEACHING AMERICA'S "GOLDEN AGE"

Source: Herb Block, *Washington Post*, April 24,
1949: A 1949 Herblock Cartoon, © The Herb Block
Foundation

The Memory Hole: The U.S. History Curriculum Under Siege, pages 65–86.
Copyright © 2014 by Information Age Publishing

This Herb Block political cartoon from 1949 illustrates brilliantly many of the themes highlighted in *The Memory Hole*. We see a nameless citizens' committee intruding in the school classroom, armed with the tools to change the curriculum. One prepares his scissors to eliminate from the map the offending letters "USSR," readying the evil acronym for history's dustbin. The State and Local Anti-subversives committee berates and interrogates the hapless teacher, clearly dictating to her what should and should not be taught. An anti-subversive kneels down to rifle through the garbage can, locating to his chagrin a radical (a wonderful little math joke from Block). Another even foreshadows the Texas school board controversy of 2010, as he suspiciously scrutinizes the visage of Thomas Jefferson, seemingly ready to pull the portrait off of the wall, erasing the enigmatic Jefferson from the potential gaze of the students.

The Block cartoon also serves as the perfect introduction to an entire era of American history, the 1950s, which some twenty-first century politicians, pundits, and educational "reformers" wish to re-invent. One of the many ironies of this cartoon is that for many years, this part of the 1950s seemed hidden behind a screen of nostalgia for an American "golden age." During the decade itself and for some years after, many Americans sought to portray the fifties as an era of American perfection, prosperity, happiness, and social calm. They touted the period as a model, especially with reference to the family and the ideology of "traditional family values." The era of *Leave it to Beaver* and *Father Knows Best* served as a guide for social and cultural perfection.

As the twentieth century progressed, cracks appeared in this vision of social perfection. Following in the wake of the civil rights movement, historians pushed to study the lives of the less powerful and disenfranchised and learned that life was far from perfect in the 1950s for African Americans, women, Hispanic Americans, gays, and the poor. Many attacked the perceived social conformity of the era, arguing that part of the problem was the Cold War push against dissidents.

There is often an ebb and flow in the study of different eras, and this is a fundamental part of the discipline of history. Different questions are asked, and often they are answered differently because new sources have been discovered. As we shall see, there is very good reason to add context and complexity to the study of the 1950s, moving beyond the one-dimensional caricature of the era as a "golden age." Some politicians, pundits, and "educators," however, seem to quite like this vision. They demand a return to teaching the 1950s as the era of social and cultural perfection. They are not doing this because of new questions or new sources. Instead, they are doing it because it fits their vision of a desired social order in the twenty-first century. Even today, as historian Susan Jacoby argues, "there are few more revealing indicators of any American's overall politics than his or her assessment of McCarthyism."[1] They ignore newly found sources and new interpretations merely because they do not accept conclusions that clash with their own political beliefs.

Those who wish to change the era's history have their sights set on a few specific targets as they attack the more contextualized history of the 1950s. Perhaps the main area of concern regards the role of women and the family, because the "family values" supposedly so central to the "golden age" remain centrally important for those who wish to retell the history of this era. One strategy they have hit upon to attack the entire feminist movement and to defend the family structure of the 1950s is to move Phyllis Schlafly into the pantheon of American heroes. This new hero and her goals purposefully ignore, as well as denigrate, much of the history of the era. In the telling of the history of the civil rights movement, they pursue the opposite tactic of eliminating the stories of important African American leaders such as Thurgood Marshall and Malcolm X.

We will begin by returning to the theme of the political cartoon that heads this chapter, with an examination of the movement in the 1950s to suppress dissent, symbolized by the meteoric career of Joseph McCarthy. One irony relating to the cartoon is that it was published in 1949, before McCarthy burst on the scene as the most energetic and rabid of the anti-subversives. One can find this cartoon, interestingly enough, online as part of a lesson that is designed to be used to teach about the growth of anti-subversion in the United States at the beginning of the Cold War.[2] The idea of the lesson is to point out that there was clearly a powerful movement afoot to root out non-conformist ideas a year before McCarthy took the spotlight. This primary source provides just one narrative that has become a central feature of the 1950s: the fear of the Cold War penetrated deeply into American society, causing an overreaction of anti-communist fever. McCarthy's attacks were also attacks on "liberals" and the New Deal. As the *Chicago Tribune* put it in an editorial after accused radical Alger Hiss was found guilty, "the guilt is collective...and spreads over the New Deal, which sponsored and protected this monstrous conspiracy against America."[3]

Joseph McCarthy was merely the loudest of a series of politicians who took advantage of this fear and desire to tarnish the New Deal (Richard Nixon is one who became even more prominent). McCarthy whipped up hysteria to epic proportions, leading harmful attacks on thousands of innocent citizens. Those who wish to retell America's history for their own political purposes seek to toss out this narrative about McCarthy and completely replace it with a narrative McCarthy himself could have written: McCarthy was right all along; he correctly identified anti-American communist agents and should be a hero, rather than a villain, of the 1950s story.

Starring in the crusade to resurrect Joseph McCarthy as the defender of true American values is the conservative polemicist Ann Coulter. McCarthy plays the central role in her book *Treason: Liberal Treachery from the Cold War to the War on Terrorism* as the "indispensable man" in the America of the 1950s. Coulter's core argument is contained in a diatribe attacking liberals and defending McCarthy found near the start of the book:

> The portrayal of Senator Joe McCarthy as a wild-eyed demagogue destroying innocent lives is sheer liberal hobgoblinism. Liberals weren't cowering in fear during the McCarthy era. They were systematically undermining the nation's ability to defend itself while waging a bellicose campaign of lies to blacken McCarthy's name. Everything you think you know about McCarthy is a hegemonic lie. Liberals denounced McCarthy because they were afraid of getting caught, so they fought back like animals to hide their own collaboration with a regime as evil as the Nazis.[4]

Coulter's purpose in writing about McCarthy, anti-communism, and the 1950s is clear: she wants to connect the treasonous liberals of this era with the treasonous liberals of the twenty-first century. As she said in an online essay in 2007,

> The McCarthy period is the Rosetta stone of all liberal lies. It is the textbook on how they rewrite history—the sound chamber of liberal denunciations, their phony victimhood as they demean and oppress their enemies, their false imputation of dishonesty to their opponents...."[5]

She has no desire to tease out a complex truth about the past. Instead, she tosses nuance, thoughtful analysis, and an accurate examination of the evidence down the memory hole to make her shrill and eye catching point about liberals for the past half century.

Coulter has had a staggering impact on the thinking of talk show hosts and politicians. Glenn Beck devoted almost half a dozen of his television shows to defending McCarthy, arguing that he was correct all along. Beck claims, "everything that McCarthy said was right" and that the "best thing to ever happen to communism was Joseph McCarthy and the Red Scare."[6] Beck's purpose in digging into the history of the 1950s was to provide a direct link between the communists uncovered by McCarthy and supporters of President Barack Obama in 2010. Michele Bachmann picked up on this theme:

> If we look at the collection of friends that Barack Obama has had in his life, it calls into question what Barack Obama's true beliefs and values and thoughts are. His attitudes, values, and beliefs with Jeremiah Wright on his view of the United States...is negative; Bill Ayers, his negative view of the United States.[7]

Bachmann followed this argument with a call to reprise the House Un-American Activities Committee (HUAC) to examine to what extent Obama and "certain congressmen" were or were not anti-American. This is a case of real history potentially repeating itself, all in the name of incomplete and oversimplified history. Bachmann was joined in the House by one of her best friends, Iowa Representative Steve King, who proclaimed proudly Joseph McCarthy as a "great American hero" when accused of attempting to bring back McCarthy-style witch-hunts of the 1950s.[8]

What supporting evidence does Coulter use to support her contention about the heroic Joseph McCarthy and the need to re-invent history and rehabilitate his reputation? The story becomes complicated at this point because, in fact, Coulter claims to make use of a cache of primary source documents and secondary source monographs from credentialed historians in order to prove her point. The entire case of Coulter, Beck, Bachmann, and others rests on a set of documents from 1942–1946 decoded and declassified in 1996 and now known as the "Venona papers." The Venona Project is the last known code name for a secret code breaking operation undertaken by the United States and the United Kingdom during World War II and, to a lesser extent, the years just after the war. The U.S. and UK intercepted and decoded thousands of messages sent by Soviet intelligence to agents in the United States. Only a relatively small percentage of the papers have been decoded and published. Most of the messages are incomplete and indecipherable. What do these papers tell us? They do show that there were Soviet spies in the United States, and that many of these spies were or had been members of the American Communist Party. However, most of the messages are so incomplete that it is rarely clear whether the messages refer to actual Soviet agents or merely individuals the Soviets wanted to contact. Importantly, none of the decoded messages to date implicate any of those branded by McCarthy as Soviet agents, because the papers deal with the 1942–1946 period, not the post-World War II, early Cold War era.

What do the Venona papers "prove" about anti-Communism in general and the actions of HUAC in particular?[9] Nothing. Some historians have argued that Venona conclusively proves HUAC was right all along in their attacks on communists, although none of the scholars defend McCarthy or his actions; the leading scholars arguing this are John Earl Haynes and Harvey Klehr. Both had written extensively about communist infiltration of the U.S. government before the release of the Venona papers. In their post-Venona collaborative book, *Venona: Decoding Soviet Espionage in America*, Haynes and Klehr argue that the newly released sources prove the depth and malevolence of Soviet intentions in the United States as well as the fundamental disloyalty of American communists. It is clearly this book, and the arguments of other scholars such as Ronald Radosh, Herbert Romerstein, and Joshua Muravchik, that Coulter and others lean on in insisting that the story of McCarthy and anti-communism in the late 1940s and early 1950s be retold. It is no accident that Haynes and Klehr have written scathing attacks on "liberal historians" and have argued for years that the liberal, or even radical, "establishment" of historians have shut them out of discourse on McCarthyism.

Interestingly, even the historians who place emphasis on the belief that the Venona papers prove significant Soviet infiltration of the American government in the mid 1940s caution against using this same evidence to exonerate McCarthy. At the wonderfully named "Raleigh Spy Conference" in 2005, Harvey Klehr gave a speech entitled "Was Joe McCarthy Right?" He began describing the Venona Project and then argued that the intercepted cables show that a significant number (dozens, perhaps in the low hundreds) of Americans served as Soviet spies during World War II, including both Alger Hiss and Julius (but probably not Ethel) Rosenberg. Yet his answer to the main question of his speech is that not only was McCarthy wrong, he was "wildly wrong." He continued by discrediting McCarthy in the strongest terms possible:

> Many of his claims were wildly inaccurate; his charges filled with errors of fact, misjudgments of organizations and innuendoes disguised as evidence. He failed to recognize or understand the differences among genuine liberals, fellow-traveling liberals, Communist dupes, Communists and spies—distinctions that were important to make. The new information from Russian and American archives does not vindicate McCarthy. He remains a demagogue, whose wild charges actually made the fight against Communist subversion more difficult.[10]

Klehr emphasizes the complexity of the situation and criticizes McCarthy precisely because of his oversimplification. As self-described liberal historian Susan Jacoby puts it, Klehr and Haynes make a "careful distinction between what they describe as legitimate efforts to protect government secrets from Communist espionage" and the bloviating anti-New Deal, anti-liberal smear tactics pursued by McCarthy.[11]

Other historians debated the value and conclusions to be drawn from the Venona papers long before Klehr gave this speech. Most famously, Ellen Schrecker, perhaps the most prolific long-term scholar of McCarthyism and anti-communism in the United States, rejects the conclusions reached by scholars such as Haynes and Klehr. Schrecker disputes neither the documents nor the specific examples of American communists acting as Soviet spies. She maintains, for example, that most historians accept that the new evidence points to the guilt of Julius Rosenberg. She also points out that so far, the Venona papers have only implicated about 100 people in the United States as one form or another of Soviet spy (Haynes and Klehr argue that the number was just over 300). Schrecker argues further that historians cannot, and should not, move on to the further conclusion that all American communists were inherently evil or that the actions of McCarthy and HUAC were defensible. As she states:

[Their] simplistic, black-and-white approach is profoundly ahistorical. Not only does it ignore years of serious scholarship; it also denies the complex reality of human activity in which, for example, the nation's founding fathers can create a framework for democratic freedom while, at the same time, holding nearly a million fellow beings in bondage.[12]

Shrecker centers this statement on the idea of the "ahistorical" nature of an argument. This is precisely correct: those who defend McCarthy and insist that the Venona papers prove that he was correct ignore the rules of doing history. In this case, they ignore "years of serious scholarship," but as we have seen, this is common for those who wish to re-invent the history of an era. They believe that since historians are elitist, they need to be ignored. They also ignore complexity, another common trait of those who are re-inventing the past.

This historiographical debate points to the fundamental flaw of the structure and basis of the entire Texas Standards document and of the understanding that too many have about history education. The standard connected to McCarthy requires students to "describe" that the findings of HUAC were confirmed by the Venona papers. Yet we don't actually know that. Historians are still arguing about the meaning of Venona and the relationship to the findings of HUAC. How can we require that students "describe" only one side of an argument, and that their description is the definitive history? A sole reliance on one set of primary sources is a sin very few historians would commit, because such a dependency ignores both issues of context and questions of reliability inherent in all primary sources. Historians are trained to examine point of view and the milieu of the time in which a document is created in order to ascertain the extent to which the document might be trusted. This case is even more problematic, because the Venona documents were created by the KGB and other Soviet intelligence services at the height of the double-crossing, secretive, and distrustful Cold War competition. Or, as Susan Jacoby puts it, "The problem with...an absolute reliance on the Venona files, is that to consider [them] credible, you must accept the assumption that movement of spies and their handlers are accurately reflected in documents compiled by spies and their handlers."[13]

At the very least, what we see here is another historical controversy. However, many politicians, pundits, and education policy makers followed the lead of Coulter, Bachmann, and others and decided that the story of Joseph McCarthy and anti-communism in the 1950s must be retold. According to Phyllis Schlafly, herself a historical figure who first became significant in the 1950s,

In the early 1950s, Joe McCarthy was one of the most popular men in America. Average U.S. citizens recognized him as Horatio at the Bridge battling against our nation's sworn enemies, the Soviet Communists. McCarthy understood, long before Reagan, that the Soviet Union was an evil empire, one of whose strategies was to infiltrate agents into our government in order to guide our policy to favor Communist goals.[14]

This is exactly the line followed by Don McLeroy and the Texas school board. In early discussions of the standards, McLeroy told the curriculum writers to "read the latest on McCarthy—he was basically vindicated."[15] McCarthy is only vindicated if Coulter's rantings stand as the guidepost to the history of this period. Even the tone and wording of McLeroy's admonition conflict with the central tenets of the historical method. History should not seek vindication, and the pursuit of an understanding of the past should not be a single-minded attempt to locate such vindication.

Historians and history teachers cannot move from the existence of the Venona papers to a conclusion that the actions of HUAC were correct and that students need to be able to describe the fact that HUAC was correct on future Texas assessments. But McLeroy, as we have seen, is not a historian, but a politician who holds a single-minded worldview that he sought to impose on the students of Texas in the standards writing process. In a speech to an explicitly conservative educational forum, McLeroy proclaimed proudly that "it is the conservatives who stand on the moral high ground" and that he and five other conservative school board members created standards unappealing to the "leftist mind." Continuing, McLeroy highlights his "Venona standard," declaring in underlined, highlighted, and italicized text that "we touched the Holy Grail of leftism on this one."[16] His motivation is clearly political, without even much of an attempt to pretend to be following the ideals of history as a discipline. McLeroy believes that to vindicate McCarthy is to vindicate the conservative right, proving to all the fundamental truth of his beliefs.

How has a political demagogue and a historical controversy from more than half a century ago become fundamental to the twenty-first century political debate? In part, the controversy over the dangers of communism have always been central in the conservative mind. McLeroy, Coulter, Beck, and others seek to return to the first principles of their ideology, and, interestingly, they choose to do so by once again relying on the writings of W. Cleon Skousen. Before writing and speaking on the religiosity of the founding fathers, Skousen made a name for himself as a rabidly anti-communist writer and lecturer. His book *The Naked Communist*, published in 1958, outlines a set of principles that Skousen claimed were the goals of communism. His credibility derived from stints as an FBI agent and police chief in Salt Lake City. Skousen claimed, among other things, that communists sought to "discredit the founding fathers by presenting them as selfish aristocrats who had no concern for the 'common man'" and to "belittle all forms of American culture and discourage the teaching of American history on the ground that it was only a minor part of the 'big picture,'" giving "more emphasis to Russian history since the Communists took over." Communists also worked to "support any socialist movement to give centralized control over any part of the culture—education, social agencies, welfare programs, mental health clinics." In Skousen's world, all liberal goals and all progressive politicians become communist enemies of the states. This is a black and white world, an either-or world, a world with no complexity, ambiguity, and very little connection to evidence. In other words, it is an ahistorical world.

A conservative minister named David Noebel of Summit Ministries appeared on Phyllis Shlafley's radio show in January 2012 and declared:

> If you read the *Communist Manifesto*, written in 1848, Marx and Engels come out with no God, no private property, no family—traditional family—no inheritance, graduated income tax, etcetera, etcetera, etcetera. In fact, if you read the ten planks of the *Communist Manifesto*, you'll be surprised at how we have nearly moved into every one of those areas. And later on, about 1958, Cleon Skousen came out with a book called *The Naked Communist*, and he listed 45 goals in 1958 of the communists and today we have nearly fulfilled every one of them.[17]

Shlafley and Noebel continue the discussion with a caller into the program by bemoaning that McCarthy is no longer being taught in schools in the correct fashion. McCarthy should be taught as a hero, rather than being "demonized" as a villain.

Skousen and his claims might easily be dismissed as relics from a bygone era if they had not re-emerged recently as a political rallying point. In fact, Skousen's anti-communist ideas seem to have as much currency in the Tea Party movement as his ideas on the religion of the founding fathers encountered in Chapter One. The ideas of Oak Norton, a Tea Party leader and educational activist from Utah, provide a case in point. Norton's extensive website and blog are littered with Skousen citations, but the clearest connections surface in a presentation he prepared for the Utah legislature entitled "planned illiteracy." In this document, Norton attacks a number of perceived problems of Utah education, yet a central object of his attack is the Utah standard that asks the students to study the impact of McCarthyism. Norton's response is to cite the Texas Venona Standard, implying, of course, McCarthy's vindication. Left unexamined is the fact that regardless of the extent to which McCarthy was or was not correct, one cannot deny the historical impact of the controversy over McCarthy and his actions. It is clear that Norton is not really concerned about students learning history; Norton is concerned about the evils of communism. Earlier in the document, Norton includes a slide that outlines the differences between communism and the American republic, with information culled directly from

Skousen. His argument is clearly that any deviation from his desired path towards good education is communist inspired.[18]

So how should Texas have handled this issue, and how might teachers in other states integrate the Venona papers into their lessons on the early Cold War? The Venona papers should be examined by students. First, they are fun and engaging; students love reading about decoded intercepts and the secret world of spies.[19] Second, whenever we get a chance to use primary sources in the classroom, we should do it. History needs to be about studying the actual records of the past. Yet studying these records devoid of context is ahistorical and potentially harmful. Students need to be encouraged to ask questions about the role of these papers in the context of the times, instead of being ordered to "describe" a particular version of the past. Students could be encouraged to discuss and engage some of the following questions:

- To what extent do the Venona papers reflect Soviet infiltration of the American Communist party?
- How do the Venona papers relate to the anti-communist actions taken by McCarthy and HUAC in the late 1940s and early 1950s?
- The findings of the Venona Project were highly confidential...neither Harry Truman nor the CIA was even aware of their existence until 1953 (and neither McCarthy nor HUAC knew about them). In what ways should the twenty-first century knowledge of the Venona papers change our understanding of actions taken in the 1950s by people unaware of the existence of Venona?

The case of the Venona Standard illustrates exactly why historians and history teachers, and not ideologically driven politicians, should write history standards. It appears as if Don McLeroy merely read some of the writings by Haynes and Klehr, was sympathetic to their attack on liberal academia, and so decided independently to include this new requirement for hundreds of thousands of future Texas students. This ignores the contentious historiography and the complexity of the issue. Oversimplification led to blacklists, the squelching of thought, and the overwrought and inaccurate attacks of Joseph McCarthy. We need to avoid such oversimplification, and we need to strive to teach students how to wrestle with contentious issues rather than asking them to memorize an oversimplified and incomplete story of the past.

McLeroy and the Texas school board followed the lead of conservative textbook writers in their crusade to rehabilitate McCarthy in the secondary school classroom. *Heritage of Freedom* argues that "*McCarthy's conclusions, although technically unprovable, were drawn from the accumulation of undisputed facts*" (emphasis in original). So even though no one can prove McCarthy to be correct, since he used facts, he must have been correct. Left unsaid is what, exactly, these facts were. This book then defends McCarthy because of the fact that "left-wing liberals" did, indeed, infiltrate the government in the 1950s. This, of course, is true, since both left-wing liberals and right-wing conservatives serve in the government at any given time. Left unexamined is the question about what the crime is with liberals in the government. The McCarthy section concludes with a brief discussion of his methods, which were "not always the wisest," and criticism of his "sarcastic tone," leaving the impression that the whole affair was a minimally important unresolved controversy.[20]

In their textbook *A Patriot's History of the United States*, historians Larry Schweikert and Michael Allen are more subtle in their defense of McCarthy. The textbook admits some of McCarthy's failings, pointing out in one sentence that he was "given to both overdrinking and overwork." Yet in the very same sentence, the book defends McCarthy as one who had a "strong record on Civil Rights and support of Wisconsin's farmers." The book admits that "McCarthyism subsequently became a term synonymous with repression and terror—an amazing development considering that not one of the people subpoenaed by the senator to testify lacked legal counsel..." *Patriot's History* concludes that McCarthy's investigations *underestimated* the problem, basing this conclusion on the Venona Project evidence. The subtlety of this text fails to mask its overly simplistic conclusions, conclusions it seeks to impart on the nation's secondary school students.[21]

The new narrative of the 1950s is much, much broader than the rehabilitation of Joseph McCarthy. Those who wish to re-invent history wish to return to a narrative that presents the entire 1950s as an idyllic time, a mythical golden age of American values and moral rectitude. In this story, McCarthy defends traditional American ideas and values, and is only occasionally criticized for his methods that crossed the lines of decency in this well ordered world. At the heart of this narrative is the perfect American nuclear family of the 1950s, with dad at work, mom at home, and the kids living safely in the cocoon of American family values. Although this image flies in the face of the historical record of the time, it is the image of the 1950s that some want to reinsert into America's classrooms.

This idyllic domestic world of the 1950s needs to exist to complete the story of the fight against radical communism. According to conservative textbook author Larry Schweikart, looming issues such as the "threat of atomic annihilation" forced Americans to "crave stability and reliability in other areas of their lives. They found comfortable reassurance in housing (Levittown), fast food chains (McDonalds), motels (Holiday Inns), and even in the explosion of AM radio...." So they created a morally upright culture to contrast with uncomfortable enemy culture.[22] Or, to put it another way, "Fear of communism, socialism, and progressivism forced many mothers to educate themselves on popular topics and spurred them to become involved in Parent Teacher Associations (PTA) and political organizations to protect their children's vulnerable minds from radical ideas."[23] In the world imagined by these re-tellers of the past, Americans clung to conservative values to protect the nation and in so doing created a society and culture that can serve as a model for future American generations. As one conservative blogger phrases it, "There is a stark difference in teachings here; and undoubtedly, the 1950s taught morals that were generally better than those taught today."[24]

As with the other topics examined in this book, conservative politicians and pundits believe in this version of the 1950s and consistently refer to it as part of their worldview. Rick Santorum, 2012 Republican presidential candidate, phrased it this way during an online interview with the *Washington Post*:

> One more point: growing up in the 1950s and 1960s was far different from growing up in this decade. The culture, the neighborhoods, the values that were being fed through the popular culture and the educational establishments were far different from now. The world was different and far more nurturing to families. Can you imagine a show today entitled *Father Knows Best?* It's a culture that undermines the family as opposed to a culture that supported the family.[25]

For Santorum, *Father Knows Best* represents a true depiction, rather than merely being one cultural artifact from the era.

The women who compose the conservative blog that call themselves the Network of Enlightened Women would agree. This group argues that the 1950s was a time to admire because it is when

> conservative women placed an emphasis on traditional family values while embracing conventional roles of women in the private sphere and expanding on them in the public sphere. Rather than focusing on gender roles and anti-male sentiment, conservatives turned their attention to protecting the future of the nation, the education of their children.[26]

Perhaps the most significant political figure espousing this view of the 1950s is a person who was herself a significant historical figure from the 1950s and 1960s, Phyllis Schlafly. Schlafly cites a different 1950s sitcom, *Ozzie and Harriet*, in a blistering attack on any who see the history of the 1950s in a different light than she sees it:

> The feminist movement started its attack on traditional marriage with Betty Friedan's 1963 book, which urged wives to leave their homes (called a "comfortable concentration camp"), join the workforce, and become independent of men. *Ozzie and Harriet*, a traditional-couple sitcom of the 1950s, became an epithet, and it became *de rigueur* to speak of different kinds of "families" instead of "family." *Wikipedia* now considers the traditional family a relic of

the 1950s and defines it as "usually considered conservative or reactionary by its critics who argue that it is limited, outmoded and unproductive in modern Western society."[27]

In fact, no single individual better exemplifies both a model of the image and a leader of those who want a return to this image than Phyllis Schlafly. Called by the right leaning *Washington Times* the "conservatives first lady" and "arguably the most important woman in American political history," Schlafly began her political career during the 1950s.[28] Ironically, she earned a law degree and helped to raise six children in the 1950s, in fact belying the typical stereotype (for which she became the leading defender) of the 1950s stay-at-home mom. It is no accident that her first political role was as a virulently anti-communist defender of McCarthy and opponent of anything she believed radical in the United States. After rising to political prominence in local Republican circles, she made a national splash in 1964, authoring a political pamphlet in support of Barry Goldwater entitled "A Choice, Not an Echo." She built on this national following by becoming the leader of the successful national movement in opposition to the Equal Right Amendment in the 1960s and 1970s, and she has been recognized as a powerful and significant leader of conservative causes ever since.

Schlafly's main line of argument is that the "traditional" American family needs to be defended at all costs. Fundamental to her vision of this family is a mother who stays at home to serve as the backbone of the nuclear American family. For Schlafly, the ultimate enemies are "feminists," which she appears to define as anyone who has a different view of the role of American women and a different view of a successful American family. She attacks the "women's liberation movement" for its support of "unilateral divorce" and argues that feminists are "at war with Mother Nature."[29] It is a critically important part of this worldview that the family image of the 1950s is upheld as the model image for American family life. According to Schlafly,

> The *NY Times* liberals seek to destroy the American family of the 1950s, as symbolized by *Ozzie and Harriet.* The TV characters were happy, self-sufficient, autonomous, law-abiding, honorable, patriotic, hard-working, and otherwise embodied qualities that made America great. In other words, the show promoted values that *NY Times* liberals despise.[30]

This is the world of the 1950s that Schlafly thinks is critical to teach to America's schoolchildren.

She obviously has a political motive, as she continues by stating, "the USA is being transformed by immigrants who do not share those values, and who have high rates of illiteracy, illegitimacy, and gang crime, and they will vote Democrat when the Democrats promise them more food stamps." Children should be taught in schools that the United States in the 1950s was a homogeneous, White, honorable society, and this contrasts with her view of a twenty-first century culture in disarray.

Don McLeroy and the Texas school board certainly had this in mind when they decided to include Phyllis Schlafly as a name for students to memorize in the study of post-World War II America. In a somewhat odd but telling anachronism, the Texas school board places Schlafly as an important name to know in the study of the 1980s and 1990s. Yet, as we have seen, Schlafly is important in symbolizing the life and role of American women in the 1950s. Her work is also historically important because of her lead role in the fight against the ERA in the 1970s. Whether or not she represents one of the *most* important Americans of the 1950s or the 1970s, one can make the case about her importance in those eras. But why is she included in the section on the "conservative resurgence" of the 1980s? It is because political leaders of the twenty-first century categorize her with Ronald Reagan and a set of particular political views I will discuss in the final chapter of this book. In essence, however, McElroy and the re-inventors of the past believe Schlafly symbolizes a golden age for Americans and the American family. To tell her story is to tell about a woman who prioritizes values that they consider traditional American values. To tell the story of the 1950s using Schlafly as the example makes the 1950s a model era of family morals and values.

This may be the image that Schlafly and McElroy remember from the 1950s, but it is not an image that conforms to reality. Conservatives extol the values of the 1950s as quintessential American family values, and claim that Americans' "most powerful visions of traditional families derive from images that are still delivered to our homes in countless reruns of 1950s television sit-coms."[31] In reality, however, the roles and trends depicted in these sitcoms were "qualitatively new" in the 1950s, a new invention that were, in fact, a "historical fluke."[32] The "traditional" American family of the pre-1950s had a different size, different roles, and different values. And, as it turns out, most actual families of the 1950s also differed from those depicted in *Ozzie and Harriet* and *Father Knows Best.* For example, almost all African Americans were excluded from the comforts of middle class life depicted in the 1950s sitcoms by "systematized legal segregation and…consistent brutality" in the South.[33] Some women experienced electric shock treatments in order to accept the domestic roles they were being fit into, and "beneath the polished facades of many 'ideal' families, suburban as well as urban, was violence, terror, or simply grinding misery."[34] Teen pregnancy rates of the 1950s were almost double those in the 1980s, belying the notion that this was an era of sexual purity and abstinence. The 1950s was, in many respects, a troubled and turbulent time, just as many other eras in American history.

Reuters blogger Jack Shafer summed up this problem best in a blog regarding the presidential campaign of 2012. Shafer points out that

> the Republican campaign ad imagery and its language of "renewal," popular since the Age of Reagan, concentrates on tree-lined streets and carefree kids riding their bikes, church socials, pickup baseball games, sunny days, and smiling snowmen. It's no coincidence that Newt Gingrich and Mitt Romney spent some of their teen years in this imagined utopia.[35]

Shafer rightly connects this re-invention of a utopian 1950s with politics, because the biggest difficulty with this imagined era is that it is reimagined in the service of politics. Because of this, students are cheated out of learning about important aspects of the time, all in order to serve a political ideology:

> This idealization of the 1950s persists because few who invoke the decade bother to remember it correctly. Yes, it was a wonderful decade for some, but it doesn't take a McGovernite to point out that Jim Crow, segregation, Little Rock, and the mistreatment of women and homosexuals should strike those years from the utopia registry.

The 1950s does not deserve any special note as a "golden age" of family values and domestic tranquility. It should be taught in all its confusion and contradiction, rather than an idyll to be blindly admired by students in the history classroom.

One significant actual change of the 1950s that should not be ignored when teaching about the decade is the growth in suburbanization and the national demographic move to the south and west. Suburban communities around Atlanta, Dallas, Houston, Phoenix, San Diego and especially Orange County, California boomed after World War II, spurred on by technological advances (especially the advent of home and office air conditioning and the invention of the "tract" home) and government policies such as the GI Bill, the interstate highway system, and the huge growth in defense contractors.

Yet these changes did not create a utopia: the results of this growth were varied and complex. For example, the building of huge suburban tract developments exacerbated racial tensions and caused a backlash against those African Americans who wanted to take advantage of the less expensive and comfortable new form of housing. Redlining, the practice of denying non-Whites the opportunity to purchase houses in all-White neighborhoods, was both the practice and the rule in the newly developing suburbs of both the north and the south. From the case of Henry Clark, an African American veteran who tried to move into a neighborhood in Cicero, Illinois and had his furniture set on fire, to the story of the middle class Myers family, who faced down mob violence in an attempt to move into a home in Levittown,

Pennsylvania, it is clear that the suburbs of the 1950s were for Whites only.[36] Levittown was the very symbol of the 1950s suburb, the ultimate example of the modern tract home, sporting all of the conveniences and family values so lauded by conservative anti-historians. Yet, according to an editorial in a Philadelphia newspaper in 1957, "Levittown was conceived and built as an all-white community by William Levitt without any concern of the social implications involved. From the beginning all Negro applicants were turned down on the sole basis of color."[37] Only lawsuits and new government rules integrated these suburbs as the 1950s came to a close.

In many suburbs, a backlash against such government interference and in defense of "individual rights" grew into a strong exclusionary and anti-government ideology. This happened most famously in Orange County, where many residents railed against "government-sponsored 'collectivism,' the erosion of traditionalist values, and a growing communist threat."[38] Interestingly, and not accidentally, this is the very same movement that spawned many of the very people who wish to retell the history of the 1950s as a golden age of American morality and decency.

Phyllis Schlafly believes that children should be taught that "women's magazines of the 1950s and 1960s were helpful and hopeful."[39] This is a belief that is at the minimum debatable, if not clearly dubious. Nancy Walker, editor of a collection of articles from women's magazines of the 1940s and 1950s, points out "the very existence of mass-circulation periodicals designed largely to instruct women in their appearance, duties, and values reveals fundamental differences between attitudes toward female and male gender roles."[40] By necessity, the magazines "promoted the status quo," a status quo that many at the time questioned, yet a status quo that Schlafly insists be taught as a desired status quo in the twenty-first century.[41] Reading these magazines as primary sources "opens a window on this period of history that no other single source can provide." Yet this window often reveals women struggling with a society cut in two by gender roles that many failed to see as either "helpful " or "hopeful."[42]

Perhaps the most surprising sleight of hand by those who want to re-invent the history of the 1950s is the attempt to re-teach the history of the civil rights movement. Teachers focus their attention regarding this era on the civil rights movement, from President Truman's order to desegregate the army in 1949, which often marks the beginning of what historians consider to be the "1950s," to Martin Luther King Jr.'s " I have a dream" speech at the March on Washington in 1963, which, along with the Kennedy assassination, serves as the endpoint of the era. With the *Brown v. Board* decision of 1954 as the centerpiece, strong history teachers introduce their students to the critical concepts and struggles of the movement. Civil rights has become such a hallmark topic that it would be nearly impossible to completely re-invent or eliminate it, as conservative politicians and educational pundits seek to do with McCarthyism and the social structure of the era.

Instead, they have been working to shift the narrative by accepting only part of the story. According to the narrative of the re-inventors of history, Martin Luther King, Jr. crusades only for individual rights, while ignoring the problems of class in America; other leaders and groups, most notably Thurgood Marshall, are completely erased from the historical landscape. It is this quite literally whitewashed narrative that the re-inventors seek to foist on schools, once again eliminating a complex, contested, yet fascinating and informative story.

One of the leading figures in this attempt to retell the story of the movement is Glenn Beck, who argues that the story needs to be retold because "We can't change our history into something it wasn't, but it's happening. We've got to grab on to the truth and cling to it."[43] Beck continues, insisting "the truth about the Civil Rights movement isn't the Black Panthers and the threats causing Congress to pass the Civil Rights, that's bull crap [um, yes]." In part, he is of course correct. The Black Panther Party did not exist in 1964, when civil rights legislation was passed. His point, I think, is that Black radicalism had nothing to do with the civil rights movement and, therefore, should not be taught as part of the story.

This ignores the very radical nature of much of the movement, exemplified by everything from the Student Nonviolent Coordinating Committee and sit-ins beginning in the late 1950s to the protests of the Mississippi Freedom Democratic Party in 1964. Ignoring the radical nature of part of the civil rights movement is his goal. For Beck, civil rights change occurred only because "God did it, by through working through people and inspiring people like Martin Luther King, and C. L. Jackson, and, yes, white people like Bobby Kennedy, and dare I say it, I'm going to set the world on fire with this...Roger Ailes." Here is a story that the re-inventors of history are comfortable with: God (not radicals) helped change American racial relations, and some leaders, especially Martin Luther King, are acceptable to teach about because of their undeniable Christian credentials. But we see how far Beck stretches credulity when he claims that Ailes (later the mastermind of the conservative *Fox News*) was central to the passage of civil rights legislation, as his job in 1964 and 1965 was as a production assistant on *The Mike Douglas Show*. Perhaps it is possible that Beck is trying to take a longer view and connect Ailes to the policies of Richard Nixon, but then, of course, one also needs to bring the Black Panthers back into the narrative. The important point is that Beck's story, which is the story the re-inventors of history wish to put into America's classrooms, is a story that seeks to eliminate some undeniably important aspects of the movement while adding individuals who had little to no connection with the movement. Down is up, and up is down.

Beck brought his new narrative to a national stage in an event he organized in Washington, D.C. for August, 28, 2010 called the "Restoring Honor" rally. This rally fit his overall strategy for re-inventing history: "I told you this summer that we are going to concentrate on restoring history. The history of our nation, the founding, the twentieth century, the Depression era, um, and the Civil Rights Movement, which has been co-opted by progressives."[44] He chose as the site for this rally the Lincoln memorial and held it in August for the express purpose of connecting himself and his ideas to the ideas of Martin Luther King and the celebrated March on Washington on August 28, 1963.

One of the featured speakers was even Alveda King, Martin Luther King, Jr.'s niece. The attendance for the event was very large, even "enormous" in the words of the *New York Times*, although exact estimates vary widely, from a low of just under 100,000 to a high of half a million. Regardless of the exact number, there is no question that Beck was able to teach a large number of Americans his new view of the place of the civil rights movement in American history. One attendee who had attended earlier speeches phrased it this way: "I have learned more from Glenn Beck—learned more about American history and government, from Glenn Beck—than in the previous 40 years of my life."[45] Glenn Beck is comfortable with the King that did indeed call for a rededication to inalienable individual American rights, and this is the King he wished to teach people about in his "Restoring Honor" rally.

However, as best phrased by reporter Will Bunch, "The only problem is that what they're learning is bunk. It's not history as it happened, but rather a Beck-scripted, Tea Party rewrite of history that demonizes Obama, Democrats and progressive activists."[46] Beck and the other re-inventors of this history focus only on King, and the King they focus on is an incomplete King. Most significantly, they miss the important fact that King was striving for both economic and political equality, and he was doing so by attempting to enlist government aid in doing so. In fact, the formal title for the March on Washington was the "March on Washington for Jobs and Freedom."

King and other speakers dreamed up the event to put pressure on, yes, to even threaten the government in an attempt to force its hand to change the political and economic lives of African Americans. As John Nichols states in *The Nation*, "Beck's attempt to associate himself with the Rev. Martin Luther King Jr., a radical critic of not just racism but of an economic system left tens of millions in poverty, would be comic if it was not so sad."[47] Beck's crusade rankles none more than the community of civil rights historians. Gabriel Winant, then a graduate student in history at Yale, argued in a guest column on Salom.com "It's hard to imagine a more up-is-down, freedom-is-slavery rendition of American history. Because if the struggle for racial equality under the law was anything, it was radical."[48] Winant maintains that the civil rights movement had been "radical" since its inception, citing as one example the leadership exercised by the Communist Party in defending the African American "Scottsboro boys" in the 1930s because no one else would.

Winant draws inspiration from a seminal article entitled "The Long Civil Rights Movement," written in 2005 by the then president of the Organization of American Historians, Jacquelyn Dowd Hall. She chastises conservatives in 2005 for their search for a palatable, non-radical civil rights movement to teach about. She rightly finds the motivation for the re-inventing of civil rights history in contemporary politics, noting that "Like all bids for discursive and political power, this one required the warrant of the past and the dominant narrative of the civil rights movement was ready at hand."[49] This narrative focused only on the goal of King and others to eliminate racial classifications and end segregation. Yet Hall points out that the goals of the movement were much larger than that, as the re-inventors of history changed the narrative for their own purposes and "ignored the complexity and dynamism of the movement, its growing focus on structural inequality and its radical goals."

Beck and others admit that racism did exist, in the far distant past, but that it is a grave error to focus on this racism when telling the story of the past. Instead, Beck thinks the focus should be on aspects of the movement that can be connected to "free market individualism" and the providential and exceptional nature of the American experience, narratives we have encountered before in this book. However, Hall argues persuasively that this is not only an insufficient and incomplete story of the movement; it is inaccurate. For "the link between race and class lay at the heart of the movement's political imagination." Hall marshals impressive evidence to demonstrate that the 1950s civil rights movement was just one moment in a "long Civil Rights Movement" that lasted for most of the twentieth century and at all times called for both racial and economic change.[50] To tell the story of the movement without discussing the economic inequality faced by African Americans is to tell an incomplete and inaccurate story. Such a story might connect more clearly with the goals of political conservatives, but it is not history, as it ignores the complexity and mixed motives of the people of the past.

There is no question that this new narrative of civil rights is creeping into American classrooms and that students are the worse off because of it. In an evaluation of curricula throughout the nation, the Southern Poverty Law Center (SPLC) noted this trend, which they identified as "the reduction of the movement into simple fables," with alarm. According to the SPLC, a well respected and long standing civil rights organization, this narrative of "fables" is most problematic because in it ignores the "breadth of social and institutional changes" wrought by the movement.[51]

The movement was also more than the seemingly random and coura-geous individual action of not sitting in an assigned seat by Rosa Parks. Parks took her action as part of an institutional decision to protest segrega-tion, and the result of her action was a radical boycott against Montgomery businesses. Parks had just attended a training session at the Highlander Folk School in Tennessee, a center focused on training generally disempowered people to fight for workers' rights. But the story of Rosa Parks most often taught to American schoolchildren is the story of "Rosa the tired," the story of a brave, stubborn, heroic seamstress who fought the system by herself and won. This is only part of the story, and a minor and misleading part at that. Parks was a trained and dedicated member of what was viewed at the time as a radical group of left wing agitators.[52]

The aspect of civil rights history the re-inventors of the era want to most shockingly distort or eliminate is the role of Thurgood Marshall. At first glance, Marshall seems to be a figure who fits into even the re-invented narrative of the time because he first walked onto the national stage as the lead lawyer for the NAACP in *Brown v. Board of Education* of Topeka in 1954. He epitomizes the civil rights leader who worked within the system to effect change. No one has argued that the *Brown* decision is an unimportant event from the era, because it symbolizes how the American system can work to improve the legal rights of individuals.

However, the re-inventors of history are working to erase Thurgood Mar-shall's name and legacy from the era. Why? Because they believe that in his later role as U.S. Supreme Court justice, his views were much too politically radical, and he exemplifies their definition of an inappropriately "activist" judge. In Texas, the history re-inventors successfully eliminated his name from the list of important names of the era, even though he was the lawyer for one of the most important Supreme Court cases in history and served as the nation's first African American justice.

The issue with Marshall came to light during the confirmation hearings for Elena Kagan, confirmed as a Supreme Court justice in the summer of 2010. Conservative senators lobbied against confirmation, arguing that Ka-gan was too radical and activist to be on the Court. Rather than attacking her statements or even attacking her as a White House advisor to President Clinton or as the solicitor general for Barack Obama, they decided to at-tack her because she had served as a clerk for Thurgood Marshall and had expressed her admiration for him. Conservative radio host Michael Savage called Marshall "an outright communist" and declared that the "Marshall Court almost destroyed America."[53] Conservative senators attacked Mar-shall for being "beyond the mainstream" and "activist."

Many took their talking points from a variety of online reports about the radicalism of Marshall. Most of these reports tarnished him via guilt-by-association, such as one right-wing blog that pointed out that

> at the all black, Lincoln University in Chester County, Pennsylvania in the 1930s, Marshall's classmates included future socialist President of Ghana, Kwame Nkrumah and poet and author Langston Hughes, later a close associate and fellow Communist Party comrade of Barack Obama's teenage mentor Frank Marshall Davis.[54]

Thus Marshall is connected to communism, which in an ironic twist looks very much like a tactic of Joseph McCarthy. Conservative bloggers had been arguing in this red baiting vein for years, as when *Front Page Magazine* asserted "almost from the NAACP's birth, the color it advanced was not so much black as red."[55] Of course, this connects to the conservative argument in the 1950s when conservative leaders such as Ezra Taft Benson (not coincidentally, a close friend and ally of W. Cleon Skousen) "charged Friday night that the civil-rights movement in the South had been 'formatted almost entirely by the Communists.'"[56] Another expose at the time of the Kagan nomination dug up this nugget that it considered to be important: "In 1946, according to communist linked historian Herbert Shapiro, Marshall was saved from a probable lynching near Columbia Tennessee, by a passenger in his car—Communist Party journalist Harry Raymond." It is of course disturbing that this article portrays Mr. Shapiro in a negative light because he was a "Communist Party journalist," even though Mr. Shapiro helped save a future Supreme Court justice from torture and probable death.[57]

And so we have come full circle in my story of those who want to re-invent the history of the 1950s. According to the re-inventors, the heroes of the story of the 1950s are those who fought communists and opposed structural change in society, from Joseph McCarthy to Phyllis Schlafly. Those who worked and fought to change the structure of society, from Betty Friedan to Thurgood Marshall, need to be eliminated and erased. Even the story of Dr. Martin Luther King, Jr., a leader who unquestionably fought for change in both the political and economic system, needs to be changed and whitewashed.

A strong history classroom would investigate the complexity and tension embedded in 1950s America. Students need to engage the career and actions of Joseph McCarthy and discuss his role in this contentious time. Yet he should not be taught as a hero just because the re-inventors of history wish it to be so. Similarly, the 1950s should not be taught as the "golden age" of the twentieth century just because it is politically convenient and palatable for twenty-first century politicians and critics to make this assertion. Most important, though, undeniably important figures should not be erased from history just because it fits a contemporary political ideology. Deciding on which names to include is nearly impossible, but to base decisions in this area on political considerations instead of the canons of the discipline of history is dangerous. And as we shall see in the next chapter, the guilty re-inventors of the history of the 1950s may be political conservatives, but political liberals have been guilty of attempting to re-invent history as well.

CHAPTER 5

ANTI-HISTORIANS OF THE LEFT

History Is A Weapon

"…we must seek out the tools we will need. History is just one tool to shape our understanding of our world. And every tool is a weapon if you hold it right."

—From opening statement, *http://www. historyisaweapon.com*

The website "historyisaweapon.com" serves as a most outrageous example of thinking about the teaching of history from the radical left. So far, this book has examined efforts on the political right to toss history down the memory hole. Many of these right-wing inventors of a new past, from Larry Shweikart to Kyle Olson to Glenn Beck, claim in their defense that they are merely countering the efforts of the radical left to re-invent American history. They see a left-wing conspiracy to take over the nation's history classrooms.

Although they vastly overestimate the power and reach of these efforts and most egregiously conflate the efforts of radical history educators with the entire history teaching "establishment," these right-wing critics have a point in identifying a group of influential left-wing educators who seek to erase history. The clear hero of this movement is Howard Zinn, whose *A People's History of the United States* is the best selling book purporting to be a U.S. history textbook. Zinn has many disciples, those who self-consciously seek to promote Zinn's arguments and spread them into America's classrooms: prominent teachers such as Bill Bigelow, revolutionaries such as the anonymous creators of "historyisaweapon.com," and an entire coterie of educators who promote "social justice education" in the nation's history classrooms. All of these radical educators share a similar disdain for the actual discipline of history, believing it to be merely a weapon to promote their agenda rather than a broader, more valuable way of thinking that has the ability to improve students' ability to think.

The radical re-inventors of the past are not shy about their goals, nor do they attempt to mask the political nature of their classrooms. Bill Bigelow seeks nothing short of "occupying the curriculum, " as his blog on the "re-thinking schools" site proclaims:

> We don't need to take tents and sleeping bags to our town squares to partici-pate in the Occupy Movement—although it would be great if more of us did. We can also "occupy" our classrooms, "occupy" the curriculum. At this time of mass revulsion at how our country—our world—has been bought and bullied by the one percent, let's join this gathering movement to demand a curricu-lum that serves humanity and nature, not the rich.[1]

Such an argument is perfectly consistent with the idea that history is a "weapon" rather than a way of thinking.

Bigelow and others all gratefully, even reverently, acknowledge they are following in the footsteps of Howard Zinn, an academic historian who spent most of his career at Boston University. Zinn has become more than merely a historian; he is, as Sam Wineburg puts it, a "cultural icon."[2] Matt Damon's character in the critically acclaimed film *Good Will Hunting* trum-pets the importance of Zinn's work, and a character in the popular prime time soap opera *The Sopranos* similarly sings its praises. Zinn's most famous work, *A People's History of the United States*, with more than two million copies in circulation, begins from the premise that that "the American system is the most ingenious system of control in World History." Zinn wrote pur-posefully, with the goal of awakening the people to their plight so that they could take action against their oppressors: "The memory of oppressed peo-ple is one thing that cannot be taken away, and for such people, with such memories, revolt is always an inch below the surface."[3]

History is a tool to be used by these oppressed people, and revolution should never be far away. The classroom should be a place where the people can learn about revolution, civil disobedience, and protest so that they can use it when necessary. Zinn and his followers argue consistently that since history cannot be objective, historians and history teachers should not even try. "None of us can" stay above or beside the fray, we must "take sides" and "help move the world in one direction or another." In such a classroom, complexity is erased, historical context is ignored, and any attempt at a judicial weighing of evidence is an unaffordable luxury.

An entire cottage industry within social studies education has grown up based on Zinn's ideas, beliefs, and arguments. This industry creates lesson plans, unit plans, websites, blogs, and even its own online periodical, *Rethinking History*. *Rethinking History* is part of the Zinn Education Project, a collaboration between "Rethinking Schools" and an organization called "Teaching for Change." *Rethinking History* asked Zinn, "How can a progressive teacher promote a radical perspective within a bureaucratic, conservative institution?" Note that the goal is not necessarily to open students' eyes to different perspectives; it is not necessarily to introduce them to buried historical ideas, facts, or people; it is quite clearly for teachers to *promote* a radical perspective.[4] And, according to Bigelow, schools and teachers must offer a pedagogy that allows them to promote and promulgate Zinn's ideas. A "people's pedagogy" needs to "engage students in explicitly critiquing traditional approaches to history" because these approaches remain too conservative, traditional, and too focused on those who have power. According to Bigelow, the problem with traditional history is not necessarily that other historians and textbook writers have presented false or even incomplete history. Instead, the problem is that the other history is not radical enough.

Many historians are sympathetic with the arguments of Zinn and his followers because Zinn does seek explicitly to be more inclusive in his writing of history. Zinn first began his career as a historian in the 1960s and 1970s, a time when the state of academic history was in turmoil. Historians of many different political stripes, but most especially left-wing historians, began to argue convincingly that the history told in both books and classrooms was incomplete. Social movements and changes of the 1950s and 1960s, most especially the civil rights movement, pushed historians to ask new questions about the past. Before the 1960s, rare was the historian or history that included voices and perspectives of women, African Americans, immigrants, the working and non-working poor, or any powerless group in their stories and classrooms. History as taught at every level was indeed history from the "top down," a history of the elite and powerful.

Zinn was originally part of a very much larger movement to make history more inclusive and to attempt, at least occasionally, to tell the story of the past from the "bottom up." The study of history blossomed, some would say splintered, into an infinite number of directions. These new "social histori-ans" discovered a wonderful array of new topics to study and teach about, providing new perspectives on the history of those previously ignored and neglected groups. According to Peter Stearns, a leading social historian, this is an

> approach to the past that carefully examines the conditions and contribu-tions of groups of ordinary people, alongside the greats; and that, as a second attribute, expands the topics covered from staples like politics, high culture, and trade to the range of concerns by which, in fact, people live their lives and evaluate them—from family to crime to emotions or the senses.[5]

Yet the history and pedagogy of Zinn and his followers is both much more and much less than adding the teaching of social history to the more traditional "political" history in the nation's classrooms. Zinn explicitly fo-cuses his history on teaching from the bottom up, arguing often that simply grafting the history of the "oppressed" onto the traditional history of the "oppressors" merely muddies the water and makes the story too broad and too complicated. His focus narrows the classroom, eliminating important ideas and issues, only to be retrieved if a particular teacher has the ability and background to teach Zinn along with other curricular materials. Yet Zinn and his followers have broadened the goals of a history classroom in a way that is much more insidious than the way in which they narrow the classroom. They seek to make the history classroom a forum for explicit po-litical indoctrination, moving beyond the purpose of history to teach about ideas such as continuity and change, complexity and historical context. The problem with Zinn and his followers is not only the "what" of history, but the "how."

Historians and history educators have noted this about Zinn and his work ever since his book became a runaway best seller in the mid 1980s. Luther Spoer, historian and history educator from Brown University, put this critique of Zinn most articulately as early as 1980:

> In the past decade, many historians have written history "from the bottom up," bringing to light the lives of the inarticulate and the downtrodden. Hap-pily, Zinn compiles many of their findings. Unhappily...Zinn is interested almost exclusively in portraying naked exploitation. History for him is a one-cylinder engine. His book has no notion of process or complexity, no sense of how the terms of argument and weapons of battle have changed over time.[6]

Predictably, historians from the right have had a field day attacking Zinn. Daniel Flynn, at the time executive director of Accuracy in Academia, blasts Zinn's work as "cartoon anti-history," pointing out correctly: "History serv-ing 'a social aim' other than the preservation or interpretation of a histori-cal record is precisely what we get in *A People's History of the United States*."[7]

Self-described conservative historian and analyst Ron Radosh also does not mince his words: "Zinn sees history as a tool to be utilized on behalf of radical politics—not as a way to understand our country's growth and development."[8]

The critiques of Zinn, however, are not confined to historians on the right. Most interesting perhaps is one written by Larry DeWitt, when he wrote as a graduate student, fully immersed in the latest debates over the scholarly direction of history. Zinn's work and the tireless efforts of his followers to insert this work into the classroom led DeWitt to ask the following question:

> Has Howard Zinn been paying attention to developments in the history profession for the last thirty years or so, or did he take his snapshot of the world sometime in the 1950s, and waving this fading Polaroid before his own eyes, he is in perpetual rebellion against a past that no longer is present?[9]

DeWitt then takes Zinn to task because Zinn failed to follow the central rule of historical questioning: rather than working to "find out what happened in the past and why…, the discipline of history is merely a tool to be used in pursuit of a political cause."[10]

Perhaps the most scathing critique of Zinn came from the most influential pen, that of Michael Kazin, professor of history at Georgetown University. Kazin was described in *Newsweek* as a historian of the "broad left," and is a historian of social movements, thus of course putting him firmly in the broad camp of "social" historians. Kazin, clearly sympathetic with Zinn's topic and even his desire to tell history from the "bottom up," nevertheless proclaims that "Zinn's big book is quite unworthy of such fame and influence. *A People's History* is bad history, albeit gilded with virtuous intentions."[11] Zinn's most important failing, according to Kazin, is his reliance on oversimplification and his consistent failure to contextualize the past. Kazin objects to this not because Zinn portrays political and economic leaders of the past in a bad light, but because "the ironic effect of such portraits of rulers is to rob 'the people' of cultural richness and variety, characteristics that might gain the respect and not just the sympathy of contemporary readers."[12] In short, Zinn's myopic, oversimplified story fails to adhere to even the most basic tenets of historical thinking, failing even to attempt an accurate rendering of the past and, even more dangerously, serving as a very flawed template for curriculum in the schools today.

The leading researcher and theorist of historical thinking today, Sam Wineburg, echoes many of Kazin's arguments about the work of Zinn and his followers. Wineburg argues that in ways that "strike at the heart of the discipline," Zinn's book fails as history and fails students.[13] Zinn does not allow readers to check his sources, for he supplies no footnotes. Zinn relies mostly on secondary sources, rather than patiently building his case with primary source material, as students should be taught. Wineburg painstakingly analyzes a single chapter from Zinn's book, the chapter on World War II, and finds that Zinn based all his conclusions about African Americans and the war on two pages from one secondary source work. In other words, just as right-wing historians cherry-pick evidence to "prove" their contentions about the religiosity of George Washington or the innocence of Joseph McCarthy, Zinn cherry-picks his evidence on this topic. Using this as a classroom text, then, teaches exactly the wrong lessons about historical thinking. Wineburg, citing historian Aileen Kraditor, refers to this as a "yes-type" question, sending "the historian into the past armed with a wish list."[14] The historian wants to find an answer for a contemporary question in the past and hunts in the past until that answer is found, rather than examining the past with no set agenda in mind.

Zinn and the Zinn Education Project is neither an isolated nor the most radical example of those who wish to transform history students into cadre' of activists for social justice. Radical re-inventors of the past, such as Ward Churchill, are all too common. Very few historians would accept Churchill, a former ethnic studies professor, as a historian, but he nevertheless insists on writing about the past as if he was a historian, and he clearly hopes his readers accept his view of the past. At various times, Churchill compares Americans to "severe alcoholics" in their stubborn adherence to patterns of repression and as "a cadre of faceless bureaucrats and technical experts who had willingly (and profitably) harnessed themselves to the task of making America's genocidal world order hum with maximal efficiency."[15]

Churchill's views do not appear to be penetrating the curricula of the K–12 school system to the extent that Zinn's ideas have, but there is no question about the importance of "social justice education" in the nation's social studies classrooms. The goal of "social justice education" is for "teachers who believe their students and create meaningful social change." It is a "vision of teaching for liberation," with clear underlying assumptions that twenty-first century America is a land of oppression requiring students and teachers to fight for the liberation of the underclass. Social justice curriculum materials provide the tools to "teach for justice."[16] "Social justice" educators begin with a set of answers about both the past and the present. Many of these answers are very simple, straightforward, and clear, which makes them both attractive and woefully inadequate in teaching history. "Social justice education" is by definition antithetical to strong and effective history teaching, which, by definition, needs to begin with questions, not answers, and needs to teach the past messy, complex, and difficult to fully comprehend.

So let's revisit the topics examined by the book so far and see how radical left-wing anti-historians have attempted to insert their history-free narrative into the schools. Have these radical inventors of history been as guilty as conservative inventors of history in attempting to insert their ideas into the nation's American history curriculum and hence into the nation's classrooms? The answer is yes.

I would argue, however, that the problem is not as serious and dangerous. In the case of the right-wing anti-history discussed so far in this book, the re-inventors seek to erase historical truth and then retell the story in their own image. As we have seen, the right-wing anti-historians have also demonstrated their hold on local political power in many parts of the country. On the other hand, the left-wing anti-historians generally do not attempt to erase truth. They see their role as providing an antidote, an argument with existing history that cannot be erased but instead should be viewed in a new perspective. Also, in an unsurprising irony, radical anti-historians are generally powerless, except in a very narrow sense, in convincing some teachers of their program, teachers who are often overruled by more powerful political forces. But in the end, the differences don't really matter. Anti-historians of both the right and the left fail to adhere to the tenets of historical reasoning and historical thinking, and so both seek to warp the minds of history students in their own particular way.

Just as with the right, the anti-historians of the left are extraordinarily concerned with America's founding. It seems that both groups believe that in order to tell the story in the (correct) way they want, it is critical to begin in the right place. For the anti-historians of the left, that beginning is before the beginning as posited by the anti-historians of the right. As we saw in Chapter One, the right begins the American story with the coming of the Puritans to the shores of North America and then collapses all of colonial history on this event, moving directly from the Puritans to the Revolution. The radical left begins much earlier, with the landing of Columbus, and then collapses all of colonial history on this event, moving directly from a genocidal Columbus to an equally morally dubious Revolution.

For anti-historians of the radical left, the story of Columbus is problematic because "...the Columbus myth is only the beginning of a winner's history that profoundly neglects the lives and perspectives of many 'others.'"[17] Bigelow, Zinn, and others are correct in introducing the concept of the "Columbus myth," for much of what we think we "know" about Columbus is incorrect. From the use of the word "discovery" (how did the inhabitants of Hispaniola feel about being "discovered"?) to fighting against the flat world beliefs of the time (most educated men in Columbus' day believed the world to be round), the mythic understandings about Columbus cannot withstand the test of historical evidence.

Yet the re-inventors of this myth move far beyond the historical record in an attempt to "repair" our understanding of this time in order to achieve twenty-first century objectives. For example, Bill Bigelow crafted a lesson that asks "students to step inside (Columbus') worldview and talk back to the materialistic and exploitative values imported to the Americas by Columbus and those who followed."[18] In truth, students need to understand that "talking back" to history is not possible, nor should we want it to be. We need to try to understand the worldview, not merely criticize and belittle it. Next, Bigelow brings the lesson to the present, comparing a controversy over native fishing rights on the Columbia River at the end of the twentieth century to the battle of the Tainos with Columbus. This lesson ignores the context of time, ignoring the change in worldviews over half a millennium. It ignores place, ignoring the differences between the Tainos of the fifteenth century and the twentieth century Native Americans of the American Northwest, as well as differences between the Spanish and the Americans. It completely ignores and flattens context and complexity. But it succeeds for Bigelow, because it allows students to become activists, even if they become activists by making uncomplicated, almost comical, comparisons between times and places that just should not be compared.[19]

In Zinn's alternative past, the next 250 years of colonial America between Columbus and the "founding era" rush past in a virtually undifferentiated blur, compressing a gigantic amount of time and a complex era of tremendous change into a simplistic story of Europeans killing Indians and stealing and raping their land. Zinn, Churchill, and those who wish to create this radical curriculum emphasize that the United States was born violent, rapacious, and undemocratic. Of course, this is analogous to how conservative fabricators skip most of this same time period in order to emphasize the religiosity of the founding. Howard Zinn sums up the European colonial interaction with the Native Americans with the following very clear and succinct sentence: "Not able to enslave the Indians, and not able to live with them, the English decided to exterminate them."[20] Zinn does concede "For a while, the English tried softer tactics. But ultimately, it was back to annihilation."[21] "A while" is actually forty years here, a generation there. Historians cannot simply annihilate or wish away time willy-nilly in order to make an argument more believable, credible, or convincing. Time must be central in the historian's toolbox. Ironically, perhaps, Zinn's rush to his point also oversimplifies the very people he seeks to bring to more importance, the Native Americans.

Historians who have spent a lifetime studying European-Native American relations in the seventeenth and eighteenth centuries have found the story to be much more complex than the narrative of rape and murder told by Zinn and other anti-historians of the left. In *Dominion of War*, Fred Anderson and Andrew Cayton outline the very complex nation-to-nation relations among the new European settlers and the Native American nations of the time. During the first century after contact, in fact, "European contacts had altered but not transformed native patterns of war and trade." After 1700, however, the "creation of colonies in North America intensified the long-standing competition among native groups and make the Indian wars more violent and uncontrollable than they had ever been before."[22] This was a complex and ever changing relationship, one that does not put Europeans in the most favorable light yet at the same time does not argue that Europeans were merely unthinking killers.

To add even more complexity and context to the story, Anderson and Cayton discuss the story of William Penn, who they argue was "the most successful Imperialist of all." The founder of Pennsylvania pioneered a set of "cultural strategies" in 1682, strategies that offered the most "efficient means to extend Britain's sway." But these strategies did not include the brutal genocidal tactics that Zinn argued characterized American interaction with the native peoples. Instead, Cayton and Anderson argue persuasively that "peace, fair trade, and liberality in dealing with Indians on terms that Indians found acceptable" characterized Penn's strategy.[23] Cayton and Anderson are not alone in following this line of argument. Richard White, in *The Middle Ground*, presents much the same line of argument, insisting that both Europeans and native peoples were forced to come to the middle in order to make their lives work in an every changing and ever more complex cultural stew of the late seventeenth and early eighteenth centuries. These historians certainly do not act as apologists for the Europeans and are very comfortable tagging them with the term "imperialist." Yet they seek to understand them in the terms of their time, not in politicized terms of the twenty-first century.

For both the radical and reactionary anti-historians, the whole point of the 1600–1750 period is as a prologue to the "founding era," the era from approximately 1750–1800 that witnessed the crafting of the Declaration of Independence, the American Revolution and the creation of the American Republic. The radical re-inventors seize this era as an opportunity to attack the founders at every turn and to show that, rather than being heroes, these men are to be disparaged for not being twenty-first century progressives. Gone is any attempt at contextualization, any impulse to understand the motivations of these historical figures through a reading and understanding of their own words.

George Washington, evangelical Christian hero of a false conservative past, endures an equally incomplete and inaccurate rendering in the eyes of radical anti-historians. In one version of the story, found in a social justice lesson, Washington is merely a greedy land speculator who is only prevented from gobbling up vast tracts of native land by the "great" Ottawa leader Pontiac. Pontiac is actually dubbed as "great" with every mention, while not a single positive adjective is used for Washington. While "Washington was free to profit from his illegal land deals" and ordered a "harsh military campaign" and "tricked the Iroquois," the Iroquois "fought in vain" against the American invasion.[24] This article "is to be used during Washington's Birthday celebrations." Yet just because the positive Washington myth might not portray all of Washington's multifaceted, complex actions does not mean that the correct method to teach Washington is to present an equally incomplete, falsified, and purposefully biased anti-myth. As Sam Wineburg eloquently argues, "Pitting two monolithic narratives, each strident, immodest, and unyielding in its position, against one another turns history into a European soccer match where fans set fires in the stands and taunt the opposition with scurrilous epithets. Instead of encouraging us to think, such a history teaches us how to jeer."[25]

Central to the radical critique of the founding era is an attack on the crafting of the American Constitution. In analyzing those who created this document, Zinn demands, "But why hold up as models the fifty-five rich white men who drafted the Constitution as a way of establishing a government that would protect the interests of their class-slaveholders, merchants, bondholders, land speculators?"[26] Asking questions is, of course, central to historical thinking. Yet Zinn's question here is not really a question at all; rather, it is a rhetorical flourish, meant to lead to a very narrow, misleading answer. We study the drafters of the Constitution because they drafted the Constitution, an unavoidable historical fact.

At least in this case, Zinn's facts are not invented. The framers of the Constitution were wealthy, many were slaveholders, and others were merchants. Yet should the focus of teaching in the secondary school classroom be narrowed to such a narrow economic analysis? Do we do right by our young people to demand an attack on this group in such a fashion? Zinn believes that history must be ideological, so he chooses to tell history from the point of view of the oppressed and previously ignored. A laudable goal in the opinion of many, but a goal that deliberately ignores actual events and the actual historical record. So, for example, Zinn chooses to teach the "Constitution from the standpoint of slaves."[27] A clear choice, and a choice that allows Zinn to accurately show certain deficiencies in the Constitution, yet a choice that is not history. History needs to rely on the primary sources connected to the event, and there are virtually no primary sources that can view the Constitutional Convention from the standpoint of slaves. Zinn might choose, then, to leave out the story of the Constitution altogether, but as we have seen, such a decision is another example of stamping out the past.

Zinn disciple Bob Peterson takes this further in creating what he insists is an authentic lesson about the Constitutional Convention. Peterson insists that the study of the Constitution and the Constitutional Convention is "boring" and not "relevant." Central to Peterson's role-play is the belief that the questions asked by the actual attendees of the Convention are neither interesting nor pertinent to the students of today. This ignores the words and the debates of the Constitutional Convention itself. Erased are debates about the executive power, a need for a Bill of Rights, or the relative power of the states. It is actually unclear how these topics are uninteresting or irrelevant. Of course, history teaching that forces a memorized set of facts through an overly dry and didactic traditional lecture can fail to engage students. Yet the actual topics of the Convention were and are intrinsically interesting and naturally engaging: power, the relationship between different kinds of people, the amount of liberty each person should be allowed.

The experience of Carol Berkin, the author of *A Brilliant Solution*, a book admired by historians and history teachers alike as one of the most interesting and accessible books on the Constitutional Convention, offers a valuable counterpoint to Peterson's perspective. Berkin relates that she is often asked about "What would the founding fathers think of" events of the present. She answers, honestly, "any answer, no matter how expert the historian, would only be conjecture." Historical events and historical figures cannot simply be ripped from the complex context of their time in order to solve a contemporary problem. Instead, historians need to ask questions of the context of the past that might be instructive in answering questions in the present. She focuses her book on questions like, "What political crises had the founding fathers faced, and how did they react to them? What problems did they hope to solve, and how did they react to them…What dangers did they think lay ahead for their nation?"[28] These questions are rooted in the past and demand a careful examination of the sources from the past for their answers. They are fascinating, intricate questions that do bear on issues of the present.

Instead, Peterson believes these issues to be dull and archaic and so crafts a role-play with what he believes *should have* been the central topics of the Convention. His instinct to create a role-play is admirable, for a role-play should be designed to create empathy for people of the past. Peterson also seeks to "develop strong oral presentation skills, including both persuasive and argumentative skills," an important and often overlooked skill that should be a fundamental part of the history curriculum.

Yet "Rethinking the U.S. Constitutional Convention: A Role Play" creates a new past that bears little relation to the actual past in its misguided effort to engage students in debating issues Peterson believes are relevant and important for the students to learn. Peterson's main objectives are the following:

- Should slavery and slave trade be abolished, and should escaped slaves be returned to their owners?
- Who should be allowed to vote in our new nation, especially what role should gender, race, and property ownership play in such a decision?"

Unfortunately for the historical record, the actual evidence shows that virtually none of these issues interested people of the late eighteenth century, and consequently few of them were discussed at the actual Convention. The framers did discuss, briefly, the slave trade. No one at the time dreamed of discussing gender, race, or property qualifications for citizenship, nor did any of them discuss the federal abolition of slavery. In part, this is because no one at the Convention dreamed that the federal government *could* have the power to make pronouncements on these issues. Any history lesson that ignores these issues ignores one of the central issues of the time and the central area of disagreement at the Convention. In an effort to bring modern sensibilities about race, gender, and class, Peterson tosses the issues that were actually pertinent down the memory hole, doing a disservice to his students in the process.

Peterson claims as another of the objectives for this class "to learn about the social forces active during and immediately following the American Revolution." The social forces he examines, though, did not exist at this time. For example, the first inkling of a social force that pushed for gender equality in voting did not surface for three generations. Peterson insists that the role-play explores "two burning questions that confronted the new American nation: slavery and suffrage."[29] Yet, for those who created the new American nation, these were not burning questions. Neither elicited the slightest debate at the Convention. Should they have been questions? Do we wish they were questions? Perhaps, but the historical record proves they were not. Does this mean we condemn the men (and, yes, they were all men) at the Convention for not discussing these issues, as Zinn would argue? While it is appropriate to observe that they did not discuss these issues, condemning everyone in the past for not thinking more like us leads to the very kind of self centered and myopic thinking that are anathema to twenty-first century progressives. Peterson and his anti-historian colleagues seem to forget that "these men (the delegates at the Constitutional Convention) inhabited a world alien to modern Americans, a world in which the United States was a fragile, uncertain experiment, a newcomer...."[30]

Peterson's role-play includes participation by an indentured servant and an Iroqouis Indian. Of course, neither type of person attended. There is didactic value in pointing this out, and in displaying how the interests of these two groups were not reflected in the decisions made at the Convention. Yet in the descriptions of these two characters, Peterson invents beliefs he thinks these people *should have* had. In relation to voting qualifications, the indentured servant believes "No property, no vote, they say. Who do they think they are?" Yet the Constitution says nothing about voting qualifications, and we have little evidence that indentured servants thought in these terms in the 1770s...voting qualifications became an important debate two generations later. As a matter of fact, at least one former indentured servant, Benjamin Franklin, did attend the Convention, and there is no evidence that Franklin wanted a change in voting qualifications.

The Iroquois Indian's first thoughts on the matter are "You know that your Native American relatives have suffered as slaves ever since the time Columbus came to this part of the world."[31] Did the Iroquois feel affinity for all Native Americans in 1776? Did they feel affinity for the Taino? Were the Iroquois treated as slaves? Until 1776, the Iroquois believed themselves to be a free and independent empire, and acted as such. Were many mistreated by Europeans? Yes. Were many the victims of European brutalities? Yes. But there is very little evidence that they felt as Peterson would have them feel, as powerless victims of a persistent and consistent three century European land grab.

It is clear that radical storytellers have, in a way very similar to the conservative re-inventors of the past, retold the history of the founding era. In both cases, ideologues have taken goals of the present and inserted them into a new and false narrative of the past. They both violate fundamental rules about that must be followed if our study of the past is to have credibility and believability. Historians should not be allowed to simply throw up their hands and say all history is political. This is especially important for history in the schools, where students need to learn about sourcing, context, authorship, and perspective. All of these are ignored as the conservatives tell of an era dominated by religious fundamentalism, while the radicals tell a story of unrelenting racism, classism, and violence.

Radical historians, led again by Howard Zinn, also deliberately distort the economic history of the nineteenth century. We saw in Chapter Two the story of how conservative anti-historians paint the era as a story of heroic captains of industry building the United States into the envy of the world. The radical historians tell quite the opposite story, portraying an era dominated by the depravity and immorality of a gaggle of greedy, power hungry, selfish capitalist power brokers. And, just as in the tale of the founding era, the conservative and the radical anti-historians seek to insert their version of this history into the nation's classrooms, distorting the actual record of the past and the purpose of history and providing students with no guidance on how to understand the reality of the past.

As usual, Zinn best exemplifies this view, neatly synthesizing the radical anti-historical view of this time period in the opening of Chapter 11 of *A People's History of the United States*:

> In the year 1877, the signals were given for the rest of the century: the blacks would be put back; the strikes of white workers would not be tolerated; the industrial and political elites of North and South would take hold of the country and organize the greatest march of economic growth in human history. They would do it with the aid of, and at the expense of, black labor, white labor, Chinese labor, European immigrant labor, female labor, rewarding them dif-

ferently by race, sex, national origin, and social class, in such a way as to create separate levels of oppression—a skillful terracing to stabilize the pyramid of wealth.[32]

The remainder of the chapter provides an unremitting series of anecdotes about the repression, oppression, horrors, death, and destruction of this era.

Conservative anti-historians are quick to pounce on radical anti-historians for their misrepresentation of this era. In his book *Indoctrination*, conservative education activist Kyle Olson rails against "useful idiots," insisting that "the truth is that progressives want to discredit standard American history as much as possible, while bringing singular attention to American figures who fought for collectivism and the redistribution of wealth."[33] Olson's arguments are almost universally simplistic, but in this case, he has a point, because the "progressives" he attacks use almost the exact same language to describe their curriculum. In his introduction to a lesson about a strike at the turn of the twentieth century, Norm Diamond, writing a lesson for the Zinn Education Project, straightforwardly insists "Corporate producers of school curricula are not interested in the collective efforts of ordinary people to better their lives."[34] The very purpose of the lesson is to bring attention to those who attacked the capitalist system. Even beyond this, the purpose of this lesson and many others by the followers of Howard Zinn is to lionize those who fought the system and demonize those who did not, in order to "prove" that the capitalist system of the twenty-first century is dangerous, elitist, even evil.

Diamond is not alone in championing ideological goals as the purpose of teaching labor history of the late nineteenth century. Bill Bigelow puts it this way:

> Proponents of corporate-driven globalization argue that adhering to principles of "free trade" will solve the world's economic ills. …However, history shows that what actually makes people's lives better is people themselves working to make them better. Thus it was not the magic of the marketplace that greatly reduced the incidence of child labor in the United States, but organized efforts to stop it.[35]

Bigelow's purpose is not, then, to learn about conditions of a particular time period in order to earn an appreciation for the difficult and challenging lives of that period. It is not for students to understand the complexities of labor/capital relations, nor is it even for students to encounter a world different from their own in order to learn the facts that laborers were mistreated. Instead, it is to celebrate the effectiveness and necessity of organized labor, with the clear implication that such efforts are critically important today. This is a shame, because Bigelow's actual lesson asks the students to examine the very powerful child labor photographs of Lewis

Hines, a wonderful primary source, providing a rare window into a different world. Many students examining the photographs might draw exactly the conclusions Bigelow wants them to, but in forcing his ideas on the students in these lessons, Bigelow dilutes their power and destroys their didactic potential.

The debate on how to portray the history of labor came to a head in Wisconsin beginning in 2009. In December of that year, Governor Jim Doyle signed into law Wisconsin Assembly Bill 192, requiring teachers to include instruction in "the history of organized labor and the collective bargaining process." On the face of it, this law is not especially problematic from the point of view of teaching history. Over the years, many legislatures have required adding topics to the K–12 history curriculum. In many cases, including this one, these laws require the inclusion of topics that were already being taught. An overwhelming consensus of teachers and historians would agree that one could not teach U.S. history without teaching about the history of organized labor and the collective bargaining process. And, in this case, it is true that in many classrooms, the history of labor is being ignored, as argued by historian Kenneth Germanson: "But who is aware of this [the contributions of organized labor] today?" Germanson asked. "Very few persons, and it's a result of an education system that has overlooked a key part of American history. It's precisely this omission that AB 172 seeks to overcome."[36] Yet this law became problematic for the teaching of history in Wisconsin when the Wisconsin department of education provided links to approved lesson plans to fulfill the law.

One of these approved plans was created by "Teaching Tolerance," a project of the Southern Poverty Law Center. This lesson, entitled "Labor Matters," centers around the debate over the Employee Free Choice Act. Two of the objectives of the lesson do well to teach students to think historically and to learn about the events of labor history in historical context. Students are asked to identify major leaders in the labor movement and their major tactics and strategies. Some might dispute the importance of labor leaders and labor movements in U.S. history, but such disputes ignore almost half a century of important historical scholarship on the centrality of the labor movement and the changes it brought to the United States in the late nineteenth and early twentieth century.

However, the first objective of the lesson points in a completely different direction: "Students will understand their connection to the history of organized labor." Students must see this connection; presumably if they do not, they will perform poorly on any assessment that evaluates what the students learned from the lesson. Further, the lesson plan asks students to "consider ways to apply these or other tactics to improve working conditions today."[37] The point of the lesson, then, has little to do with the past. Aiming instead at the present, the lesson takes labor history out of context, replacing that context with a ham-handed attempt to make students into activists. And at the time that this lesson became the curriculum recommended by the state department of education, the issue became much more dangerous. In essence, the state has put its imprimatur on the idea that it is acceptable to study history out of context and that it is not only acceptable, but preferable, for teachers to promote activism in support of unions in a class that is supposed to focus on understanding the history of organized labor.

The area where left-wing radical anti-historians have worked hardest to reinvent the curriculum is in relation to America's role in the world. We have seen how right-wing anti-historians seek to tell a story where the U.S. becomes the exceptional nation in world history, standing above all other nations in its dedication to moral purity, peacefulness, the promotion of liberty, and the rejection of any pretense at empire. In Chapter Three, we saw how that completely distorted the events of the time and had much more to do with a twenty-first century right-wing worldview rather than any sort of reality that might be gleaned from a complete reading of the sources.

Ironically, left-wing anti-historians also believe that the history of the U.S. is an exceptional one. In this story, however, the United States has been exceptionally bloodthirsty, avaricious in its attempt to grow an empire, and warlike. And just as the right-wing anti-historians, those from the left have attempted to push their version of American empire into the nation's schools, thus potentially cheating students out of an opportunity to think with the past. And again, their vision begins not with a desire to understand the past on its own terms, but rather "as a call to action" for a "flurry of political activity" to end the "ceaseless wars" of the American present.[38]

Radical anti-historians go to great lengths in attempting to prove that the United States is not, nor has it ever been, exceptional. One example is a lesson in *Rethinking Our Classrooms* entitled "A New U.S. Bill of Rights" by Larry Miller. In holding up the Bill of Rights to analysis, Miller aims at the heart of American exceptionalism. Those who trumpet the positive form of American exceptionalism hold the Bill of Rights as the ultimate example of justice, freedom, and individual rights. Miller's lesson plan, in contrast, creates a role-play asking students to write a new U.S. bill of rights based on the United Nations' Declaration of Human Rights and the South African Bill of Rights. In outlining the basic tenets of the lesson, Miller asks the following questions of the U.S. Bill of Rights:

- Does the U.S. Bill of Rights offer protection against racism, male chauvinism, and homophobia? Which of these documents comes closest to the list that students brainstormed earlier?
- Do we in the United States have the same protections as the South African Bill of Rights?

- Does our Bill of Rights have the same environmental guarantees as those stated in the South African Bill of Rights?
- Are the rights stated in the South African Bill of Rights for children comparable to children's rights in the United States?
- Does the U.S. Bill of Rights deal with past discrimination?[39]

Miller's intent is to prove to the students that the American Bill of Rights not only falls short of perfection, it falls significantly short of the rights afforded citizens in other countries. Significantly, nothing is said about the historical context of these documents, nor about the fact that the American document was created more than two centuries before the South African version. History is subsumed into a point Miller wishes to make about America's shortcomings. Also importantly, nothing is said about the implementation of these rights over time, and because of this, Miller loses credibility in arguing that the South African legal system reaches closer to perfection than the American one.

We saw in Chapter Three another attack at the core of the right-wing anti-history in the CSCOPE (the Texas lesson plan "bank" until 2013) lesson plan on terrorism. This lesson, you will recall, asks students to consider the extent to which the Boston Tea Party, an iconic symbol of the American Revolution, was an act of terrorism. Such a lesson is ahistorical in much the same way the Constitutional Convention role-play discussed earlier is ahistorical. The Tea Party of the late eighteenth century and the attack on the World Trade Center at the dawn of the twenty-first are in no way comparable, and any assumption that they could be ignores the importance of chronology, geography, culture, technology, and philosophy in the understanding of history.

The radical anti-historians begin their story of American empire with a discussion we have already encountered, the mistreatment and even genocide of other peoples. That is the story of Columbus, a story that prefigures and foreshadows the entire American experience in the world of Zinn and other left-wing anti-historians. Bill Bigelow declares that "the traditional Columbus myth has conditioned children to accept without question imperial adventures like the Iraq war."[40] Bigelow provides no empirical supporting data for this claim, a claim that is anti-historical on its face, as it conflates two events, more than five hundred years apart, ignoring context, complexity, sources, and geography, just as a start.

For the anti-historians, the next chapter in the ugly saga of American empire is the Mexican-American war. Bill Bigelow points out that most Mexicans know that the war against Mexico was another chapter in U.S. imperialism—a "North American invasion, as it's commemorated in a huge memorial in Mexico City's Chapultepec Park." Bigelow continues by pointing out that abolitionists opposed the war as a land grab for the slave power.

Once again, if Bigelow had stopped there, he would not be off the mark. Any historian delving deeply into the primary sources from the time of the war would indeed find criticisms of President Polk and his land grab by a variety of critics, including famously a young and soon to be unpopular Representative from Illinois, Abraham Lincoln. No, the problem with Bigelow's lesson begins with his purpose. We need to teach the negative lessons of this war because this country's military is still being sent to invade and occupy—and murder—people with silent, invisible drones. "The rich and powerful poison our atmosphere, our water, our food, and our children. So, yes, let's have a curriculum that gets emotional—and that tells a fuller truth than is offered in our textbooks."[41]

Thus begins the argument that the United States is now, because it has always been, an avaricious empire bent on consistently smashing any opponent in its way. Of course, some of the most significant evidence in support of this narrative is that of American government actions towards the Native American nations in the nineteenth century. For this argument, this is low hanging fruit, because the story of American attitudes and actions towards Native Americans in the nineteenth century is indeed ugly. Replete with stories of massacres of Native Americans, unprovoked attacks on Native American villages, governmental mistreatment of entire tribes, to say nothing of massive forced relocations such as the Trail of Tears, the record is clear about the mistreatment of Native Americans and the march of American imperialist expansion in the nineteenth century, sustained by White American greed and violence.

The radical anti-historians, however, insist that this record is erased when history is taught at the K–12 level, arguing for a radical change in curriculum. Kathleen Wooton and Christopher D. Stonebanks, for example, argue that

> Accounts such as "Sand Creek," "Great Swamp," or "Wounded Knee" are strangely absent from the nonnative-controlled curriculum, and when Native issues are brought into the class, children are usually taught of an oversimplified cooperation between Native peoples and settlers.[42]

The purpose of ignoring these issues in the curriculum, according to these anti-historians, is that "in order to ensure passivity in regard to continued empire building and conquest, this is an essential part of education." They praise Bigelow and Zinn: " How many teachers do we have who have the courage to take the next step and admit that, really, we are not living in a postcolonial world?"[43] For these authors, the key is making a point about the world today, not attempting to understand the world of yesterday, even if that means distorting the world of yesterday.

As the evidence makes clear, however, Wooton and Stonebanks did not do very much research on the world of schools today in making their argument that curricula ignore atrocities towards Native Americans such as Sand Creek, Great Swamp and Wounded Knee. Even a cursory look at state curriculum standards points out the fallacy of their argument. The seventh grade Kansas history standards explicitly require the study of the Sand Creek massacre, and the South Dakota High School history standards explicitly require the study of Wounded Knee.[44] The story of White American mistreatment of Native Americans also earns important billing in nationally available curriculum, such as can be found on the web site of the Gilder Lehrman Institute of American History. In a section devoted to U.S./Native American affairs in the nineteenth century, Gilder Lehrman includes both a lesson plan on Sand Creek and an essay about Indian removal, written by well respected historians and history educators.[45] It is also worth noting here that both of the benefactors of the organization, Dick Gilder and William Lehrman, are conservative politically, but the organization they support focuses not on right-wing anti-history but on following the sources towards a logical conclusion, the skills of a true historian.

Why do Wooton and Stonebanks insist that there is some sort of cover-up connected to the twenty-first century teaching of the history of American imperialism? We can find a hint in the title of their article, which focuses on "roosting chickens." As they freely admit, their article starts from the premise of a book entitled *On the Justice of Roosting Chickens: Reflections on the Consequences of U.S. Imperial Arrogance and Criminality* written by academic Ward Churchill. This book became infamous and a national cause célèbre, because Churchill calls those who died in the attack on the twin towers on 9-11 "little Eichmanns," insisting that they were "faceless bureaucrats who willingly harnessed themselves to the task of making America's genocidal world order hum with maximum efficiency."[46] Churchill faced withering criticism for this statement and calls for dismissal from his post as an ethnic studies professor at the University of Colorado. This pressure did lead to a university investigation, which in turn led to the discovery of a general pattern of sloppy scholarship and specific instances of plagiarism in Churchill's work, which ultimately led to his firing.

Churchill specializes in hyperbole, painting a picture of the "seething, bleeding psychic wastelands spawned by the unspeakable arrogance of U.S. imperial pretension."[47] Later, Churchill compares American thought patterns to those of "severe alcoholics."[48] His central thesis is that "far from 'fighting for freedom and democracy,' the U.S. has with equal consistency fought to repeal it anywhere and everywhere...."[49] Churchill's single-minded focus on attacking the history of U.S. policy leads him into the trap of making the past enemies of the U.S. into heroic defenders of freedom. This includes North Korea, merely "responding to U.S. initiatives" and dedicated to reunifying their country in 1950; Cuba under Castro, where the nature of any human rights abuses is "ambiguous at best;" and even the Soviet Union under Stalin, which "fortunately" served as a "political counterbalance" to post World War II American ambitions.[50]

It is amazing that anyone has ever taken Churchill seriously at all, whether to publish his work or attempt to defend his ideas in the school curriculum. For a supposed defender of the rights of the oppressed to ignore the millions killed under Stalin's purges, the hundreds of thousands starved in North Korea or the thousands jailed under Castro is historical malpractice of the highest order. Churchill also invents (or at best exaggerates) facts, as when he claims that the Japanese "had been attempting to surrender for many months" before Hiroshima in 1945, a claim supported by only the very slimmest of evidence.[51] Evidence matters little for Churchill. He intends to blow up what he perceives to be the status quo of historical scholarship, a point emphasized by his AK-47 toting picture on the back cover of his book. Such books have no place on the bookshelf of school classrooms, not because of what he argues, but because of the way in which he argues.

At least Howard Zinn does make use of historical evidence and does not make negative flippant generalizations about his readers. However, Zinn is clear in his argument about the consistent historical depravity of American actions towards the rest of the world. The nadir of this activity was, in Zinn's view, the era of U.S. overseas expansion in the late nineteenth century. Again, he picked an easy target, for many Americans at the time, most famously Mark Twain, also criticized American imperial overreach. Yet Zinn takes advantage of the situation, pushing this era to the forefront in order to fully illuminate his thesis on a different kind of American exceptionalism. In events leading to the Spanish-American War, Zinn intones "The taste of empire was on the lips of politicians and business interests throughout the country now. Racism, paternalism, and talk of money mingled with talk of destiny and civilization."[52] Zinn continues, asking, "Was that taste in the mouth of the people through some instinctive lust for aggression or some urgent self-interest? Or was it a taste (if indeed it existed) created, encouraged, advertised, and exaggerated by the millionaire press, the military, the government, the eager-to-please scholars of the time?"

Zinn then inverts the usual discussions of the Spanish-American War. He ignores the Battle of Manila Bay and the Battle of San Juan Hill. Actually, he ignores almost the entire war in his rush to get to the Filipino-American War. In this he does have a point, because this war is ignored by most textbooks and school curricula and is an empty spot in the American memory. The Filipino-American War lasted longer than its precursor, the Spanish-American war, and it resulted in more American casualties (to say nothing of the staggering casualties experienced by the Filipinos). More American troops fought in the Philippines, and the result of the war led to a half-century of American occupation. The war was brutal, and primary sources reveal a clear and unmistakable strain of racism in the American prosecution of the war.

Yet Zinn completely ignores contrary facts about the American occupation. Americans embarked on a serious and sustained medical program in the islands, inoculating thousands of Filipinos against disease and building the islands' first sanitary system. Thousands of American volunteers, known as the "Thomasites," traveled across the Pacific to volunteer in Filipino classrooms, and the United States promulgated a new judicial system that allowed for much more Filipino autonomy than the Spanish system. This is not to deny the fact that the United States ignored and imprisoned Filipino independence advocate Emilio Aguinaldo, nor is it evidence that freedom, democracy, morality, and the rule of law always followed the American flag. It is evidence that suggests, however, that the U.S. involvement in the Philippines was complex and an integral part of the "progressive" context of the times. Understanding involvement in the Philippines should help students understand America at the time, including both what we might now see as the positive and the negative aspects of the involvement. After all, the first governor of the Philippines was future president and chief justice William Howard Taft, symbolizing the centrality of this era in American history. Zinn is right to put the conflict front and center in our understanding of the past, but he is too simplistic in his depiction of the era as one of unmitigated U.S. brutality and greed.

For the radical anti-historians, not all has been bleak in U.S. history, and just as the reactionary anti-historians, they have focused on one particular era in American history as the "golden age." As we saw in Chapter Four, conservatives believe it is critical to portray the 1950s as this golden age, seeking to defend their forgotten heroes such as Joseph McCarthy while purging misbegotten heroes such as Thurgood Marshall. In doing so, they take the actual understanding of the complexities of the era out of history, instead viewing the 1950s as a grab bag of goodies, the goodies being the heroic examples of right-wing political ideology. Radical anti-historians attempt the same trick, yet their golden age is the 1960s, and their heroes the leaders of radical movements of the time. Just as Phyllis Schlafly is both a historical figure and a conservative anti-historian writing about her own era, so Ward Churchill and Howard Zinn are figures from the radical history of the 1960s, seeking to reincarnate themselves and their ideological programs in the twenty-first century.

This chapter has already examined and criticized the ideas of "social justice educators" in connection with teaching history. This branch of social studies, which came to the forefront beginning in the 1960s, views the ideas of radical groups of the 1960s as central to their ideology and openly seeks to promote these ideas in their understanding of the teaching of history. A core idea in this ideology is the argument that history cannot be objective, so teachers should not even attempt to teach objectively. Actually, such a belief does not even accurately criticize the work of historians, for historians in the twenty-first century understand the impossibility of "true" objectivity and seek instead to be open to new evidence and new interpretations. Yet in social justice education, students should not be taught how to ask their own questions of the past and then search for evidence to answer those questions, as professional historians attempt to do. Instead, "Students… critique historical and contemporary texts not just as academic historians do, but as critical minded citizens do, noting whose facts are presented as 'what happened' or as 'the truth,' as well as who benefits and who is silenced by particular interpretations of the past and present."[53] Beneath and behind this argument is the fundamental belief that, of necessity, everyone is and always has been *biased* and seeks to twist the facts to *benefit* themselves, and that is what students need to look for. Yes, everyone does have a unique perspective, but such an understanding of a biased world is overly simplistic and pessimistic. Nevertheless, the key concept in teaching the past becomes not understanding it, but giving voice to the voiceless and power to the powerless.

Social justice educators see the teaching of the social movements and leaders of the 1960s as a prime opportunity for this kind of teaching. Radicalism, oppressed people working for complete change in a hierarchical society, becomes not only a political, but a pedagogical goal. By definition, leaders of radical movements of the 1960s became heroes because they serve as models for action in the twenty-first century. No attempt need be made at understanding historical context, complexity, or even in engaging primary documents in order to gain a complete understanding of a person or era.

A prime example of this is teaching about the Black Panther Party. A Zinn Education Project lesson on the Black Panthers introduces the group as one that

> sought social justice for African Americans and other oppressed communities through a combination of revolutionary theory, education, and community programs. Their party platform, better known as the Ten Point Program, arose from the Black Panthers' assessment of the social and economic conditions in their community.[54]

This is a start for understanding this group, and it is not inaccurate. This provides a partial understanding of the Black Panthers, but it neither presents their complete set of ideas nor places the group in the context of the time. For social justice educators, the point of teaching about the Panthers is that they can serve as a model for twenty-first century groups fighting for social justice. One educator trumpeted putting the Panthers as the center of her curriculum in order to "connect the movement to today's issues" so that "they can review the Black Panther Party's Ten Point Program and develop their own personal versions of the program." The context of the times is ignored, as well as the understanding that students today live in a world far removed from the 1960s, which was, after all, the world of their grandparents, a world without personal computers, MTV, facebook, or cell phones. Students, who can easily learn more about the Panthers online, will simply dismiss such myopic teaching about a group that has been so roundly criticized (rightly or wrongly) as a negative, rather than positive, force in U.S. history.

Similarly, Gilda Ochoa has created a lesson that makes Chicano activists of 1968 the heroes of a golden age in American history. The main purpose of the lesson is not to introduce students to a little known part of American history, or to broaden the context of understanding of the civil rights movements, both of which would be important goals in the context of history education. Instead, the goal is to "provide teachers and students with the tools to make historical-contemporary connections that enhance critical thinking skills. We must ground contemporary schooling in the legacy of injustice."[55] The focus is on the present, to prove that there is a legacy of injustice. Ochoa is straightforward in her disdain for what she views as traditional education, arguing that students "socialized in today's schools, they had neither been encouraged to see systemic injustices nor to unmask romanticized images of the U.S." The concluding lesson of this teaching unit is "By thinking about how Chicana/o history has been left out of schools and the ways that students were mistreated in the 1960s, they seemed better able to understand the importance of exposing such injustices." History must be yoked to awakening student consciousness to current injustice; otherwise it is not especially valuable. In the end, Ochoa dreams of the time when more students raise their hands into a collective fist when asked about the history of inequality and resistance in schools.

In the world of radical anti-historians, anti-Vietnam protestors also receive the hero treatment. One surprising hero is Daniel Ellsberg, the bookish researcher who leaked the Pentagon Papers to the *New York Times*. Yet the purpose of studying him is not to gain a deeper appreciation of the tensions of the time, nor even to understand the injustices of the war itself. Instead, based on a lesson plan from the Zinn Education Program, Ellsberg is valuable to understand in order to comprehend the twenty-first century issue of the WikiLeaks controversy. Daniel Ellsberg is "a hero because he was a whistleblower…not merely an important person to study, but important because he is a model, a template that should be followed by kids."[56] At least this lesson plan is straightforward in its call for social activism. The lesson provides "ideal resources for students trying to understand the news about WikiLeaks today." As a conclusion, the promotional materials for the teaching guide insist that "in the spirit of Howard Zinn, this teaching guide explodes historical myths and focuses on the efforts of people—like Daniel Ellsberg—who worked to end war." Left unclear is which myths are exploded, because the lesson really focuses on twenty-first century activism rather than saying anything whatsoever about the Vietnam War itself.

Just as the conservative anti-historians, the radical anti-historians campaign to insert their version of the past into the nation's classrooms. We have now seen both stories, American exceptionalism and American evil. What is a student to do with them? Take some of both? Ignore them both? Or start from scratch, making use of evidence from both stories in order to craft a new story that is not something halfway between, but something brand new?

Importantly, the sin of the radical anti-historians has generally not been as egregious as the sin of the reactionary anti-historians. The problem is not as severe because the narrative and the curriculum is in some ways expanded. Topics of social history do need to be included in the curriculum, and teachers do need to craft lessons examining the lives of the previously ignored and the oppressed people of the past, because otherwise we are fooling ourselves into thinking we are providing for a feel of life in previous times. And it is often precisely these stories that reactionary anti-historians are so keen to make disappear from the nation's classrooms. But the real problem with both incorrect and incomplete versions of the past is that they ignore the basic rules for working to understand the past: rules of evidence, perspective, inclusiveness, context. The rules of the discipline are once again erased.

In neither case do these crusaders focus on what history actually is and can be, and in neither case are they doing much of a service for the nation's schoolchildren. As Matt Taibi argues in a critique of a book on the Reagan presidency, these two versions of the past pit "social conservatives' unshakeable faith in American exceptionalism against the progressive insistence that there's something dark and violent at the core of American hegemony. These two sides have painstakingly constructed competing versions of recent American history, leaving us without even a common set of historical facts to debate."[57] And understanding the era of Reagan is precisely the best place to go in order to examine the failure of both the reactionary and the radical branches of anti-history.

CHAPTER 6

TEACHING RONALD REAGAN

Two contrasting images of Ronald Reagan, one depicting him as one of America's greatest presidents, the other portraying him as an embattled failure. The differences could not be more stark. They portray in the sim-

The Memory Hole: The U.S. History Curriculum Under Siege, pages 111–135.
Copyright © 2014 by Information Age Publishing

plest terms two different narratives about Reagan the man and Reagan the president. Both ideas have some connection to fact, yet they are for the most part divorced from fact and historical evidence. Both are products of conscious, politically-motivated mythmaking, and neither helps teach about the past. And, just as for all of the topics of the book, there are concerted efforts to put both of these contrasting views of Reagan into the nation's classrooms. Politicians and pundits from the left and right crusade to shape the history of the Reagan era, threatening to so distort this past that the idea of actual history in relationship to this era may disappear.

The first image depicts Ronald Reagan as the fifth stone face on Mt. Rushmore, forever joining Washington, Lincoln, Jefferson and Theodore Roosevelt in the pantheon of iconic and heroic American leaders. Jack Kemp, former Republican vice presidential candidate, says that this image of Reagan is a "classy work that just might ignite a successful movement to put Ronald Reagan up on Mount Rushmore, where he belongs among America's beloved great leaders."[1] Kemp offered this support to the organizers of a movement to not only memorialize Reagan on Mt. Rushmore, but to somehow memorialize Reagan in every state or even every county in the union. There is a strong and well-organized national movement to ensure that Reagan is remembered in the twenty-first century as one of the greatest presidents of the twentieth century. This movement is led by politicians and political operatives much more interested in twenty-first century political debates than in the teaching and learning of accurate history.

At the same time, many politicians and policy analysts from the left seek to demonize Reagan, sculpting a story that makes him America's worst president. Iconic left-wing writer and journalist Christopher Hitchens said of his only personal encounter with Reagan that he "was looking at a cruel and stupid lizard" and that "Reagan was as dumb as a stump." Hitchens concluded his scorching article on Reagan with the comment that "I could not believe that such a man had even been a poor governor of California in a bad year, let alone that such a smart country would put up with such an obvious phony and loon."[2]

There is often discussion and debate about figures in the relatively recent past, and the reputations of presidents often endure reassessment and new analysis. The records, policies, and reputations of presidents have often been reassessed long after their presidencies. Perhaps the most instructive example is the presidency of Dwight Eisenhower. When Eisenhower was president, many critics derided him as being aloof and detached from the day-to-day policy machinations of the government. They skewered him as being out of his depth, more interested in golf than policy, a political and intellectual lightweight who attained the presidency only because he was a famous general. Beginning in the late seventies, historians began to reassess both Eisenhower as a leader and his leadership style. Some of the impetus for this did indeed come from a desire for a post-Vietnam, post-Watergate president who was honest, respectable, and clear headed on military matters.

Yet these desires only guided the questions, not the answers. New answers only emerged as new evidence surfaced. For this is the time when most the records of the Eisenhower administration became declassified, and historians could finally evaluate Eisenhower based on a relatively complete record rather than on political opinion. What emerged was a school of thought known as "Eisenhower revisionism." In this narrative, Ike is depicted as an experienced delegator, a subtle and nuanced manager, and a leader with firm control of a potentially rogue military. For example, the evidence from previously confidential internal government records shows Eisenhower preventing war in Vietnam in 1954, overruling zealous generals who proposed using nuclear weapons to save the French in Dien Bien Phu. Views of presidents do change and should change as new historical evidence comes to light.

Reagan is different. For the most part, the campaigns to either canonize or demonize Ronald Reagan have not been undertaken by historians. These calls for change have actually bubbled up from society and are not drawn from a sober reassessment of record. The impetus is to teach people an ideology, rather than trying to get the history right.

Media outlets with an explicit tilt towards the right or the left provide the strongest examples of attempting to invent a new narrative about Ronald Reagan. This was especially true on the 100th anniversary of his birth. According to the conservative *Washington Times* on February 6, 2011, Reagan was "the 'George Washington' we actually knew, the 'Thomas Jefferson' we respected, and he was the 'Andrew Jackson' the enemies of the United States came to respect and trust."[3]

Those who wish to teach the positive Reagan myth are much more organized and systematic in their defense of Reagan than those who attack Reagan. Reagan aide and anti-tax crusader Grover Norquist started the Ronald Reagan legacy project to rename roads, bridges, and buildings after Reagan. The clear purpose was that "these are teaching moments...The reason we do this is so children turn to their parents and... have conversations about who Reagan was and why he was important."[4] Norquist's deputy at the legacy project in the 1990s (and later COO of the California Republican party), Michael Kumburowski, made even more clear the purpose of the organization's efforts: "The left had been far better at rewriting history. Conservatives just haven't paid much attention to this kind of thing."[5] Conservatives believe strongly that they need to lead a focused effort to reinvent the history of the time and then to make sure that this history enters the nation's classrooms.

There are a number of areas on which Reagan's defenders and attackers focus most closely in the reinvention of his history. These aspects of his presidency are ripe for the retelling not because new evidence has emerged or because we know more about the context of the times. All of them relate to a narrative of the past that suits certain political needs of the present. Norquist and his allies on the right have crafted a narrative where Reagan is the hero of late twentieth century history, ushering in a new era of conservative thought and policy that Americans today need to uphold and reaffirm. Especially important to this narrative is Reagan the leader, a Reagan that embodies all of the leadership and character traits that need to be adhered to by future conservative political leaders. In this narrative, Reagan displayed this leadership most clearly in three main policy areas: his foreign policy, especially the ending of the Cold War; his tax policy and dedicated work to eliminate the national debt; and his social policy.

The counter-narrative of Reagan's presidency attacks exactly these same policy areas. The counter-narrative begins by attacking Reagan as a leader, arguing that he was completely ill suited to the presidency and lacked any of the qualities of a successful leader. Due to this, the liberal narrative continues, his international policy was disastrously narrow-minded, his tax and debt policy was both ineffective and selfish, and his social policy was ignorant and cruel. Neither narrative allows for an acceptance of even the smallest part of the other, and neither takes into account all of the historical evidence or the historical context of the times. Yet these are the narratives that many are desperate to foist on America's schoolchildren, endangering both a thoughtful understanding of the past and useful connections of this past to the present.

Both narratives begin with an assessment of Reagan's leadership. In a speech at the Reagan Library, New Jersey Republican governor Chris Christie made the following declaration:

> Ronald Reagan believed in this country. He embodied the strength, perseverance and faith that has propelled immigrants for centuries to embark on dangerous journeys to come here, to give up all that was familiar for all that was possible. He judged that as good as things were and had been for many Americans, they could and would be better for more Americans in the future.[6]

To say that Reagan is a hero for Christie and the twenty-first century conservative movement is clearly an understatement. Reagan is more even than a saint—his character and leadership ability becomes the touchstone against which all twenty-first century political leaders must be judged. Journalist Richard Herman might be even more effusive in his praise:

> President Reagan's grandfatherly and folksy wisdom, though decades old, can be our blazing lantern in these dark times....He inspires us with his reflections on the "Shining City on the Hill," a confident, wind-swept, God-

blessed city, that becomes stronger by welcoming immigrants from around the world...President Reagan reminds us that we must constantly nurture this delicate flame of American patriotism.[7]

2012 Republican presidential candidate Mitt Romney may have synthesized the accepted dogma on the right most succinctly during a speech in South Carolina in 2005: "Ronald Reagan is also my hero and a friend of all of ours...I believe that our party's ascendancy began with Ronald Reagan's brand of visionary and courageous leadership."[8]

Journalist Herman, as Christie and Romney, places Reagan in a pantheon, a leader who through his very character and presence should inspire the nation. Most importantly, the purpose of this Reagan should be to inspire our children. As Herman puts it, "informed patriotic culture must be cultivated first and foremost at the dinner tables—but also in our schools, media and entertainment."[9] Conservative historian Larry Schweikart even goes as far as to attach an almost messianic character to the Reagan presidency. He titles his chapter in *A Patriot's History* that covers the 1974–1988 era "Retreat and Resurrection," arguing that the nation retreated after Watergate in the failed presidencies of Ford and Carter but was "resurrected" during the presidency of Reagan.[10] Another textbook titles its chapter on Reagan "The Reagan Magic," as opposed to Jimmy Carter's "Ineffectual Presidency."[11]

This view of Reagan's leadership is indeed beginning to gain a strong foothold in the nation's schools. At Reagan Elementary School in Brownsburg, Indiana, teachers weave information about Reagan into class projects when students study U.S. history, says Carla Hubbard, principal of the school: "It doesn't have anything to do with political viewpoints," she says. "It is more about the model he set as a good American, and so we try to emphasize that in the curriculum with the students."[12] The point here is not that Reagan was not a good American. The point is that the starting point for the lesson is that Reagan must have been a good American, because that is what the right-wing punditocracy has told us. This lesson does not start from an examination of the evidence, or even a historical question.

We also see this sort of backwards understanding of history in the educational section of the Heritage Foundation's website. The Heritage Foundation, a conservative think tank, is dedicated to advancing "free market" conservative ideas and introducing those ideas to America's students. They argue that

Reagan lifted the country out of a great psychological depression induced by the assassinations of John F. Kennedy and Martin Luther King, Jr. and sustained by the Vietnam War, Watergate, and the Jimmy Carter malaise. He did so by appealing to the best in the American character. As he explained in his

Farewell Address, quoting the Constitution, "We the People" was the underlying basis for everything he tried to do as President.[13]

No historical evidence is provided, and of course many of these statements are historically debatable if not dubious. But the Heritage Foundation wants these ideas to be central in the nation's classrooms.

A national essay contest sponsored by the Ronald Reagan Educational Foundation and promoted by Texas governor Rick Perry best exemplifies this attempt to teach the "great" leadership qualities of Ronald Reagan. Essay contests should promote strong writing and reward the abilities to analyze and support an argument with strong evidence. The essay, in fact, is a central aspect of an effective history classroom. But this essay contest was different and did not promote the qualities of analytical thinking and argumentation. As Richard Herman, a liberal writer for the *Austin Statesman* and frequent critic of Perry, wrote, the point of the essay contest is that "entrants must love a president who left the White House before they were born."[14] The essay contest itself required the students to craft an essay that "describe how Ronald Reagan's leadership qualities influence the applicant's life." Even before this prompt, the result of the essay is made clear to potential entrants: "This year, Americans are celebrating the 100th anniversary of the birth of America's greatest president, Ronald Reagan, remembering a man who reminded us of our nation's boundless potential." Those who might believe that Reagan's influence was negative need not apply. Essays were to be kept under 100 words, again clearly showing that educational quality and rigor were not central to this teaching exercise. One of the finalists gushed "His example of humility, patriotism, and determination in every area of life, grounded upon strong religious principles, is a standard for which I strive." Perry's clear desire is not for history students to think about Reagan, or even to think with Reagan, as should be the goal in a history classroom, but to love Reagan.

Others, rather than seeking to enshrine Reagan in the minds of America's schoolchildren, seek to either erase any memory of Reagan from these minds or to create a wholly negative version of Reagan in America's schools. Many pundits at the time of Reagan's presidency attacked him and stood confused about his popularity, as we see by essayist Lance Murrow from 1986: "If F.D.R. explored the upper limits of what government could do for the individual, Reagan is testing the lower limits. Reagan's opinions and policies would be enough in another time to have protesters marching in the streets, or worse. And yet something about Reagan soothes and unites—even though the effects of his programs may repel."[15] *Newsweek*'s Jonathan Alter got into the game not long after Reagan left office, pointing out that "Reagan's approval ratings never put him in the top rank of most popular Presidents; that was always a myth. And his confectionary, heavily scripted presidency tended to lead the country backward."[16] Bob Herbert from NBC and later the *New York Times* said in 1994 that Reagan "should have been covered as a clown."[17] Liberal journalists wrote consistently and insistently about Reagan's failings, lack of qualifications, and ineffectiveness as a leader.

Many historians have since joined ranks with these journalists in their incessant attacks on Reagan's leadership. According to Michael Schaller, who has written a short synthesis of the Reagan-Bush years intended by his publisher Oxford Press to be the definitive college text about the era, "off screen or off script, Reagan often lacked focus, clarity and direction."[18] In examining Reagan's leadership in the area of international affairs, Schaller is even more damning, insisting that "With few exceptions...Reagan initiated nothing and gave few orders."[19] At various times in the book, Schaller attacks Reagan for the "moral morass" in El Salvador and then a "comic opera" operation in Grenada, and then even criticizes Reagan because his choice for the director of the Office of National Drug Control Policy, William Bennett, was a "chain-smoking 'nicotine addict' and compulsive gambler."[20] There is a fine line between a historian choosing engaging vocabulary to connect to the reader and a polemicist who eviscerates his subjects merely for explosive effect, but Schaller clearly crosses the line.

So what is the real story of Reagan's leadership? The temptation would be to try to split the difference between saint and devil and perhaps list the positive and negative factors, coming up somewhere in between. Yet this is an intellectually vapid answer. One can't be part saint and part devil. Neither the explanation of the Reagan hagiographers nor the explanation from the Reagan haters connects to historical evidence, so why should we choose some from each side?

Rather, the answer is to both look at the actual historical record and then to try to find the qualities, characteristics and policies that elicit such polarized feelings. For example, although right-wing supporters view Reagan as a strong, no compromise defender of conservative ideology, it turns out that his record reflects something different in the area of leadership. "The rest of the story is that Reagan was a guy who cut deals," argues biographer Lou Canon. "He was practical on the margins," a president willing to compromise some of his conservative principles to enact others.[21] Author Will Bunch, often a detractor of Reagan and his myth, points out "It was the president's often practical side that ruled the day, and it was this, not his radical conservative instincts, that had the lasting positive impact."[22] The right in the twenty-first century wants to paint Reagan as a no-nonsense, principled conservative, and so this is the picture they try to convince the schools to promote. He was, instead, a politician for most of his life, very close to being the "career politician" that has become anathema to so many on the right.

At the same time, it is clearly incomplete and inaccurate to argue that Reagan was an utter failure as a leader. Too many people believed and believe in him. The fact is that he was elected to two terms and is still revered by a large segment of the American population. To ignore this is to ignore evidence, just as it is to ignore evidence to argue that Reagan did no wrong in his leadership of the country. Will Bunch was on to something when he stated that "Ronald Reagan had a God-given gift for connecting with the American people."[23] That fact alone needs to be taught, but then the analysis needs to go further. Bunch, a critic of Reagan believes that Reagan "abused this gift," and that what is really important is that "Reagan was a transformative figure in American history, but his real revolution was one of public-relations-meets-politics and not one of policy."[24]

Those who wish Reagan to be enshrined on Mt. Rushmore go beyond his leadership style in their positive assessment. They argue that Reagan's policies fundamentally changed and helped the nation in many different areas. First and foremost is their argument that Reagan won the Cold War. Conservatives of the twenty-first century now take it as a given that Reagan, and Reagan alone, was responsible for the disappearance of the Berlin Wall and the crumbling of the Soviet Union. Larry Schweikart, conservative author of *A Patriot's History of the United States* and *48 Liberal Lies about American History*, phrased it this way in answer to a reporter on Fox News: "the majority of books credit former Soviet President Mikhail Gorbachev with ending the Cold War, and not Reagan. That's 'a joke,' Schweikart says. ' lived through the Reagan years, I remember.'"[25] His very answer, of course, points to a major flaw in Schweikart's thinking. He ignores critical differences between his memory, which is of course individual, particular, and concentrated on his perspective of the world, and history, which needs to be collective, informed by general context, and concentrated on multiple and varied sources.

Most conservatives move beyond their personal memory in insisting that Reagan ended the Cold War. According to the Heritage Foundation, "Reagan's military buildup and competition with the Soviet Union not only kept America safe but also won the Cold War without firing a shot."[26] The conservative *Washington Times*, in a tribute issue to Reagan, enlisted the leader of a conservative think tank in the Czech Republic to make the case that Reagan ended the Cold War in an article entitled "To Eastern Eyes, a Liberator":

> Then Ronald Reagan appeared on the scene. He terrified the brutes, scared the hell out of them, compelled them—for the first time in their lives—to entertain a terrible thought: "What if Athens (Western democracy) is not conquered by Sparta (Soviet militarism) after all? What if, this time, Athens defeats Sparta? With that man in the Oval Office, it's possible. Nay, it's likely. Inevitable...'"[27]

The argument goes something like this: due to Reagan's steadfastness of purpose and uncompromising attitude towards the Soviet Union, his prescient build-up of the American military forced the Soviet Union to give up the arms race; and because of his determination to speak truth to dictatorial power in his speeches, the Soviet Union gave up attempting to compete with the United States and retreated into defeat in the face of Reagan's determined stance. Key to this narrative is not only Reagan's single-mindedness, but also the single-handedness with which this task was accomplished. There is little room in this story for other actors, whether it is the reform minded leader of the Soviet Union Mikhail Gorbachev or even George H. W. Bush, who was president when the wall came tumbling down and two years later and when the Soviet Union actually dissolved.

Perhaps the clearest picture of this story, and one that is most pertinent as we examine the changing of history in America's classrooms, is the one that emerges in a lesson plan Joy Hakim wrote as an accompanying text for *Freedom: A History of US*. Hakim, originally a teacher, first gained prominence in the U.S. history curriculum world with a very readable survey of U.S. history for young readers. Such a series was sorely needed because so many textbooks are written by committee and so are virtually unreadable, and Hakim is a gifted storyteller with a knack for making history engaging and interesting. Her story on Reagan and the Cold War focuses on a speech Reagan made in Berlin in 1987, where

> he said bluntly to his new friend, "Mr. Gorbachev, tear down this wall!" Two years later, in 1989, the Soviet Union, rent by internal forces, fell apart, a victim of inefficiency, huge military expenditures and a flawed political system. The Russian people repudiated communism. Ronald Reagan said, "Let us move toward a world in which all people are at last free to determine their own destiny."[28]

It is important to note that Hakim does mention factors other than Reagan in the fall of the USSR, factors which we shall examine below. Yet the clear focus of this discussion, and of the entire lesson, is on Reagan and the speech he made in Berlin. This speech is always cited in the story of the end of the Cold War, as if the mere utterance of the words caused the wall to actually tumble to the ground.

The history that conservative politicians, pundits, and educators want taught in the classroom is a history that gives Ronald Reagan sole credit for winning the Cold War. The "tear down this wall" speech is always given center stage in this narrative. We see an example in a teaching unit created by teachers from Nebraska entitled "Ronald Reagan and the end of the Cold War (1947–1988)." This unit includes important strengths, in that it asks students to engage in depth a variety of primary source material. Yet the very title is problematic...the Cold War did not end when Reagan left office at the end of 1988. No one took a hammer to the Berlin Wall until November of 1989, a full year after the election of George H. W. Bush, and the Soviet Union fell two years after that. The unit centers on a number of speeches given by Reagan, of course highlighting the "tear down this wall" speech. Students are also asked to read an important 1983 Reagan speech where he calls the USSR an "evil empire." Significantly, students are also asked to read Reagan's speech from 1964 entitled "A Time for choosing" as well as Reagan's speech to HUAC in 1947 condemning communists in Hollywood. The hero of the story of the Cold War, then, becomes Ronald Reagan and only Ronald Reagan, a lone voice of steadfast determination against the evils of communism. With this focus, the story of the Cold War is not a story of leaders from both parties standing firm against a dictatorial enemy but instead a story of a home grown American hero who finally gains power in the 1980s and can finally speak clearly to America's foes in 1987.[29]

The "tear down this wall" narrative also takes center stage in an educational video produced by 2008 Republican presidential hopeful, conservative pundit, and former Arkansas Governor Mike Huckabee. After his presidential run in 2008, Huckabee led an effort, which he calls "Learn Our History." "Learn Our History" produces animated videos depicting a group of schoolchildren traveling through time to find out what really, truly happened in the past, presenting "true American history facts without bias." In explaining how these products are unbiased, Huckabee argues that he feels compelled to bring "real" history to America's schoolchildren, because "Learn Our History's products have been developed to correct the 'blame America first' attitude prevalent in today's teaching." It is difficult to understand how he does not see that this in itself is a bias, a different point of view that brings a clear political agenda into the classroom. Be that as it may, Huckabee believes that one of his main audiences is homeschoolers and that his videos "will get them excited about learning history, social studies and current events. Plus, as they watch the videos, they'll be developing a deep appreciation for America and a strong sense of national pride."[30] Huckabee's goal is to retell much of American history in a way that will excite American schoolchildren and inculcate the values he feels are important, rather than examining history for history's sake. It is no accident that Larry Schweikart is the most significant historical advisor for these videos.

Perhaps the most interesting of all of the videos is the one entitled "The Reagan Revolution." This video is mostly a story of Reagan's domestic economic and social policies, which we will examine later, but a key point in the video is when the time traveling students get to be witness to the "tear down this wall" speech. During the discussion, Carter is condemned because he does not understand that "the Soviet Union wants America destroyed," and he is cutting our military "so we can't fight them as well." We are taught that it is called a "Cold War" because "our side ain't doing so hot." Huckabee then can't resist returning the audience to 2011 and the real political purpose behind the video, having one of the students not so obliquely criticize Barack Obama by exclaiming "sounds like how Iran and Russia treat us today…I guess history can repeat itself."

Luckily, we then get transported to September 1980, and we meet the hero of the video, Ronald Reagan. He declares that "My strategy for the Cold War is we win, they lose." And, in respect to the Cold War, that is how the video plays out—the U.S. wins because of the efforts of Reagan, and the USSR is indeed confined to the "dustbin of history." One of the students even marvels that "Reagan made the wall come down." Of course there is nothing in the video about the Iran-Contra affair, to say nothing of Reagan's dubious dealings with South Africa or the tragedy that befell the American marines in Lebanon—those incidents are simply erased. The speech itself becomes the central event in the Cold War for these students. Not the establishment of containment under Harry Truman, not the Cuban Missile Crisis under John F. Kennedy, not détente under Richard Nixon—the argument of the video is that Reagan's speech and demeanor are the only central lessons about presidential leadership and policy that need to be learned regarding the Cold War.

As history, the weaknesses of presenting Reagan as the sole American Cold War champion are legion. First, as already mentioned, the story violates chronology in ignoring when the Cold War actually ended, which happened between one and three years after Reagan left office. Second, the facts don't match the argument that Reagan bankrupted the Soviet Union. After a careful study of the numbers, Jeffrey Knopf of the Naval War College rhetorically asked, "Did Reagan win the Cold War? The Soviet Union never increased its military spending to match the Reagan buildup and hence avoided exacerbating the defense burden on the Soviet economy."[31] Reagan defenders, and even many with less of an ideological axe to grind, often argue with some justification that Reagan set up the conditions that led to the collapse of the Soviet Union, as Ted Koppel did in a discussion with Phil Donahue in 1987: "Ronald Reagan may have won the Cold War by forcing the Soviet Union to realize that it could not compete financially or technologically with a revitalized United States."[32]

Historians needs to look at the big picture, and taking the big picture into account, it is important to note that Reagan's policies differed very little from his predecessors, all of whom followed the policy outline first set out by Harry Truman in the late 1940s. All of the presidents sought to contain the Soviet Union and their communist allies. All of the presidents sought to negotiate arms control deals to keep the threat of nuclear war at bay (including Reagan in his discussions with Gorbachev in Reykjavik in 1986). All of the presidents made speeches in defense of freedom and opposition to tyranny, even if Reagan's "tear down this wall" speech was more eloquent than most. But chronologically, the only president in office when the Cold War ended was George H. W. Bush, not Ronald Reagan.

The story of Reagan the Cold War hero also ignores at least two other critical components of history: context and multiple perspectives. In order to come to an approximate understanding of what happened in the past, it is the duty of the historian to examine as much of the context of the time as possible and as many of the perspectives of the time as possible. Merely sending children back in a time machine to see Reagan's speech is not sufficient because, at the very least, the children can't see nor know anything about Gorbachev and what he was attempting to do in a Soviet Union that was in economic trouble long before Reagan became president. Strobe Talbott, international policy analyst and journalist, declared in 1991 that

> The Soviet Union collapsed, the Cold War ended almost overwhelmingly because of internal contradictions and pressures within the Soviet Union and the Soviet system itself. And even if Jimmy Carter had been reelected and been followed by Walter Mondale, something like what we have now seen probably would have happened.[33]

Perhaps Talbott has gone too far in the other direction in not giving Reagan any credit, and we shall examine that issue later. The point is that virtually anyone that has studied the Soviet Union during the 1970s and 1980s has found that it was very near to internal collapse. They also note that without a reform-minded leader like Gorbachev, no changes would have even been discussed, no matter how many times Reagan called for them. Gorbachev himself insisted "We were increasingly behind the West, which was achieving a new technological era, a new productivity."[34] As Matthew Dallek colorfully argues in *The American Scholar*, "the idea that Reagan 'won' the Cold War reduces the story to the myth of a lone cowboy riding to the rescue when the world was on the eve of nuclear annihilation."[35] Specialist in Soviet history Stephen Kotkin insists that "too many analysts credit President Reagan with having helped bring down the evil empire," but the real reason for the collapse of the USSR was astronomical military spending in the 1970s and the failure to keep up with western capitalism.[36]

Many historians argue today that it was American soft power, or the ability of western consumer goods and consumer culture to "conquer" the people of the east bloc and Soviet Union that led to the demise of the Cold War. In other words, it was the personal computer, rock and roll music, and blue jeans that deserve the credit, not a speech given by Reagan in Berlin. Historians must look for context and background such as this, and students of history need to be encouraged to look this deeply as well, rather than settling for the simpler answer that the entire Cold War was ended by a single speech. Historians and history students must also look at this issue from the perspective of Soviet history and the Russian people, rather than being satisfied that the only viewpoint that matters is the viewpoint from Washington, DC.

Interestingly and disturbingly, critics of Reagan often take an extra step beyond debunking the myth of Reagan as Cold War hero. In this narrative, Reagan becomes the villain, and many Reagan critics are working very hard to make this narrative central in America's classrooms. As Eleanor Clift, left-wing journalist from *Newsweek,* put it, "People who want to give Ronald Reagan the entire credit for the collapse of the Soviet Union ignore the fact that the Soviet economy was collapsing and the Reagan Administration covered it up...The CIA concealed what was happening over there so they could keep the defense budget over here high."[37] She starts from a historically reasonable premise, yet follows it up with a claim that is not substantiated with any evidence. Ted Koppel ridicules this sort of attack, one that he sees as common in the American media: "But to the American media, the Reagan defense buildup seemed like a plot designed to deny government aid to poor and hungry people."[38]

In this narrative, the purpose of Reagan's defense spending build-up was merely to allow Reagan to sound tough and to reward his wealthy defense industry supporters. As NBC anchor John Chancellor put it, "Some say Ronald Reagan won the Cold War by spending so much on defense that the Kremlin went bankrupt trying to keep up. That won't wash. During Reagan's presidency the United States itself became a bankrupt country." In 1991, PBS's Juan Williams put it this way: "When you talk about the spending during the Reagan years on defense, you're talking about absolute abdication of responsibility to domestic policy and issues in this country, and it's totally without regard to the fact that these people were spending hundreds of dollars on toilet seats, not even this advanced technology."[39] In this narrative, any possible contribution Reagan made to the ending of the Cold War is either ignored or buried in criticism of his domestic policy. The key point is that all complexity is swept aside in the attempt to demonize Reagan. Without an acceptance of complexity, historical thinking is impossible, either in public debate or in the classroom.

Critics of Reagan continue by arguing that because of his narrow-minded focus on the Cold War, Reagan committed a number of errors in the international arena that belie the belief that he was a defender of freedom and model foreign policy leader. Thomas Friedman, in a conversation with former Secretary of Education and staunch Reagan loyalist Senator Lamar Alexander, argues that Reagan's lack of experience scared him and then implied that it was exactly this lack of experience that led to 245 marines being murdered by terrorists in Beirut.[40] Will Bunch points out in relation to the bombing in Beirut that "withdrawing Marines after bombing was exactly the same type of response that would be lambasted by conservatives today...'as cutting and running'" and that such an action from Reagan's predecessor Jimmy Carter would have and still would evoke calls of cowardice from conservative critics.[41] Staying in the Middle East, Reagan's critics also attack him for supporting the Taliban in their war against the Soviet Union in the 1980s (Reagan even went so far as to dedicate a 1987 space shuttle mission to the Taliban). Such support, the critics argue, set up and supplied a future dread enemy of the United States. Of course, such a criticism is also problematic from the point of view of a historian, criticizing a leader for not foreseeing a situation a generation in the future that almost no one at the time anticipated.

One area where Reagan did receive tremendous criticism while he was in office is the Iran-Contra scandal. Reagan's administration, in an attempt to release hostages held by extremists in Lebanon, sold sophisticated weapons to Iran. This violated traditional U.S. policy and Reagan's own statements on the matter. The administration then took the money from these arms sales and secretly funneled the money to fund the Contra rebels in Nicaragua, violating the will of Congress and a law Congress passed to prevent the funding of the Contras. Journalist Michael Kinsley provides a brief but scathing critique of Reagan's actions:

> One Reagan foreign policy initiative almost no one tries to defend is trading weapons for hostages in Iran-Contra. It was morally contemptible, it violated one of the central principles that got Reagan elected, it trampled the very value of democracy it was ostensibly designed to promote. And it didn't even work.[42]

The uproar almost led to impeachment proceedings against Reagan and dominated the news and the tenor of the final three years of Reagan's presidency. Yet the scandal only receives scant attention, if any at all, from conservative defenders of the Reagan hero myth. In the twenty pages on Reagan in Schweikart's *A Patriot's History of the United States*, one paragraph is devoted to the scandal, and that one paragraph taunts Reagan's critics for allowing Oliver North to take the blame and get away without prosecution.[43] An important component of historical thinking is empathy, attempting to come to grips with the thoughts and feelings of people at the time. Iran-Contra dominated the news of the nation and the focus of Washington for two years, and ignoring it is to sweep the actual events of the period under the rug.

On the other hand, for left-wing critics of Reagan, the Iran-Contra scandal *is* Reagan's foreign policy and dominates the narrative of his term. Will Bunch declares it "can't be ignored that 1987 was a year of low poll numbers and very low esteem for Reagan."[44] On Iran-Contra: "Any information about Iran-Contra or how the 1979–1981 hostages were released that didn't fit the new official story line was being metaphorically clipped out of the newspaper and tossed down the "memory hole.'"[45]

Reagan also comes under fire from the left for his policy towards South Africa. Examining it from the South African perspective, Reagan's policy was at the very least problematic. On a trip to the United States after winning the Nobel Prize in 1984, Bishop Desmond Tutu memorably declared that Reagan's policy was "immoral, evil and totally un-Christian." Reagan did retain a close alliance with the Apartheid government, which he thought was a bulwark against communism. He vetoed any legislation that would impose sanctions against South Africa and at times displayed a remarkable ignorance about South Africa, as when he told a radio interviewer in 1985, "They have eliminated the segregation that we once had in our own country—the type of thing where hotels and restaurants and places of entertainment and so forth were segregated—that has all been eliminated."[46]

Such facts about the Reagan policy and administration are important to tell and should not be brushed aside in a rush to tell a story about Reagan's uniformly heroic foreign policy. At the same time, should teachers *only* teach about Iran-Contra and Reagan's policies towards South Africa? Of course not, because the context would be incomplete. One cannot understand Reagan on South Africa if one does not understand Reagan on the USSR. Students should be encouraged to ask about choices that need to be made by presidents. Should Reagan have viewed South Africa as a battleground in the Cold War? Our schools are getting shortchanged because the only curriculum students are being exposed to is either an argument that Reagan's foreign policy was heroic or an argument that Reagan was an evil villain in his relationships with the rest of the world.

We see a similar depressing dichotomy in the narratives about Reagan's economic policies. One story portrays Reagan as the heroic champion of free enterprise, low taxes, and controlled government spending. The other story portrays Reagan as the intellectually vacuous champion of supply side voodoo economics, causing reliance on budget deficits and inhumanely slashing the American social support system. As with an examination of Reagan's foreign policies, an examination of his domestic policy shows that both arguments miss the mark. Both stem more from later political views than an examination of the full context of the 1980s. Both shortchange history, in the process shortchanging students of history and helping to exacerbate an every growing gulf in twenty-first century American politics.

As in so many other examples, conservative historian Larry Schweikart leads the way in his hyperbolic treatment of Reagan's tax and economic policy. In his textbook *A Patriot's History of the United States*, he titles the section on Reagan's economic policy "Tax cuts revive a nation."[47] Schweikart opens the section defending the effectiveness of supply side economics and the Laffer curve, a very dubious line of argument that runs counter to the thinking of most economists. Regardless of this, such a defense is a very odd argument in a history textbook, especially a textbook that Schweikart and his co-author insist presents "just the facts." The important aspect of supply side economics in this text is that "Reagan knew in his soul the tax cuts would work."[48] Schweikart admits that two years of deep recession and high unemployment followed the tax cuts, but because Reagan was patient and persistent, he allowed them time to succeed because "average Americans could see by their wallets that the economy was growing by leaps and bounds."[49]

Schwiekart is similarly effusive in his praise of Reagan's economic policies in *48 Liberal Lies about American History*. The title of the book, of course, trumpets the political tone and purpose of the book, giving lie to any belief that Schweikart is attempting to begin with the evidence to reach his conclusions. "Lie #47" is entitled "The Reagan tax cuts caused massive deficits and the national debt." In a six-page essay, Schweikart attacks everyone who criticized Reagan, directing especially severe attacks on historians who "don't even bother to consult the most rudimentary facts." The next paragraph includes some of those facts, including the fact that government tax revenues rose in the 1980s despite the 1981 tax cut. To use his own term, such a "rudimentary" look at the facts ignores the reasons for the economic growth that caused this rise in revenues, many of which were completely disconnected from the 1981 tax cut. However, Reagan did raise taxes many more times than he lowered them, bringing the supply side argument into even greater question.

Schweikart then moves into a discussion of the deficit, which many have blamed on the tax cutting, because, he argues, these textbook authors have a "deep-seated hostility to tax cuts." The answer is simple, according to Schweikart. The deficits were caused not by tax cuts or defense build-up, but by "*The Democratic congress, with its pork-barrel spending*" (italics in original). Yet he provides no statistics on how much this spending was, even after he dismissed the rise in defense spending as un-important because it represented less than 1% of GDP.[50] The bottom line is that Schweikart's arguments read more like the political "spin" from a twenty-first century presidential race than a work of history. He does not even make a nod towards objectivity, apparently believing that objectivity is not possible, even though striving for objectivity needs to be a central goal for historians and history students. He makes no attempt to examine a variety of evidence, even though searching out a variety of evidence needs to be a central goal for historians and history students. And he makes no attempt to frame questions in the context of their time, rather than in the political context of a later time, even though asking contextual questions needs to be a central goal for historians and history students.

Others have taken the ideas of Schweikart and brought them directly to students. Nothing better exemplifies this than a statement written by Kate Obenschein, the vice president of the Young American's Foundation

(YAF), a group dedicated to teaching American students the "right" history. Obenschein is a leader of the Republican party in Virginia and an on-again off-again staffer for one-time Republican governor and senatorial candidate George Allen. Her bio at the YAF website proclaims that as "a regular guest on Fox News, Kate Obenshain is an articulate, fearless defender of conservative principles."[51] In an effort to discount the ratings given to Reagan by "liberal" history professors, she argues,

> The facts are that President Reagan ended the Cold War and generated the greatest period of peacetime economic growth in US History. Under President Reagan, the misery index (inflation plus unemployment) fell nearly 10 points and youth unemployment dropped more than 5%. Revenues doubled, and the country pulled out of two economic recessions. Professors can't say the same about FDR or any other president.[52]

It is not clear where she found her facts, but they are clearly distorted. Moving beyond her problematic discussion of the Cold War, we see her misuse statistics merely to prove her point. The most fascinating aspect of this is her focus on "the misery index" in comparing FDR and Reagan. This is a completely nonsensical and ahistorical comparison. Because FDR took office in a time of rampant and destructive *deflation*, any measurement of the growth of inflation while he was president would show a large increase in inflation, and thus a larger "misery index." Yet FDR, and virtually everyone in the United States in the 1930s, *wanted inflation*, and so applying the misery index to that time period makes no sense. Ms. Obenschein's arguments masquerade as history but really present political spin.

Those who fervently believe in the Reagan economic miracle also fervently believe that young history students need to be taught about it. This is clear in Schweikart's textbook, designed for high school history students and is perhaps even more clear in Mike Huckabee's "Learn Our History" videos. The time traveling teens travel back to Washington DC in 1977 so they can get an understanding of how terrible life was in the United States before Reagan's election. The DC they arrive in is crumbling and frightening, complete with garbage on the streets and graffiti on every wall. One of the students immediately comments on what an "icky place America is in the 1970s," immediately following the comment with "Jimmy Carter is still president." Although it is not entirely clear why a teenager would immediately make a jump from "icky place" to a president she had not heard of before, the purpose of the comment is clear. They are saved from an evil gang by a teen (of course, a father of one of the teens in his teenage years) who tells them that everything is so "icky" because of "the recession...the downturn in everything is killing us...and some of their morals are gone." He continues by saying the problems include high taxes and inflation.

The cartoon children watch as Reagan fixes the disastrous economic problems brought on (in the argument of the video) by Jimmy Carter. At one point, the students return to the dilapidated street in DC that they originally visited and note that the "changes are amazing." Huckabee introduces the traveling teens and the audience to supply side economics, and we all learn together that this is the basis for the change. One of the children actually challenges this, meekly questioning, "Didn't the rich get richer and the poor get poorer." (It is unclear why she would ask this question, since she supposedly knows nothing at all about the era, but the audience is meant to suspend disbelief in a cartoon, I suppose.) The answer is disturbing: "No, actually, income for Blacks is growing faster than Whites." The question was about the poor, and the answer was about race, which might be confusing, except that all are meant to assume that to be Black meant to be poor. By the end of the video, everyone is economically well off. The legacy of Reagan is that "President Reagan's policies of tax cuts and limited government led to a quarter century of growth."

Of course, this completely erases the presidency of Bill Clinton with a moderate rise in taxes and an increase in a variety of government programs. Reagan is the hero here, and the clear and transparent purpose of the video is to make the "Great Communicator" into a saint. Not a near saint, but actually a saint, as we hear him declare after the assassination attempt in 1981, "It was God who saved me from that bullet. I'm here because there is work for me to do." Huckabee's video seeks to make students see Reagan as America's most effective president, painting him as a hero who rid the world of communism and saved the American economy. The sins against historical thinking contained in this video are legion. Of course, we encounter an overly simplistic narrative that avoids all complexity. Huckabee moves beyond oversimplification by inventing evidence and ignoring counterevidence. Further, he implies a cause and effect relationship for which there is no basis in fact.

However, just as with the Cold War, there are many historians, left-leaning pundits, and analysts who seek to teach students that Reagan's economic policy made him anything but a saint. First, critics are fond of dismissing the Reagan mystique by pointing to a number of statistics that belie the essence of the myth. For example, in "seven of his eight years in office," Reagan raised taxes rather than lowering them. Significantly, most of these tax raises did not impact the marginal income tax rate, but instead applied to other taxes such as the payroll tax, the gas tax, and even corporate tax. As historian David Brinkley put it, it "is a myth" that Reagan was an anti-tax zealot. As it turns out, Reagan was not especially focused on attacking the deficit either. As a "progressive" web site happily points out, "during the Reagan years, the debt increased to nearly $3 trillion, roughly three times as much as the first 80 years of the century had done altogether."

This counters the "conservative myth" that supply side economics would be able to both lower taxes and lower the deficit.[53] We have already seen the conservative retort to this argument, that Democrats in congress forced Reagan's hand in domestic spending, and this caused the deficit instead of lower taxes. The point here, though, should not be to reargue the policy debates of the 1980s.

This provides little opportunity for history students to learn. The left and the right are talking past each other in their efforts to prove a point about the past that they believe will help them in the present. Students need to learn both that marginal tax rates went down while Reagan was president and that the deficit went up. Students need to encounter the arguments of both sides during the 1980s in the form of primary documents from the time period. They need to attempt to understand the policy arguments of the time, rather than arguing over the extent to which the policies "worked" in the eyes of those in the twenty-first century. For historical thinking to occur, students also need to understand the extent to which Reagan and his policies polarized people at the time.

Not surprisingly, it was many in the media who most directly attacked the Reagan myth and mystique in the 1990s. Of course, this fits well into the conservative mantra that the elitist media were obsessed with tearing down Reagan at any opportunity. However, to be fair, the media did consistently focus on facts. As Tim Russert of "Meet the Press" put it, "Our viewers remember from '80, from 1980 to 1988, Ronald Reagan said he could cut taxes, increase defense, and still balance the budget. The deficit under Ronald Reagan doubled. The debt tripled, and home mortgage rates were 12 percent. It didn't work then. Why would it work now?"[54] Sam Donaldson framed it this way:

> For ten years Ronald Reagan taught us there was a free lunch. "Folks," he said, "we're going to cut your taxes and we're going to spend like there's no tomorrow and you don't have to pay for it." Folks, we're now paying for it and it's bitter medicine...We're going to have to raise taxes to get some sort of fairness here...For ten years the great wizard sold us that idea, that we could grow our way out of the deficits and we bought it, and we didn't.[55]

The fact that Donaldson and Russert, as leaders in the media, could not understand the creation and acceptance by a majority of Americans of a packaged and pointed story is a wonderfully interesting irony. For the important legacy of Reagan's economic and tax policy is not be found in economic statistics but in political memory. Historian and political analyst Will Bunch, often very critical of Reagan, is not hesitant to attack him about his economic policy, noting that the federal deficit grew exponentially, the federal work force grew even while tax revenue from all sources went up. Bunch believes that this was "because a turnaround from the abnormally bad 1970s was inevitable. Because Reagan allowed Carter's unpopular pick for Federal Reserve chairman, Paul Volcker, to squeeze the money supply, and because oil prices plummeted in the Reagan years."[56]

But Bunch understands that this is not the entire story, and if teachers attempt to focus on only this point as the entire story, they will be short-changing their students of the full context of the times. As Bunch puts it,

> Undoubtedly, the Reagan 1981 tax cut—and the notion that cutting top tax rates and all taxes on corporations is the only acceptable policy direction—is the enduring legacy he has bequeathed, at least in terms of public debate, to our modern politics…it was, quite accurately, a revolution…A political turning point, not an economic one.[57]

There must be a reason that Schweikart and others so doggedly hold to the myth of Reagan as saint and a reason why so many Americans cling to the myth and wish to use the myth as a foundation for the building of their political personas. Analyzing the extent to which the Reagan economic policies worked as promised is only part of the analysis students need to undertake. Students must also study political attitudes and the political mood of the country and must attempt to discern whether there was any change that took place during the Reagan years, and there is no doubt that a political change did occur between the landslide defeat of Goldwater in 1964 and the landslide victory of Reagan in 1984.

Another fundamental shift that students of history need to examine is the shift in social policy and attitudes towards social policy that took place while Reagan was president. In this area, too, the fawning pro-Reagan myth-makers and the shrill anti-Reagan myth busters dominate the interpretative landscape, drowning out real thinking about the era's history. In the right-wing story, Reagan is saintly first because he recognized the Christian character and history of the nation. The homeschool textbook *America's Providential History* takes special note of this, commending Reagan for his National Day of Prayer Proclamation in 1982, when he insisted "The most sublime picture in American history is of George Washington on his knees in the snow at Valley Forge."[58] Of course, we have already examined the questionable veracity of the Washington story, but it is a critical starting point in understanding the role of traditional morality in the narrative of the Reagan presidency. In this story, Reagan was one of, if not *the*, greatest presidents in history only partly because he ended the Cold War, lowered taxes, and fixed the American economy. Most importantly, in this story, he returned the United States to a time of moral clarity and purpose, rescuing it from the drift and degradation of the Carter years. This is the clear intent of the Huckabee video "The Reagan Revolution" we examined earlier, as we viewed the Carter years as years of dirt, decay, and criminals running amok on the streets of DC and the Reagan years as ordered and peaceful.

Most Reagan hagiographers see the return to "traditional values" as a centerpiece of his presidency. For example, in a travel book of tourist sites in Washington DC connecting God and America, Newt Gingrich and his third wife Calista Gingrich praise Ronald Reagan for his "evil empire" speech challenging the Soviet Union because Reagan attacked government efforts to "water down traditional values" and declared that "freedom prospers when religion is vibrant and the rule of law under God is acknowledged."[59] Conservative speaker T. Kenneth Crib, in a speech entitled "Ronald Reagan and the Moral Imagination," declared that, "Ronald Reagan began his life learning from the Bible at his mother's knee. At his death, he still owned that Bible, with its well-marked passages in her hand and his. He said once that his mother gave him a great deal, but nothing more important than the special gift of his life-long practice of intercessory prayer. And he spoke of the happiness and solace to be gained by talking to the Lord."[60] In this story, Reagan was the model example of the moral Christian, and this morality infused every single thing he did as president.

The pro-Reagan mythmakers seek to take this narrative of Reagan morality into the schools. One of the most popular homeschool textbooks, *Heritage of Freedom*, expresses clear support and approval for Reagan's stance on social issues and morality. In the words of the text, "As he campaigned for the Presidency, he expressed a sincere desire to return America to the traditional values (Biblical values such as moral purity, honesty, respect for human life) that made America great. The nation's moral decline, particularly the problem of abortion, greatly concerned him." Of course, this text presents an absolute moral code, and those who do not follow the tenets of this code contribute to the nation's "moral decline." According to this textbook, after being elected, Reagan fulfilled his promise to try to lift uplift the nation, for example hiring William Bennett to be Secretary of Education. Bennett "argued strongly for the return of morality and discipline to the classroom" but was thwarted by the "American educational establishment."[61] Bennett himself, in his own right-leaning textbook of U.S. history, argues that he sought to "stress the importance of character development."[62] In the story these right-wing politicians and pundits wish to tell in the schools, Reagan halted the moral decline of a nation.

This story is crystal clear in a fascinating set of flashcards published by a homeschool teacher on a program called "Quizlet." "Quizlet" is a template that anyone can publish on, and anyone can access the cards, with the assumption that they are accurate. These materials are flashcards, designed to quiz homeschooled children on the "facts" of the Reagan presidency. The very first card asks, "What did Ronald Reagan stand for?" The answer is "traditional values and military strength."[63] Card number five reinforces the idea of the moral and economic failures of the 1970s by asking what public schools were like in the 1980s, the answer being "there was theft, drug use and violence." So any unsuspecting student hoping to improve his or her understanding of the Reagan presidency is apt to learn these as "facts" about the Reagan presidency.

Those on the left who seek to discredit and attack Reagan at every turn seek to do so by relating a very different narrative about Reagan and morality. This Reagan was cold, selfish, and narrow minded in his view towards others. First, his economic policies allowed the rich to get richer and the poor to get poorer, showing that Reagan really did not care about the poor. As Will Bunch put it, "Reagan's true lasting gift to American society is the ever widening gulf between the wealthy and the middle class."[64] *New York Times* Washington Bureau chief Howell Raines was much more biting and direct in his criticism:

> I was a correspondent in the White House in those days, and my work which consisted of reporting on President Reagan's success in making life harder for citizens who were not born rich, white, and healthy saddened me. My parents raised me to admire generosity and to feel pity. I had arrived in our nation's capital [in 1981] during a historic ascendancy of greed and hardheartedness.[65]

In other words, Reagan created the "decade of greed," and how can such a leader be viewed as a "moral" leader?

The criticism of Reagan's morality becomes even more strident when anti-Reagan analysts examine specific social policies, or lack of social policies, during the Reagan administration. Reagan displayed a rare tin political ear in his treatment of racial and civil rights issues. Historian Matthew Dallek relates a story about a Reagan comment about Dr. Martin Luther King, Jr., when Reagan said in answer to a charge from conservative and one time strident segregationist Senator Jesse Helms that King was communist. "'We'll know in about 35 years, won't we,' Reagan replied. 'I almost lost my dinner over that,' David Gergen (White House communications director at the time) told biographer Lou Cannon."[66] In a 2002 article in *Time*, columnist Jack White wrote "It's with Reagan, who set a standard for exploiting white anger and resentment rarely seen since George Wallace stood in the schoolhouse door, that the Republican [party]'s selective memory about its race-baiting habit really stands out."[67]

Reagan's legacy endures the sharpest criticism because of his lack of a policy on AIDS. As journalist Allen White declared in 2004, "As America remembers the life of Ronald Reagan, it must never forget his shameful abdication of leadership in the fight against AIDS. History may ultimately judge his presidency by the thousands who have and will die of AIDS."[68] AIDS first burst onto the American scene in 1981, and it is clear that the Reagan administration did very little to tackle or combat the issue until near the end of his terms in 1987. Biographer Lou Canon admits that Reagan's leadership on combating the disease was "halting and ineffective," and Will Bunch insists that Reagan's lack of leadership on this issue was "appalling" and points out that Reagan did not utter the word "AIDS" in a prepared speech until 1987.[69] Critics of Reagan reach a higher pitch of shrillness in this area as opposed to any other, insisting that "a gerontocratic Ronald Reagan took this [AIDS] plague less seriously than Gerald Ford had taken swine flu. After all, he didn't need the ghettos and he didn't want the gays"[70] and that "Ronald Reagan cares more about UFOs than AIDS."[71]

And just as the morally perfect Reagan image has crept into right-wing textbooks, the morally lacking Reagan makes an appearance in high school textbooks of the left. Howard Zinn's is worth quoting at length, with his diatribe about Reagan and his amoral treatment of the poor and minorities:

> At the end of the eighties, at least a third of African-American families fell below the official poverty level, and black unemployment seemed fixed at two and a half times that of whites, with young blacks out of work at the rate of 30 to 40 percent. The life expectancy of blacks remained at least ten years lower than that of whites. In Detroit, Washington, and Baltimore, the mortality rate for black babies was higher than in Jamaica or Costa Rica. Along with poverty came broken homes, family violence, street crime, drugs. In Washington, D.C., with a concentrated population of black poor within walking distance of the marbled buildings of the national government, 42 percent of young black men between the ages of eighteen and thirty- five were either in jail, or out on probation or parole. The crime rate among blacks, instead of being seen as a crying demand for the elimination of poverty, was used by politicians to call for the building of more prisons.[72]

For Zinn, the policies are not merely bad or unsuccessful. They show Reagan to be uncaring (ignoring babies and early death), racist (ignoring black babies and jailed black youth), and ignorant (failing to see a "crying demand").

What are students to do with such divergent views of Reagan? One temptation would be to simply ignore both views, since both are in some measure distorted and both ignore important contextual ideas form the time. Yet both also include important facts and valuable concepts, facts and ideas that students should come to grips with if they are to understand the Reagan era. We cannot simply toss everything down the memory hole and attempt to restart from scratch. It is a fact that Gorbachev and the USSR were forced to spend more because of the U.S. military build-up, and that was in part a contributing factor to the end of the USSR. Yet it is also a fact that Reagan vetoed legislation that, after his veto was overridden by congress, contributed to the downfall of a racist regime in South Africa. It is a fact that Reagan lowered marginal tax rates, yet it is also a fact that the deficit ballooned while he was president. It is a fact that Reagan's rhetoric on Christian morality buoyed the spirits of many Americans, yet it is also a fact that his silence on the AIDS epidemic angered many other Americans.

Another option might be to split the difference and present a story to students exactly half good and half bad. Of course, such a middle road is nearly impossible to navigate, because someone on one side or the other will always feel that he or she is being slighted. Many teachers in classrooms throughout the country actually take this approach, assigning, for example, excerpts from *both* Schweikart's *A Patriot's History of the United States and* Zinn's *People's History of the United States* to teach a variety of topics, including Reagan. Students are then asked to choose the best argument. This does have the merit of showing that history is constructed by historians who marshal evidence to support their own particular point of view. Yet these views are so wildly divergent, and so influenced by political ideology, that they really aren't history at all. They are stories of the past dictated by predilections of the present, so using them together actually has the potential of harming students. This happens when students throw up their hands in disgust, giving up any chance of trying to understand the past because they believe the views of historians are so incompatible that all history is just invented.

No, the answer is not to attempt to split the difference. The answer is to ignore the debate altogether, because the debate has not been crafted by those who wish to teach students to think historically. The debate has instead been created by political mythmakers. On the right, these mythmakers have the same view of history as an official in the George W. Bush administration interviewed about the invasion of Iraq in 2004. In answer to a question by author Ron Suskind, the aide claimed that Suskind and other "fact checkers" were mired in the "reality based community, which he defined as people who 'believe that solutions emerge from your judicious study of discernible reality.'" The official then went on to explain that in the new world of the twenty-first century, "we create our own reality" because "we are history's actors."[73] In other words, because the U.S. was an unparalleled empire, it and the people who worked for it could create reality and new facts, ignoring inconvenient "reality based" ideas such as history.

Suskind found a sustained, conscious, concerted effort by right-wing politicians and pundits to build a legacy for Reagan that was meant to sustain right-wing causes and ideas. In the aftermath of Ronald Reagan's funeral, a television executive, while crafting a memorial piece on Reagan, told journalist Jim Hoagland, "Today history is what we say it is."[74] So this is exactly what the Reagan mythmakers did. As Will Bunch so articulately phrased it, a "posse of political jihadists had a narrow and partisan agenda: to patch up a fractured Republican party and provide a badly needed source of inspiration that might recapture the white house for the GOP in 2000 and generations beyond."[75] The "beyond" is what this "posse" is working on now, striving to put this story into the schoolbooks and the schoolhouses, while their political enemies strive just as hard in the opposite direction.

History students must instead be pushed to examine the significance of the Reagan presidency in a dispassionate, non-political fashion. Reagan historian David Greenberg has it about right when he argues that Reagan "Was a significant president in helping move the climate of Washington politics to the right" and "he helped revitalize the Republican party after Watergate and gave conservative politicians a set of words and images and issues to use for the next decade."[76] The words and images and issues have lasted much longer than this single decade, even serving as a centerpiece in the 2012 presidential campaign. One of these images is, of course, the image of Reagan himself on Mt. Rushmore, an image that is not helpful at all in learning about the history of the era.

CONCLUSION

The Party could thrust its hand into the past and say this or that even, it never happened—that, surely, was more terrifying than mere torture and death.
—George Orwell, *1984*, Book 1, Chapter 3

The U.S. history curriculum is under attack. Politicians, political analysts, and ideologues seek to wipe clean the slate of the American past and replace it with a past of their own invention. The basis for this new narrative of the past comes from political beliefs of the present, rather than any systematic examination of the past. These anti-historians campaign to insert their version of the past into the nation's classrooms, hoping to begin a process that will forever transform our understanding of America's past.

Conservative anti-historians have crafted a long agenda of changes to the American past. They seek to reinvent the understanding of the founding fathers, nineteenth century industrialists, Joseph McCarthy, and Ronald Reagan. They hope to erase words such as "capitalism" and "imperialism" from the lexicon of American history, replacing them with ideas such as "free market entrepreneurship" and "exceptionalism," ideas more palatable to the twenty-first century conservative mind.

The Memory Hole: The U.S. History Curriculum Under Siege, pages 137–145.
Copyright © 2014 by Information Age Publishing

Radical left-wing re-inventors of the past commit the same sins as their right-wing counterparts. They have re-imagined and recreated a past that fits their own prejudices but fails to even remotely resemble a past that actually existed. From their creation of the monster of Christopher Columbus, to their overly simplistic rendering of economic history to their reinvention of the 1960s radicals and, yes, Ronald Reagan, left-wing anti-historians attack accurate understanding of the way things were in times gone by. And, just as their right-wing counterparts, radical left-wing anti-historians seek to change the curriculum of the nation's schools to better suit their own ideological perspective.

The correct thing to do is not to merely throw up our hands and split the difference between these two incorrect interpretations of the past. This is the "Sunday Talk Show" vision of history, a journalistic view of the past where we seek opinions from both sides, hoping that the correct answer is somewhere in between. Journalists are trained to give equal time to "both sides" and to be as objective as possible in providing them with equal time and equal credibility. Yet what if neither side is credible? What if neither side has actually *engaged* the past in crafting a story of the past? This is the situation with the anti-historians' versions of the past.

This is not to condemn the goals from either side of the debate. It is appropriate, especially at the younger ages, for students to learn about role models from the American past, such as George Washington, even if such positive portrayals are often oversimplified and incomplete. Beginning the road to historical learning with a positive and hopeful journey is entirely appropriate. It is also important for students to learn about social inequality and the need for social justice in a society experiencing ever-greater income inequality. But indoctrinating students in the positive aspects of our American heritage or in the negative failings of the American system is not history. In fact, such educational force-feeding is antithetical to the historical sensibility. Students required to learn a particular past as the complete truth, even in the face of readily attainable information, will reject those teachings and reject learning about the past altogether. History teaches students to think for themselves, using a set of tools that are admittedly not perfect but provide the opportunity for students to develop their own thinking abilities.

The ceaseless bickering and poisonous tug-of-war between the left and the right has actually led to a situation that is, if anything, even more dangerous than choosing one side or the other. That is the elimination of the history curriculum altogether. History is slowly but surely getting left behind in the rush of educational reform in the twenty-first century, and this is in large measure due to the perception that history is both irrelevant and politically dangerous.

A general reform movement in education began in the mid-1980s, a response to *A Nation at Risk*, a report written by the National Commission on Excellence in Education. *A Nation at Risk* argued that the United States was falling behind its counterparts the world over, in part because educational standards were lax or nonexistent. There were no national standards for what students were supposed to know and be able to do upon graduation from high school or advancement in the earlier grades, and this, the report argued, was causing the nation's education system to fail. A slew of standards in everything from math to physical education to foreign language followed the report, as states throughout the nation adopted standards to meet the call to reform.

The discipline of history followed suit, and the result was unparalleled disaster. The standards were written by the National Center for History in the Schools (NCHS), a sort of history "think tank" operated by historians at UCLA and teachers from southern California. This group spent three years writing, vetting, rewriting, and revising a set of standards and teaching examples for the nation's history classrooms. However, even before the official release of the document, it was savagely attacked by conservatives. Led by the recent head of the National Endowment for the Humanities (and wife of the future vice president) Lynne Cheney, they attacked the standards for presenting a "grim and gloomy" view of U.S. history and for overemphasizing anything in the nation's political past that was "politically correct." Cheney blamed the faulty standards on radical progressives whose "revisionist agenda no longer bothered to conceal their great hatred of traditional history."[1] Pundits on conservative radio chimed in with their agreement with Cheney, led by popular syndicated radio host Rush Limbaugh. Limbaugh attacked "historical correctness" and clarified for his audience the real problem: the historians and history teachers who wrote the standards and examples simply did not understand that "History is real simple. You know what history is? It is what happened."[2]

Historians and history teachers fought back. They pointed out that the conservatives were generally not attacking the standards themselves, but the optional examples NCHS wrote to help teachers apply the standards. And these optional examples did indeed introduce material about the past that conservatives were not comfortable with. Some lessons focused on the bullying tactics of Joseph McCarthy, and others on the shortcomings of the U.S. Constitution in protecting the rights of minorities. The debate on the examples in these standards helped set the stage for both radical anti-historians and conservative anti-historians I have discussed in this book. In 1995, political conservatives used the examples in the standards to put those they opposed to an embarrassing political defeat. This inevitable rout came in a nearly unanimous vote in the U.S. Senate decrying the standards, as the supporters of the document had little political clout, while those on the attack were politically very well connected.

The standards themselves actually focused on ideas of historical thinking I have discussed throughout this book, but the examples overshadowed the focus of the standards. Those on the right believed these examples imposed a radical narrative on the American past, and they worked to fight this, hoping that America's history classrooms would tell a more conservative story. Analysts dubbed this episode the "history war," another front in the "culture wars" of the late twentieth and early twenty-first century. Ideas of historical thinking that served as the underpinnings for the document were ignored and shunted aside in the firestorm over which story to tell. But the firestorm itself was the problem because it put the emphasis on two different yet incomplete versions of the past rather than on the ideas about *how* to study the past.

This debate made history the pariah discipline, the third rail of educational reform, as no educational reformer wishes to repeat the debacle of the history war of 1994–1995. In consequence, history as a subject has failed to connect with the world of educational reform in the schools since the turn of the millennium. School leaders and teachers are afraid to tackle the thorny problem of history for fear of getting caught in the political maelstrom. They perceive that there is no room for true compromise. So conservative President George W. Bush's "No Child Left Behind" (NCLB) educational reforms and liberal President Barack Obama's "Race to the Top" reforms both ignore history. History was not assessed in the NCLB reforms, so some schools and districts began to eliminate it from the curriculum. Thoughtful change in history education earned no extra points in "Race to the Top," so states and districts ignored it in their rush for ever-dwindling federal funding in education.

Ironically and tragically, this has left the playing field of history education open to the very politicized attacks outlined in this book. With federal, state, and school district funds going elsewhere and educational leaders focused on other areas, history classrooms have been ignored—except by the anti-historians. They are free to pursue their agendas because no one seems to have an agenda to counter them.

All need not be lost, however. The answer, as this book suggests, is right in front of us. For history is much more than a string of names, dates, facts, and figures. This is one of the first things historians and history teachers learn as they begin their journey to deeper understanding of their discipline. According to historian Edward Hallett Carr in his book *What is History?*, it is a "preposterous fallacy that historical facts exist objectively and independently of the interpretation of the historian."[3] Historians must gather and organize facts in order to tell a story and craft an argument, resulting in history becoming much more than Limbaugh's "what happened."

"What happened" for Limbaugh is not history, but a political heritage he wants taught in the classroom. This heritage is not history but is instead an incomplete, slanted, and politically motivated attempt to instill a particular kind of patriotism in the nation's students. Others, such as Howard Zinn and Ward Churchill, work to imbue students with a kind of anti-patriotism that they see as a cure to a simplistic and incomplete heritage curriculum. The left-wing anti-historians' goal is to teach about the multi-cultural past in a single-minded effort to promote socio-cultural change. But, as historian Timothy D. Slekar asks, "the question that arises here is whether teaching history as an exercise in patriotism or celebration of diversity or instilling civic values is really a study of history at all."[4] This book demonstrates that it is not. We must move above this debate and focus on history as a method of understanding and thinking if we are going to give our students any chance of understanding how to sift through the blizzard of conflicting information they face every day.

For the anti-historians, the past is propaganda rather than history. Historians need to strive to tell the story of the past with no political agenda. All historians realize this is not completely possible. And I am not arguing for burning or banning the books of anti-historians. If for nothing else than as an example of how not to "do history," a rare examination of the works of the anti-historians might be valuable in a history classroom. When the rules of the discipline are followed, the discipline can and does transcend petty, simplified, and politicized propaganda and ideally leads students to an enhanced ability to think for themselves.

While we are unlucky to live in a time that seems to be devaluing history in the schools, we are lucky to live in a time when so much thought has been dedicated to understanding and defining what history is as a discipline and what it can be in the schools. This book has utilized the insights developed by dozens of researchers and analysts in history education over the past decades.[5] In the study of each of the eras discussed in this book, I have recommended focusing attention on thinking historically about the era, rather than utilizing political ideology from the present to think about the past. Historical thinking is a way of questioning, examining, thinking about, and concluding about the past. First, and perhaps most important, is the idea that history is about *questions,* not answers.[6] Bruce Lesh argues "It all starts with questions… approaching every topic through the lens of a question" is the key concept in history teaching.[7] Sam Wineburg agrees, insisting that historical "facts are mastered by engaging students in historical questions that spark their curiosity and make them passionate about seeking answers."[8]

Every topic in this book became problematic when the anti-historians sought to teach it as an answer rather than a question. Twenty-first century religious anti-historians, led by David Barton, begin with the answer that George Washington and the founding fathers had to be evangelical Christians, and they search for evidence to prove that point, discarding other evidence as inappropriate. Economic anti-historians desperately wish to prove the efficacy of nineteenth century monopoly capitalism and so discard questions about any negative consequences of that system. Those who wish to prove that the United States is and always has been exceptional refuse to ask questions that might lead to alternative viewpoints, and those who wish to defend Joseph McCarthy stretch evidence to prove their predetermined answer.

Some social justice educators begin from the premise that the United States is not, nor ever has been, a just society, rather than asking questions that might lead to nuanced answers about the extent to which ideas of social justice were significant at any particular time. And defenders and detractors of Ronald Reagan begin with their answers about his significance and importance, fishing only for the evidence that suits their ideas. In order to effectively teach historical thinking in the nation's classrooms, teachers need to ignore narratives and arguments that begin with answers and instead begin with questions that will lead them and their students on a journey into the past. Such a classroom focus has the added bonus of making the experience more engaging, which is not accidental because it allows "teachers to introduce a sense of mystery into the most ordinary and standard lessons by raising thought-provoking questions, ones that demand answers supported by reasons, by evidence."[9]

Historical thinking also requires an examination of evidence. Historians use primary sources to understand the past and secondary sources to help contextualize our subject, and history students need to learn to do the same thing in the classroom. As we have seen, anti-historians often at least recognize the need to examine some primary sources. However, many, such as David Barton, W. Cleon Skousen, and Howard Zinn, selectively pick and choose which sources to use in defense of their stories. They only choose the evidence that will support their conclusion, ignoring all other evidence, even if the vast preponderance of the evidence points in a different direction. Others twist the meaning and significance of sources, as we saw Ann Coulter and Glenn Beck doing with the Venona Project documents.

Many of the anti-historians are outwardly disdainful of the use of secondary sources. Secondary sources are the narratives and arguments crafted by historians about the past. These narratives and arguments are not always correct. In fact, they are often proven to be inaccurate. One obvious example of this is the historical works about slavery written before World War II. These books invariably "obliterated from the record...the horrors of the slave trade, the brutality of slavery, the resistance of enchained Africans, and the struggles of free blacks...."[10] However, this example actually serves as a prime example of the dangers of ignoring the historical method in examining the past. Before World War II, historians purposefully ignored or dismissed large swaths of evidence about slavery because their own racism prevented them from examining this evidence. In other words, they began with an answer—Blacks were inferior, so any evidence from the Black slaves themselves was not worth examining. Historians after World War II began to ask different questions, and this has led to a much more complete and accurate picture of slave life. If historians do their job correctly and begin with questions rather than answers, it is a valuable and critically important exercise for students to utilize these questions in attempting to understand the past.

Both anti-historians of the right and the left insist that historians are elitist, narrow-minded and consistently inaccurate and so can be properly ignored. Yet such self-conscious ignorance fails to provide a model to follow in building student understanding of the past. Does every generation really need to start over in their study of the past? Is it not more logical to examine existing narratives for questions and ideas that will help us understand the past? Even if we disagree with a conclusion, we should not simply toss the conclusion away. We need to deal with the conclusion, examine the evidence for ourselves, and then evaluate the conclusion based on new sources or new questions.

Secondary sources provide a necessary framework to begin our examination of the past. In Chapter One, we examined the idea of morality in the time of the founding fathers, utilizing the work of historian Gordon Wood to understand the meaning of morality in a time of republican values. In Chapter Two, we looked at the work of historian David Kennedy to try to conceptualize the impact of the New Deal, rather than merely rejecting the New Deal because it did not fit our twenty-first century conception of the proper role of government. The work of historians should help guide us as we craft questions for our classrooms rather than being ignored as the anti-historians would ask us to do.

The work of doing history is and always must be *complex*. As we peer into the past, we need to look for patterns of cause and effect; we need to look at multiple perspectives; we need to look at the authorship of sources. In short, we need to appreciate the complicated context of our sources, our questions, and any answers we develop about the past. In every chapter of this book, we encountered the anti-historians oversimplifying the past in pursuit of easy answers in the present. They ignored the context of the times and ignored multiple perspectives.

There are multiple methods to use in the classroom to introduce students to the rules of historical thinking. One example is offered by Flannery Burke of Saint Louis University and Thomas Andrews of the University of Colorado, who argue "these ideas, we believe, stand at the heart of the questions historians seek to answer, the arguments we make, and the debates in which we engage."[11] Burke and Andrews outline their struggle to "think harder about the disciplinary knowledge we possessed and potential ways of training teacher candidates to communicate aspects of this knowledge to their pupils." They outline their method, which is to discuss what they cleverly dub the "5 C's of historical thinking"—change over time, context, causality, contingency, and complexity. Note that they define historical knowledge by what some might call "skills" or even "process." I would term this historical understanding and agree that it is at the very heart of what historians do and needs to be at the heart of what history teachers do. "The Five C's" provide just one example of what has become a growing literature on historical thinking and its application to the classroom.

Bruce Lesh offers a different classroom model to lead his students towards historical thinking. He begins with a deep reading of sources, asking students to examine not only the text of these sources, but their subtext and context. Jumping off from that point, he provides examples of how students might study chronological thinking, causality, multiple perspectives, change over time, historical significance, and historical empathy.[12] In *Reading Like a Historian*, Sam Wineburg, Daisy Martin, and Chauncey Monte-Sano focus on similar skills in each of their examples. The point is that there is broad agreement among historians, history educators, and history teachers that there are rules governing how the past needs to be studied and that these rules can and should be applied to the nation's classrooms.

The crucial concept here is that historical understanding entails the process of historical inquiry. It begins with questions and then follows a set of rules in developing an array of answers to those questions. Anti-historians ignore the process and ignore the questions in a headlong rush to predetermined answers. They insist that it is the answers that are taught in the classroom, not the questions, and not the method of understanding. They believe history is for teaching what to think, whereas in fact history is a discipline designed to teach students *how* to think.

The point is not to create an army of little historians that will spend their lives researching and writing works of history. As Wineburg pus it, "We're not talking about some esoteric procedure for working in an archive." Instead, following the process of "doing history" allows students to "see patterns, make sense of contradictions, and formulate reasoned interpretations when others get lost in a forest of detail and throw up their hands in frustration."[13] Looking at the past with the lens of the disciplinary structure of history allows students to stretch their minds in ways they have never done before.

This is why we can't just give up and allow the anti-historians to control the debate. If we allow them to invent a past and then insert this past into the nation's classrooms, we take one more step towards eliminating thinking from our schools. What would this mean? George Orwell provided one possible answer in *1984*. The power in his vision, and the vision of countless other analysts who have imagined a life without individual thought, is that it has provided us with an understanding of what we would be missing if the facts, ideas, and concepts of the past were ripped from our lives. All of us, but most especially young students, must be provided the opportunity to wrestle with the blizzard of information at our fingertips and must be provided a method to guide our examination. The anti-historians seek to distort the past, narrow available information, and provide a different, politicized method for understanding that past.

Eliminating thinking also means the elimination of joy, wonder, and engagement. In an educational world where reform means an ever increasing number of standardized tests and specified dictates on how and what to teach, we can not afford to allow this to happen. The memory hole will create a hole in our nation's ability to think and understand, which will ultimately result, as it did for Winston Smith in *1984*, in an inability to experience the human condition.

BIBLIOGRAPHY

BOOKS

Anderson, Fred, and Andrew R. L. Cayton. *The Dominion of War: Empire and Liberty in North America, 1500–2000.* New York: Viking, 2005.

Barry, John M. *Roger Williams and the Creation of the American Soul: Church, State and the Birth of Liberty.* New York: Viking, 2012.

Barton, David. *America's Godly Heritage.* Aledo, TX: WallBuilder Press, 1993.

———. *Separation of Church and State: What the Founders Meant.* Aledo, TX: WallBuilder Press, 2007.

Beck, Glenn. *The Original Argument: The Federalists' Case for the Constitution, Adapted for the 21st Century.* New York, NY: Mercury Radio Arts, 2011.

Beliles, Mark, and Stephen K. McDowell. *America's Providential History: Including Biblical Principles of Education, Government, Politics, Economics and Family Life,* 3rd ed. Charlottesville, VA: Providence Foundation, 2010.

Bennett, William. *America: The Last Best Hope.* Nashville, TN: Thomas Nelson, 2006.

Berkin, Carol. *A Brilliant Solution: Inventing the American Constitution.* New York, NY: Harcourt, 2002.

Bigelow, Bill. *A People's History for the Classroom.* Milwaukee, WI: Rethinking Schools, 2008.

Bigelow, Bill and Bob Peterson, eds. *Rethinking Columbus: The Next 500 Years.* Milwaukee, WI: Rethinking Schools, 1998.

Bigelow, Bill, Bob Peterson, Linda Christensen, Stan Karp, Barbara Miner, eds. *Rethinking Our Classrooms.* Milwaukee, WI: Rethinking Our Schools, 1994.

Brenner, Lenni, ed. *Jefferson and Madison on Separation of Church and State: Writings on Religion and Secularism.* Fort Lee, NJ: Barricade Books, 2004.

Bunch, Will. *Tear Down this Myth: The Right-Wing Distortion of the Reagan Legacy.* New York, NY: Free Press, 2010.

Carr, Edward Hallett. *What is History?* New York, NY: Vintage Books, 1961.

Chernow, Ron. *Washington: A Life.* New York, NY: Penguin, 2010.

Churchill, Ward. *On the Justice of Roosting Chickens: Reflections on the Consequences of U.S. Imperial Arrogance and Criminality.* Oakland, CA: AK Press, 2003.

Coontz, Stephanie. *The Way We Never Were: American Families and the Nostalgia Trap* New York, NY: BasicBooks, 2000.

Coulter, Ann. *Treason: Liberal Treachery from the Cold War to the War on Terrorism* New York, NY: Three Rivers Press, 2004.

Donovan, M. Suzanne, and John D. Bransford, eds. *How Students Learn: History, Math and Science in the Classroom.* Washington, DC: National Academies Press, 2005.

Epstein, Terrie. *Interpreting National History: Race, Identity, and Pedagogy in Classrooms and Communities.* New York, NY: Routledge, 2009.

Fea, John. *Was America Founded as a Christian Nation? A Historical Introduction.* Louisville, KY: Westminster John Knox Press, 2011.

Folsom, Burton W., Jr. *New Deal or Raw Deal.* New York, NY: Threshold Editions, 2008.

———. *The Myth of he Robber Barons: A New Look at the Rise of Big Business in America,* 6th ed. Herndon, VA: Young America's Foundation, 2010.

Gaustad, Edwin. *Sworn on the Altar of God: a Religious Biography of Thomas Jefferson.* Grand Rapids, MI: W.B. Eerdman, 1996.

Gerwin, David, and Jack Zevin. *Teaching United States History as Mystery.* Portsmouth, NH: Heinemann, 2003.

Gillespie, Susan, ed. *Perspectives on Teaching Innovations: Teaching to Think Historically.* Washington, DC: AHA, 1999.

Gingrich, Newt, and Callista Gingrich. *Rediscovering God in America: Reflections on the Role of Faith in Our Nation's History and Future,* rev. ed. Nashville, TN: Thomas Nelson, 2009.

Gingrich, Newt, and Vince Haley. *A Nation Like No Other: Why American Exceptionalism Matters.* Washington, DC: Regnery Pub., 2011.

Harris, Matthew L., and Thomas S. Kidd, eds. *The Founding Fathers and the Debate Over Religion in Revolutionary America: A History in Documents.* New York, NY: Oxford University Press, 2012.

Hodgson, Godfrey. *The Myth of American Exceptionalism.* New Haven, CT: Yale, 2009.

Holt, Tom. *Thinking Historically.* New York, NY: College Board, 1995.

Immerman, Richard H. *Empire for Liberty: A History of American Imperialism from Benjamin Franklin to Paul Wolfowitz.* Princeton, NJ: Princeton University Press, 2010.

Jacoby, Susan. *Alger Hiss and the Battle for History.* New Haven, CT: Yale University Press, 2009.

Johnson, Haynes. *Sleepwalking Through History: America in the Reagan Years.* New York, NY: Anchor, 1991.

Kennedy, David M. *Freedom From Fear: The American People in Depression and War, 1929–1945.* New York, NY: Oxford University Press, 1999.

Keesee, Timothy, and Mark Sidwell, *United States History for Christian Schools, Teacher's Edition,* 2nd ed. Pensacola, FL: A Beka, 1991.

Kushner, David. *Levittown: Two Families, One Tycoon, and the Fight for Civil Rights in America's Legendary Suburb.* New York, NY: Walker and Company, 2009.

Lepore, Jill. *The Whites of Their Eyes: The Tea Party's Revolution and the Battle over American History.* Princeton, NJ: Princeton University Press, 2010.

Lesh, Bruce. *Why Won't You Just Tell Us the Answer.* Portland, ME: Stenhouse, 2011.

Levstik, Linda, and Keith Barton. *Doing History: Investigating With Children in Elementary and Middle Schools.* New York, NY: Routledge, 2010.

Lowenthal, David. *The Past is a Foreign Country.* Cambridge: Cambridge Press, 1985.

Lowman, Michael, George T. Thompson, and Kurt A. Grussendorf. *Heritage of Freedom.* Pensacola, FL: A Beka Book, 1996.

Mack, Tara, and Bree Picower, eds. *Planning to Change the World: A Plan Book for Social Justice Teachers 2012–2013.* Milwaukee, WI: Rethinking Schools, 2012.

McDougall, Walter. A. *Promised Land, Crusader State: The American Encounter with the World since 1776.* Boston, MA: Houghton Mifflin, 1997.

Nash, Gary B., Charlotte Crabtree, and Ross E. Dunn. *History on Trial: Culture Wars and the Teaching of the Past.* New York, NY: Knopf, 1998.

Noll, Mark, George M. Marsden, and Nathan O. Hatch. *The Search for Christian America.* Colorado Springs, CO: Helmers and Howard, 1989.

Olson, Kyle, Ben Velderman, and Steve Gunn, *Indoctrination: How "Useful Idiots" Are Using Our Schools to Subvert American Exceptionalism.* Bloomington, IN: Authorhouse, 2011.

Orwell, George. *1984.* New York, NY: Signet, 1977.

Painter, Nell Irvin. *Standing at Armageddon: A Grassroots History of the Progressive Era.* New York, NY: WW Norton, 2008.

Perry, Rick. *Fed Up!: Our Fight to Save America from Washington.* New York, NY: Little, Brown and Company, 2010.

Pierard, Richard V., and Robert D. Linder. *Civil Religion and the Presidency.* Grand Rapids, MI: Academic Books, 1988.

Schaller, Michael. *Right Turn: American Life in the Reagan-Bush Era 1980–1992.* New York NY: Oxford, 2007.

Schweikart, Larry. *48 Liberal Lies About American History.* New York, NY: Sentinel, 2009.

———. *A Patriot's History of the United States.* New York, NY: Sentinel, 2007.

Sheridan, Eugene R. *Jefferson and Religion.* Charlottesville, VA: Thomas Jefferson Memorial Foundation, 1998.

Skousen, W. Cleon. *The 5000 Year Leap: A Miracle that Changed the World.* Malta, ID: National Center for Constitutional Studies, 1981.

Sokolower, Jody, ed. *Teaching About the Wars.* Milwaukee, WI: Rethinking Schools, 2013.

Stearns, Peter, Peter Seixas, and Sam Wineburg. *Knowing, Teaching and Learning History.* New York, NY: NYU Press, 2000.

VanSledright, Bruce. *The Challenge of Rethinking History Education: On Practices, Theories and Policy.* New York, NY: Routledge, 2010.

Walker, Nancy A., ed., *Women's Magazines 1940–1960: Gender Roles and the Popular Press.* Boston, MA: Bedford/St Martin's, 1998.

Warren, Wilson J., and D. Antonio Cantu, eds. *History Education 101.* Charlotte, NC: Information Age, 2008.

Widenor, William. *Henry Cabot Lodge and the Search for an American Foreign Policy*, New York, NY: ACLS Humanities e-book, 2008.

Wineburg, Sam. *Historical Thinking and Other Unnatural Acts: Charting the Future of Teaching the Past.* Philadelphia, PA: Temple University Press, 2001.

Wineburg, Sam, Daisy Martin, and Chauncey Monte-Sano. *Reading Like a Historian: Teaching Literacy in Middle and High School History Classrooms.* New York, NY: Teachers College Press, 2011.

Wood, Gordon S. *The Creation of the American Republic.* Chapel Hill NC: University of North Carolina Press, 1998.

Zinn, Howard. *A People's History of the United States.* New York, NY: HarperCollins, 1980.

WEBSITES

A Conservative Teacher Blog. http://aconservativeteacher.blogspot.com/2011/06/lessons-from-economic-recessions.html, 1/25/12.

Civil War Memory Blog. http://www.cwmemory.com.

CNN Opinion. http://www.cnn.com/OPINION/.

Crooks and Liars. http:///www.crooksandliars.com.

Daily Breeze. http://www.dailybreeze.com.

Daily Kos, http://www.dailykos.com.

Democratic Strategist. http://www.thedemocraticstrategist.org.

Eagle Forum. www.eagleforum.org.

Ed Liberty Watch. http://edlibertywatch.org.

Education News. http://www.educationnews.org.

EdWatch. http://www.edwatch.org.

Enlightened Women. http://www.enlightened women.org.

FoxNews.com: Liveshots. http://liveshots.blogs.foxnews.com.

Fox News Radio. http://radio.foxnews.com.

Free Republic. http://www.freerepublic.com.

Friberg Fine Art. http://www.fribergfineart.com/copyright.html.

Front Page Mag. http://www.frontpagemag.co.

FSTDT Refugee Board blog. http://fstdt.probprads.com.

Gingrich Productions. http://www.gingrichproductions.com.

Gulag Bound. http://www.gulagbound.com.

Hinterland Gazette. http://www.hinterlandgazette.com.

HNet On-line. http://www.h-net.org.

Huffington Post Blog. http://www.huffpost.com.

Humanevents. http://www.humanevents.com.

Investors.com. http://www.investors.com.

Kona Tea Party. http://konateaparty.com.

Learn Our History. http://www.learnourhistory.com.

Liberty University on-line syllabus GOVT 329 American Exceptionalism. http://www.luonline.com/media/3415/courseguides/GOVT329_Syllabus.pdf.

Media Research Center. http://archive.mrc.org.

Newsbusters. http://newsbusters.org.

Patriots History. http://www.patriotshistoryusa.com.

PJ Media. http://www.pjmeida.com.

Politico. http:///www.politico.com.

Real Clear Politics. http://www.realclearpolitics.com.

Rethinking Schools Blog. http://www.rethinkingschoolsblog.wordpress.com.

Reuters Blog. http://blogs.reuters.com.

Right Wing Watch. http://www.rightwingwatch.org.

Salon On-Line. http://www.salon.com.

Slate On-line. http://www.slate.com.

Statesman.com, www.statesman.com.

Talk to Action. http://www.talk2action.com.

Tea Party Patriots. http://www.teapartypatriots.org.

Teaching a People's History. http://www.zinnedproject.org.

TFN Insider. www.tfninsider.org.

The Heritage Foundation. http://www.heritage.org/initiatives/first-principles/ba-sics.

The Nation On-Line. http://www.thenation.com.

The Red Apple Project. http://redappleproject.com/2013/03/richardson-isd-oth-ers-the-public-is-concerned/.

Think Progress. http://www.thinkprogress.org.

Townhall.com. http://www.townhall.com.

Truth About IB. http://www.truthaboutib.com.

Utah's Republic. http://www.utahsrepublic.org.

Young America's Foundation. http://www.yaf.org/kate-obenshain.aspx.

Zinn Education Project. http://www.zinneducationproject.org.

ARTICLES, SPEECHES, POSITION PAPERS

Algeo, Matthew. "Forget Romney or Gingrich. In 2012, the Tea Party wants…another Grover Cleveland." *Christian Science Monitor.* May 17, 2011. http://www.csmonitor.com/Commentary/Opinion/2011/0517/Forget-Romney-or-Gingrich.-In-2012-the-tea-party-wants-another-Grover-Cleveland.

Amazon.com customer review. "About Time Someone Took on the New Deal," November 13, 2008. http://www.amazon.com/review/R3CR81GIKB1FSX.

Ayers, Ed. "The Next Generation of History Teachers." American Historical Association. http://www.historians.org/pubs/Free/historyteaching/situation.htm.

Barton, David. "2009 TEKS Review." Texas Education Agency. https://s3.amazonaws.com/s3.documentcloud.org/documents/408349/david-barton-review-of-current-social-studies-teks.txt.

Berkin, Carol. "American Indians: From the Editor." *History Now* 28 (Summer 2011). http://www.gilderlehrman.org/history-now/2011-06/american-indians.

Birkey, Andy. "Meet David Barton, Bachmann's Constitution Class Teacher." *The Minnesota Independent,* November 16, 2010. http://americanindependent.com/156775/meet-david-barton-bachmann's-constitution-class-teacher.

Blackford, Mansel. "Review of Entrepreneurs vs. the State: A New Look at the Rise of Big Business in America, 1840–1920." *The Business History Review* 63 (Autumn, 1989): 674–675.

Boston, Rob. "Texas Tall Tale." *Church and State*, July/August 2009. http://www.au.org/church-state/julyaugust-2009-church-state/featured/texas-tall-tale.

Buckett, Jennifer. "Values and Morals in American society: The 1950s versus today." September 23, 2007. http://www.stevenjthompson.com/varioustopics/culturaldecline/values_morals_in_american_society_1950s_vs_today.html.

Burns, Douglas. "Has King Left No Sense of Decency?" *Daily Times Herald*, October 5, 2005. http://www.carrollspaper.com/main.asp?Search=1&ArticleID=336&SectionID=4&SubSectionID=4&S=41.

Chancey, Mark. "Educating for a 'Christian America'? Bible courses, Social Studies Standards and the Texas Controversy." Transcript of Remarks at the Baker Institute for Public Policy, Rice University. http://bakerinstitute.org/publications/REL-pub-ChanceyEducatingChristianAmerica-022411.pdf.

———. "Textbook Example of the Christian Right." *Journal of the American Academy of Religion* 75 (September 2007): 554–581.

"Conservatives' First Lady Sparked Pro-Family Effort." *The Washington Times*. October 7, 2005. http://www.washingtontimes.com/news/2005/oct/7/20051007-120157-1091r/?page=all.

Cmods Curriculum Modules. "The American Creed." Unit one, module three. http://cmods.org/Unit1Module3.html.

Cribb, T. Kenneth. "Ronald Reagan and the Moral Imagination." *The Intercollegiate Review*, February 4, 2011. http://www.firstprinciplesjournal.com/articles.aspx?article=1480.

Dallek, Matthew. "Not Ready for Mt. Rushmore: Reconciling the Myth of Ronald Reagan with the Reality. " *The American Scholar* (Summer 2009). http://theamericanscholar.org/not-ready-for-mt-rushmore/#.Ue7VPqVFtHw.

Dowd Hall, Jacqueline. "The Long Civil Rights Movement and the Political Uses of the Past." *The Journal of American History* 91, no. 4 (March 2005): 1233–1263.

Dregni, Eric. "James J. Hill Lake Minnetonka History." *Lake Minnetonka Magazine*. September 2011. http://lakeminnetonkamag.com/article/james-j-hill-property/james-j-hill-lake-minnetonka-history.

Eckholm, Erik. "History Buff Sets a Course for the Right." *New York Times*, May 4, 2011, A1.

Epps, Garrett. "All Patriots 'Know' that Moses Wrote the Constitution." *The Atlantic On-line*, October 29, 2010. http://www.theatlantic.com/national/archive/2010/10/all-patriots-know-that-moses-wrote-the-constitution/65353.

Fischer, Fritz. "The Historian as Translator: Historical thinking, The Rosetta Stone of History Education." *Historically Speaking* 12, no. 3 (June 2011): 15–17.

———. "The Texas History Standards: The Case of the 'Venona Standard' and Effective History Teaching." *History Matters* 23 (September 2010): 4–7.

Frank, Thomas. "The Persecution of Sarah Palin." *Wall Street Journal*, November 17, 2009. http://online.wsj.com/article/SB1000142405274870478230457454205 1447849052.html.

Gould, Philip. "Virtue, Ideology and the American Revolution: The Legacy of the Republican Synthesis." *American Literary History* 5, no. 3 (Autumn 1993): 564–577.

Henninger, Daniel. "Bring Back the Robber Barons." *Wall Street Journal*, March 3, 2010. http:// online.wsj.com/article/SB10001424052748703862704575099572105775414.html.

Houston Independent School District. "America's Heritage: An Adventure in Liberty." The American Heritage Foundation (2003): 81–100. http://www.cdsar.org/AmericanHeritage/NHSL.pdf.

"Interview with Larry Schweikart, Author of *What Would the Founders Say?*" *All Right Magazine*, March 23, 2011. http://www.allrightmagazine.com/books-and-reviews/interview-with-larry-schweikart-author-of-what-would-the-founders-say-sentinel-2011-7629/.

"It Takes a Family." Washington Post live Q & A with Rick Santorum. *Washington Post On-line*, July 25, 2005. http://www.washingtonpost.com/wp-dyn/content/discussion/2005/07/20/DI2005072001515.html.

Joch, Roman, "To Eastern Eyes, Reagan a Liberator." *Washington Times*, February 3, 2011, 3.

Kaiser, Robert. "Gorbachev: 'We all lost Cold War.'" *Washington Post*, June 11, 2004, A1.

Klehr, Harvey. "Was Joe McCarthy Right?" *Raleigh Spy Conference Report*, November 7, 2005.

Konvitz, Milton. "Separation of Church and State: The First Freedom." *Law and Contemporary Problems* 14 (Winter 1949): 44–60.

Lackey, Katherine. "In Reagan's Name: 'Teaching Moments.'" *USA Today*, January 24, 2011. http://www.usatoday.com/news/washington/2011-01-24-ronald-reagan-names_N.htm.

Laub, Mike. "Quotes from Governor Mitt Romney about President Ronald Reagan." Blog post. http://myclob.pbworks.com/w/page/21959547/Ronald%20Reagan#QuotesfromGovernorMittRomneyaboutPresidentRonaldReagan.

Leonard, Frank. "'Wise, Swift, and Sure'? The Great Northern Entry into Seattle, 1889–1894." *The Pacific Northwest Quarterly* 92 (Spring, 2001): 81–90.

Lightman, David. "The Reagan Name Game." *The Courant*, December 27, 1997. http://articles.courant.com/1997-12-27/news/9712270184_1_reagan-legacy-project-ronald-reagan-tax-bill.

Locker, Richard. "Tea Parties Issue Demands to Tennessee Legislators." *The Commercial Appeal*, January 13, 2011.

Lowry, Richard, and Ramesh Ponnuru. "An Exceptional Debate: The Obama Administration's Assault on American Identity." *National Review On-Line*, March 8, 2010. http://www.freerepublic.com/focus/f-news/2457827/posts.

MacNicol, Glynnis. "Glen Beck: During the Civil Rights Movement God Spoke through MLK, RFK...and Roger Ailes." *Mediaite*, July 14, 2010.

Marqusee, Mike. "The Iron Click: American Exceptionalism and US Empire." Blog post. http://www.mikemarqusee.com/?p=865.

Marshall, Peter. "Second Version TEKS Review." Texas Education Agency. www.tea.state.tx.us/WorkArea/linkit.aspx?LinkIdentifier=id&ItemID=6276.

McGrew-King, Jason. "James J. Hill wasn't always admired by Wayzata." *Lakeshore Weekly News*, September 6, 2005, 3C.

McLeroy, Don. "Teaching Our children What It Means to Be an American in 2011?!" Speech at "Educational Policy Conference," St. Louis, MO, Jan 28, 2011.

Metropolitan Omaha Educational Consortium. "Ronald Reagan and the End of the Cold War (1947–1988)." http://www.tahg.org/module_display.php?mod_id=44&review=yes.

Morrow, Lance. "Why Is This Man So Popular?" *Time*, July 7, 1986. http://archive.mrc.org/specialreports/2004/pdf/Ronald_Reagan_PDF_version.pdf.

Neem, Johann N. "Taking Historical Fundamentalism Seriously." *Historically Speaking* 12 (November 2011): 3.

Nichols, John. "Bizarro History: The Rough Rider as Socialist Stooge." *The Nation*, December 8, 2011. http://www.cbsnews.com/8301-215_162-57339239/bizarro-history-the-rough-rider-as-socialist-stooge/.

"No, Glenn Beck is Not a Civil Rights Icon," *The Nation Online*, August 28, 2010. http://www.thenation.com/blog/154200/no-glenn-beck-not-civil-rights-icon.

Powell, Albrecht. "International Baccalaureate is Anti-American & Anti-Christian?" About.com Guide, February 22, 2006. http://pittsburgh.about.com/b/2006/02/22/international-baccalaureate-is-anti-american-anti-christian.htm.

Rae, John B. "The Great Northern's Land Grant." *The Journal of Economic History, 12* (Spring, 1952): 140–145.

Reich, Robert. "The Rise of the Regressive Right and the Reawakening of America." *Robertreich.org*, October 16, 2011. http://robertreich.org/post/11511074902.

Schonberger, Howard. "James J. Hill and the Trade with the Orient." *Minnesota History* 41 (Winter, 1968): 178–190.

Schoenfeld, William. "Separation of Church and State: A Policy or a Principle." *The North American Review* 189 (May 1909): 662–674.

Schrecker, Ellen. "History in Red—and White and Blue." *Radical History Review* 93 (September 2005): 159–169.

Schwarzenegger, Arnold. "Ronald Reagan: My Hero, and eternal light for the world," *USA Today On-Line*, June 8, 2004. http://usatoday30.usatoday.com/news/opinion/editorials/2004-06-08-arnold_x.htm.

Slekar, Timothy D. "Disciplinary History Versus Curricular Heritage: Epistemological Battle." *Journal of Thought* (Fall 2001): 63–70.

Shorto, Russel. "How Christian Were the Founders?" *New York Times Magazine*, February 11, 2010. http://www.nytimes.com/2010/02/14/magazine/14texbooks-t.html?pagewanted=all.

Siefer, Ted. "Senate Kills Anti-International Baccalaureate Bill." *New Hampshire Union Leader*, May 16, 2012. http://www.unionleader.com/article/20120516/NEWS06/705169912.

Southern Poverty Law Center. "Teaching the Movement: The State of Civil Rights Education in the United States." Southern Poverty Law Center 2011. http://www.splcenter.org/sites/default/files/downloads/publication/Teaching_the_Movement.pdf.

Spoehr, Luther. "Review: *A People's History of the United States*, by Howard Zinn." *Saturday Review*. February 2, 1980, 37–39.

Stearns, Peter. "Social History and World History: Toward Greater Interaction." College Board AP Central. http://apcentral.collegeboard.com/apc/members/courses/teachers_corner/180003.html.

Stratton, Jim. "Rep. Harris Condemns Separation of Church, State." *Orlando Sentinel,* August 26, 2006. http://www.washingtonpost.com/wp-dyn/content/article/2006/08/25/AR2006082501640.html.

Strauss, Valerie. "Protestors Call IB Program Un-American. Is it?" *Washington Post,* May 18, 2010. http://voices.washingtonpost.com/answer-sheet/apibhonors/protesters-call-ib-program-un-.html.

Street, Paul. "Sarah Palin, Corporate Capitalism, and Right Wing Nostalgia for the 'Free Market' Nineteenth Century." Blog post. http://www.paulstreet.org/?p=448.

Suskind, Ron. "Without a Doubt." *New York Times,* October 17, 2004.

Taibbi, Matt. "The Hunters and the Hunted." Book review of *Subversives: The FBI's War on Student Radicals and Reagan's Rise to Power. New York Times Book Review,* October 7, 2012, 11.

"Texas Textbook Controversy." *Religion & Ethics Newsweekly.* April 30, 2010. http://www.pbs.org/wnet/religionandethics/episodes/april-30-2010/texas-textbook-controversy/6187/.

Tooley, Mark. "Exceptional America?" *The American Spectator,* April 8, 2011. http://spectator.org/archives/2011/04/08/exceptional-america.

Tumulty, Karen. "Conservatives' New Focus: America the Exceptional." *Washington Post,* Nov 10, 2010. http://www.washingtonpost.com/wp-dyn/content/article/2010/11/28/AR2010112804139_3.html?sid=ST2010112901818.

Tyrell, I. (2008). *Empire of Denial: American Empire, Past, Present and Future.* October 14, 2008. http://iantyrrell.wordpress.com/empire-of-denial-american-empire-past-present-and-future.

Utah Education Issues. "Plus Ridiculous Paranoia about the UN Infiltrating Bountiful and Provo." February 22, 2008. http://utahedu.blogspot.com/2008/02/plus-ridiculous-paranoia-about-un.html.

White, Allen. "Reagan's AIDS Legacy: Silence Equals Death." *San Francisco Chronicle,* June 8, 2004. http://www.sfgate.com/opinion/openforum/article/Reagan-s-AIDS-Legacy-Silence-equals-death-2751030.php.

Wilentz, Sean. "Confounding Fathers: The Tea Party's Cold War Roots." *The New Yorker,* October 18, 2010, 3.

Wilkins, Steve. "A Christian Perspective of History." New Life Community Church. http://www.new-life.net/growth/other-articles/a-christian-perspective-of-history/.

Williams, Roger. "A Letter to the Town of Providence." 1655. http://www.nbu.bg/webs/amb/american/1/williams/letter.htm.

Wineburg, Samuel L. "Undue Certainty: Where Howard Zinn's *A People's History* Falls Short." *American Educator* 36 (Winter 2012–13): 27–34.

Wood, Gordon S. "The Greatness of George Washington." *Virginia Quarterly Review* 68 (Spring 1992): 193–194.

Wooton, Kathleen, and Christopher D. Stonebanks. "The Backlash on 'Roosting Chickens': The Continued Atmosphere of Suppressing Indigenous Perspectives." *Cultural Studies <=> Critical Methodologies* 10, no. 2 (2010): 112–113.

Zinn, Howard. "Unsung Heroes." *The Progressive,* June 2000. http://www.thirdworldtraveler.com/Zinn/Unsung_Heroes.html.

NOTES

INTRODUCTION

[1] Haynes Johnson, *Sleepwalking Through History: America in the Reagan Years* (New York: Anchor, 1991); Arnold Schwarzenegger, "Ronald Reagan: My Hero, and Eternal Light for the World," *USA Today On-Line*, June 8, 2004, http://usatoday30. usatoday.com/news/opinion/editorials/2004-06-08-arnold_x.htm.

[2] Most importantly Samuel S. Wineburg, who has written the central book in this field, *Historical Thinking and Other Unnatural Acts: Charting the Future of Teaching the Past* (Philadelphia: Temple University Press, 2001).

[3] See, for example, Robert B. Bain, "'They Thought the World Was Flat?' Principles in Teaching High School History," in *How Students Learn: History, Mathematics and Science in the Classroom*, ed. National Research Council (Washington, DC: National Academies Press, 2005), and Bruce A. Lesh, *Why Won't You Just Tell Us the Answer?: Teaching Historical Thinking in Grades 7–12* (Portland, ME: Stenhouse, 2011).

[4] Occams Hatchet, "So Long, Seminoles: Florida Disappears Indians—and Sex," *Daily Kos*, June 8, 2006, http://www.dailykos.com/story/2006/06/08/216984/-So-long,-Seminoles:-Florida-disappears-Indiansand-sex.

[5] Historian David Lowenthal uses the phrase as a title for his path-breaking book on the past and history, *The Past is a Foreign Country* (Cambridge: Cambridge University Press, 1985). He cites L. P. Hartley's book *The Go-Between* (New York: NYRB Classics, 1953) for the use of the phrase.

[6] Anonymous, "The Dangers of Politicized History," August 24, 2011, ISI Faculty Resource Center (blog), http://faculty.isi.org/blog/post/view/id/660/.

The Memory Hole: The U.S. History Curriculum Under Siege, pages 157–176.
Copyright © 2014 by Information Age Publishing

[7] In her book *The Whites of Their Eyes*, historian Jill Lepore documents this worldview, calling the tea partiers "historical fundamentalists" and criticizing them for their "antihistorical" belief that "time is an illusion." Jill Lepore, *The Whites of Their Eyes: The Tea Party's Revolution and the Battle over American History* (Princeton, NJ: Princeton University Press, 2010), 8–16.

[8] See the National Council for History Education website for one example of "History's Habits of Mind," http://www.nche.net/habitsofmind.

CHAPTER 1

[1] See the Wallbuilders' banner at the top of http://www.wallbuilders.com/, accessed October 27, 2011.

[2] Friberg Fine Art, "Copyright Information," http://www.fribergfineart.com/copyright.html.

[3] The Good Book Company, "The Prayer at Valley Forge by Arnold Friberg," accessed July 15, 2013, http://www.prayeratvalleyforge.com/.

[4] Richard V. Pierard and Robert D. Linder, *Civil Religion and the Presidency* (Grand Rapids, MI: Academic Books, 1988), 71.

[5] John Fea, *Was America Founded as a Christian Nation? A Historical Introduction* (Louisville, KY: Westminster John Knox Press, 2011).

[6] American Christian Heritage Blog, "George Washington in Prayer at Valley Forge," accessed July 15, 2013, http://acheritagegroup.org/blog/?p=180.

[7] Fea, *Was America Founded*, xvii.

[8] Library of Congress Teaching with Primary Sources, "Reading an Image: George Washington," accessed July 15, 2013, http://www.tpsnva.org/teaching_materials/learning_experience/all.php?experiences_key=3793.

[9] Jim Stratton, "Rep. Harris Condemns Separation of Church,State," *Orlando Sentinel*, August 26, 2006, http://www.washingtonpost.com/wp-dyn/content/article/2006/08/25/AR2006082501640.html.

[10] Mark A. Chancey, "Textbook Example of the Christian Right," *Journal of the American Academy of Religion* 75 (September 2007), 554–581.

[11] Ron Chernow, *Washington: A Life* (New York, NY: Penguin, 2010), 326.

[12] Gordon S. Wood, "The Greatness of George Washington," *Virginia Quarterly Review* 68 (Spring 1992), 193–194.

[13] Pierard and Linder, *Civil Religion*, 74.

[14] Matthew L. Harris and Thomas S. Kidd, eds., *The Founding Fathers and the Debate Over Religion in Revolutionary America: A History in Documents* (New York, NY: Oxford University Press, 2012), 23.

[15] http://www.wallbuilders.com/libissuesarticles.asp?id=126, accessed July 15, 2013.

[16] Wallbuilders, "Educating the Nation," accessed July 15, 2013, http://www.wallbuilders.com/ABTOverview.asp.

[17] W. Cleon Skousen, *The 5000 Year Leap: A Miracle that Changed the World.* (Malta, ID: National Center for Constitutional Studies, 1981).

[18] Alexander Zaitchik, "Meet the Man who Changed Glenn Beck's Life," *Salon On-Line*, September 16, 2009, http://www.salon.com/2009/09/16/beck_skousen/.

[19] Mark Chancey, "Educating for a 'Christian America'? Bible courses, Social Studies Standards and the Texas Controversy," Transcript of Remarks at the Baker Institute for Public Policy, Rice University, http://bakerinstitute.org/publications/REL-pub-ChanceyEducatingChristianAmerica-022411.pdf.

20 John M. Barry, *Roger Williams and the Creation of the American Soul: Church, State and the Birth of Liberty* (New York, NY: Viking, 2012), 394.

21 Roger Williams, "A Letter to the Town of Providence," 1655, http://www.nbu.bg/webs/amb/american/1/williams/letter.htm.

22 Barry, *Roger Williams*, 394.

23 Ibid., 11.

24 David Barton, *America's Godly Heritage* (Aledo, TX: WallBuilder Press, 1993), 8–9.

25 In a fascinating discussion of Barton's work, early American historian Johann N. Neem argues that Barton does this purposefully, because Barton wants to "slice through the layers of dogma" he associates with professional history. Neem argues that Barton wants to be the Martin Luther of historians, ignoring the high priests of history by interpreting only the primary sources of the past for himself. However, this does give Barton and others too much credit and does take him too seriously, because if they genuinely sought to understand the truth of the past, as Luther attempted to understand the truth of his religion, would they not seek to include all of the truth about the past, rather than merely picking selective truths about the past that supported their own belief system? Johann N. Neem, "Taking Historical Fundamentalism Seriously," *Historically Speaking* 12 (November 2011), 3.

26 Rev. Steve Wilkins, "A Christian Perspective of History," accessed July 15, 2013, http://www.new-life.net/growth/other-articles/a-christian-perspective-of-history/.

27 Skousen, *The 5000 Year Leap*, 15.

28 Ibid., 75–76.

29 Fea, *Was America Founded*, 68.

30 David Barton, *Separation of Church and State: What the Founders Meant* (Aledo, TX: WallBuilders, 2007), 5.

31 The text of the First Amendment pertaining to religion reads "Congress shall make no law respecting an establishment of religion, or prohibiting the free exercise thereof." For at least the past century, legal scholars have insisted that this statement should be defined by the idea of a "separation of church and state." See, for example, William Schoenfeld, "Separation of Church and State: A Policy or a Principle," *The North American Review*, 189 (May 1909), 662–674, where Schoenfeld quotes Theodore Roosevelt's discussion of the separation of church and state. Or see Milton Konvitz's discussion of the meaning of the first amendment in "Separation of Church and State: The First Freedom," *Law and Contemporary Problems* 14 (Winter 1949), 44–60.

32 Barton, *Separation of Church and State*, 9.

33 Mark Noll, George M. Marsden, and Nathan O. Hatch, *The Search for Christian America* (Colorado Springs, CO: Helmers and Howard, 1989), 73.

34 From Eugene R. Sheridan, *Jefferson and Religion* (Charlottesville, VA: Thomas Jefferson Memorial Foundation, 1998), 18, as quoted in Andrew Levison, "The Conservative 'Christianization' of Thomas Jefferson," http://www.thedemocraticstrategist.org/_memos/TDS_WP_Levison_Jefferson_Christ.pdf.

35 From Lenni Brenner, ed., *Jefferson and Madison on Separation of Church and State: Writings on Religion and Secularism.* (Fort Lee, NJ: Barricade Books, 2004), 339, as quoted in Andrew Levison, "The Conservative 'Christianization' of Thomas Jefferson," http://www.thedemocraticstrategist.org/_memos/TDS_WP_Levison_Jefferson_Christ.pdf.

[36] From Edwin Gaustad, *Sworn on the Altar of God: a Religious Biography of Thomas Jefferson* (Grand Rapids, MI: W.B. Eerdman, 1996), 37 as quoted in Andrew Levison, "The Conservative 'Christianization' of Thomas Jefferson," http://www.thedemocraticstrategist.org/_memos/TDS_WP_Levison_Jefferson_Christ.pdf

[37] Ibid., 72.

[38] Erik Eckholm, "History Buff Sets a Course for the Right," *New York Times,* May 4, 2011, A1.

[39] Rob Boston, "Texas Tall Tale," *Church and State,* July/August 2009, accessed July 15, 2013, http://www.au.org/church-state/julyaugust-2009-church-state/featured/texas-tall-tale.

[40] YouTube, "Bachmann to David Barton: You Are a Gift to our Nation," accessed July 15, 2013, http://www.youtube.com/watch?v=iZCZdoTicv8.

[41] Andy Birkey, "Meet David Barton, Bachmann's Constitution Class Teacher," *The Minnesota Independent,* November 16, 2010, http://americanindependent.com/156775/meet-david-barton-bachmann's-constitution-class-teacher.

[42] Kyle Mantyla, "Flashback: Gingrich's Presidential Campaign to Heavily Rely on Barton's Counsel and Advice," *Right Wing Watch,* March 3, 2011, http://www.rightwingwatch.org/content/flashback-gingrichs-presidential-campaign-heavily-rely-bartons-counsel-and-advice.

[43] Erik Eckholm, "History Buff," A1.

[44] Ibid.

[45] Birkey, "Meet David Barton."

[46] For the text of the bill see http://thomas.loc.gov/cgi-bin/query/z?c110:H.RES.888:.

[47] Chris Rodda, "Think the 'Christmas Resolution' Was Bad: Check Out House Resolution 888," *Talk to Action,* January 4, 2008, http://www.talk2action.org/story/2008/1/4/24725/53989.

[48] Ibid.

[49] Ibid.

[50] EdWatch, "Minnesota Legislative Report," April 22, 2004, http://www.edwatch.org/updates/042204.htm.

[51] Ibid.

[52] Cmods Curriculum Modules, "The American Creed," accessed July 15, 2013, http://cmods.org/Unit1Module3.html.

[53] The beginnings of the process resembled the process followed by other states. First, a committee of teachers was gathered to examine the standards written a decade earlier and suggest changes and, if necessary, write new standards. Then a panel of experts in history and history education were to review the standards, and then the state board would make the decision on approval for the standards after a period of public comment.

[54] Phyllis Schlafly, "Texas Kicks Out Liberal Bias from Textbooks," *Eagle Forum,* March 9, 2010, 1, www.eagleforum.org/column/mar10/10-03-19.html.

[55] Don McLeroy, "Teaching Our children What It Means to Be an American in 2011," speech at the Educational Policy Conference, St. Louis, MO, January 28, 2011.

[56] Mark A. Chancey, "Educating for a 'Christian America'?", 10.

[57] Russel Shorto, "How Christian Were the Founders?," *New York Times Magazine,* February 11, 2010, http://www.nytimes.com/2010/02/14/magazine/14texbooks-t.html?pagewanted=all.

[58] Peter Marshall Ministries, www.petermarshallministries.com.

[59] Peter Marshall, "Second Version TEKS Review," Texas Education Agency, www.tea. state.tx.us/WorkArea/linkit.aspx?LinkIdentifier=id&ItemID=6276.

[60] David Barton, "2009 TEKS Review," Texas Education Agency, https:// s3.amazonaws.com/s3.documentcloud.org/documents/408349/david-barton-review-of-current-social-studies-teks.txt.

[61] See John Fea, *Was America founded as a Christian Nation?*

[62] Barton, *2009 TEKS Review*, 11.

[63] Ibid.

[64] Philip Gould, "Virtue, Ideology and the American Revolution: The Legacy of the Republican Synthesis," *American Literary History* 5 (Autumn 1993), 565.

[65] YouTube, "Gordon S. Wood on Republican Virtue," accessed July 15, 2013, http:// www.youtube.com/watch?v=1JAkFxAsdJQ. For a complete discussion of the idea of "republican virtue," see Gordon S. Wood, *The Creation of the American Republic* (Chapel Hill, NC: University of North Carolina Press, 1998).

[66] From Brenner, *Jefferson and Madison on the Separation of Church and* State, 195, as quoted in Levison, "The Conservative 'Christianization' of Thomas Jefferson."

[67] Rob Kuznia, "Tea Party Campaigns for Constitution Education in Redondo Schools," *Dailybreeze.com*, September 19, 2011, http://www.dailybreeze.com/ news/ci_18931512.

[68] Sean Wilentz, "Confounding Fathers: The Tea Party's Cold War Roots," *The New Yorker*, October 18, 2010, 3.

[69] Garrett Epps, "All Patriots 'Know' that Moses Wrote the Constitution," *The Atlantic On-line*, October 29, 2010, http://www.theatlantic.com/national/archive/2010/10/all-patriots-know-that-moses-wrote-the-constitution/65353/.

[70] Tea Party Patriots, "Adopt a School: Tools: FAQ," accessed July 15, 2013, http:// www.teapartypatriots.org/training/constitution/adopt-a-school/tools/faq/.

[71] "Interview with Larry Schweikart, Author of *What Would the Founders Say?*," *All Right Magazine*, March 23, 2011, http://www.allrightmagazine.com/books-and-reviews/interview-with-larry-schweikart-author-of-what-would-the-founders-say-sentinel-2011-7629/.

[72] Mark Beliles and Stephen McDowell, *America's Providential History: Including Biblical Principles of Education, Government, Politics, Economics and Family Life*, 3rd ed., (Charlottesville, VA: Providence Foundation, 2010).

[73] Christine Miller, "History in the Grammar Stage," accessed July 15, 2013, http:// www.classical-homeschooling.org/grammar/history.html.

[74] Fea, *Was America Founded*, 59.

CHAPTER 2

[1] Burton W. Folsom, Jr., *The Myth of he Robber Barons: A New Look at the Rise of Big Business in America*, 6th ed. (Herndon, VA: Young America's Foundation, 2010), 16.

[2] "Texas Textbook Controversy," *Religion & Ethics Newsweekly*, April 30, 2010, http:// www.pbs.org/wnet/religionandethics/episodes/april-30-2010/texas-textbook-controversy/6187/.

[3] Ibid.

[4] Folsom, *The Myth of he Robber Barons*, 17.

[5] Ibid., 39.

[6] Mansel Blackford, "Review of Entrepreneurs vs. the State: A New Look at the Rise of Big Business in America, 1840–1920," *The Business History Review* 63 (Autumn, 1989): 674–675.

[7] The land grant was for seven million acres, the seventh largest of the original 75 railroad grants. See John B. Rae, "The Great Northern's Land Grant." *The Journal of Economic History* 12 (Spring 1952): 140–145.

[8] Jason McGrew-King, "James J. Hill Wasn't Always Admired by Wayzata," *Lakeshore Weekly News*, September 6, 2005, 3C.

[9] Frank Leonard, "'Wise, Swift, and Sure'? The Great Northern Entry into Seattle, 1889–1894," *The Pacific Northwest Quarterly* 92 (Spring 2001): 81–90.

[10] Eric Dregni, "James J. Hill Lake Minnetonka History," *Lake Minnetonka Magazine*, September 2011, http://lakeminnetonkamag.com/article/james-j-hill-property/james-j-hill-lake-minnetonka-history.

[11] Howard Schonberger, "James J. Hill and the Trade with the Orient," *Minnesota History* 41 (Winter 1968): 178–190.

[12] Folsom, *The Myth of the Robber Barons*, 134.

[13] Ibid., 54.

[14] Daniel Henninger, "Bring Back the Robber Barons," *Wall Street Journal*, March 3, 2010, http:// online.wsj.com/article/SB10001424052748703862704575099572105775414.html.

[15] See, for example, FSTDT Refugee Board blog, "Grover Cleveland, Hero of the Tea Party," accessed July 15, 2013, http://fstdt.proboards.com/index.cgi?board=pg&action=display&thread=8822.

[16] Matthew Algeo, "Forget Romney or Gingrich. In 2012, the Tea Party Wants…another Grover Cleveland," *Christian Science Monitor*, May 17, 2011, http://www.csmonitor.com/Commentary/Opinion/2011/0517/Forget-Romney-or-Gingrich.-In-2012-the-tea-party-wants-another-Grover-Cleveland.

[17] Burton W. Folsom, *New Deal or Raw Deal: How FDR's Economic Legacy Has Damaged America* (New York, NY: Threshold Editions, 2008), 77.

[18] See, for example, Nell Irvin Painter, *Standing at Armageddon: A Grassroots History of the Progressive Era* (New York, NY: W. W. Norton and Company, 2008).

[19] Kona Tea Party, "Capitalism Works, Socialism Fails," April 19, 2011, http://www.konateaparty.com/2011/04/capitalism-works-socialism-fails/.

[20] John Nichols, "Bizarro History: The Rough Rider as Socialist Stooge," *The Nation*, December 8, 2011, http://www.cbsnews.com/8301-215_162-57339239/bizarro-history-the-rough-rider-as-socialist-stooge/.

[21] Ibid.

[22] Ibid.

[23] Folsom, *New Deal or Raw Deal*, 24, 219, 221, 75.

[24] Ibid., 164, 93.

[25] Ibid., 168–193, 109–110.

[26] David M. Kennedy, *Freedom From Fear: The American People in Depression and War, 1929–1945* (New York, NY: Oxford University Press, 1999), 355–380.

[27] Ibid., 365.

[28] Ibid., 372.

[29] Ibid., 377.

[30] Amazon.com customer review, "About Time Someone Took on the New Deal," November 13, 2008, accessed July 15, 2013, http://www.amazon.com/review/R3CR81GIKB1FSX.

[31] "Interview with Larry Schweikart, Author of What Would the Founders Say?," *All Right Magazine,* March 23, 2011, http://www.allrightmagazine.com/books-and-reviews/interview-with-larry-schweikart-author-of-what-would-the-founders-say-sentinel-2011-7629/.

[32] Bill Schneider, "It's Rick Perry vs. New Deal," *Politic,* September 13, 2011, http://www.politico.com/news/stories/0911/63402.html#ixzz1jMXphRWV.

[33] Rick Perry, *Fed Up!: Our Fight to Save America from Washington* (New York, NY: Little, Brown and Company, 2010), 47–48.

[34] Thomas Frank, "The Persecution of Sarah Palin," *Wall Street Journal,* November 17, 2009, http://online.wsj.com/article/SB100014240527487047823045745420 51447849052.html.

[35] Paul Street, "Sarah Palin, Corporate Capitalism, and Right Wing Nostalgia for the 'Free Market' Nineteenth Century," Blog post, September 13, 2011, http://www.paulstreet.org/?p=448.

[36] Robert Reich, "The Rise of the Regressive Right and the Reawakening of America," October 16, 2011, http://robertreich.org/post/11511074902.

[37] EdWatch press release, "New Standards Improvement over the Profile but still Flawed," May 26, 2004, http://www.edwatch.org/.

[38] EducationLibertyWatch, "Alert! New PC Social Studies Standards are a Disaster!!," March 3, 2011, http://edlibertywatch.org/2011/03/alert-new-pc-social-studies-standards-are-a-disaster/#more-392.

[39] Todd Starnes, Fox News and Commentary, "Nebraska Educators Debate American Exceptionalism," July 11, 2012, http://radio.foxnews.com/toddstarnes/top-stories/nebraska-educators-debate-american-exceptionalism.html.

[40] Don McLeroy, "Teaching Our Children What it Means to be an American in 2011?!," January 28, 2011, http://www.scribd.com/doc/47997816/Don-McLeroy-Teaching-Our-Children-What-It-Means-to-Be-an-American-in-2011.

[41] Ibid.

[42] David Barton, "2009 TEKS Review." Texas Education Agency. https://s3.amazonaws.com/s3.documentcloud.org/documents/408349/david-barton-review-of-current-social-studies-teks.txt.

[43] Ibid.

[44] Ibid.

[45] McLeroy, "Teaching Our Children."

[46] See http://www.tea.state.tx.us/index4.aspx?id=2386 for the complete text of the proposed new Texas Economics course.

[47] The Heritage Foundation, "Who Were the Progressives and What Did They Believe?" and "What Is the New Deal and How Does It Depart from the Principles of the Founding?," accessed July 15, 2013, http://www.heritage.org/initiatives/first-principles/basics.

[48] Mark A. Beliles and Stephen K. McDowell, *America's Providential History: Including Biblical Principles of Education, Government, Politics, Economics, and Family Life,* 3rd ed. (Charlottesville, VA: Providence Foundation, 1991), 206.

[49] Ibid., 206–207.

[50] Ibid., 251.

[51] Michael R. Lowman, George T. Thompson, and Kurt A. Grussendorf, *United States History in Christian Perspective: Heritage of Freedom* (Pensacola, FL: A Beka Book, 2008), 362.

[52] Ibid., 365.

[53] Ibid., 373–374.

[54] Ibid., 536.

[55] Ibid., 544.

[56] Young America's Foundation, "Our Mission," accessed July 15, 2013, http://www.yaf.org/Mission.aspx.

[57] Young America's Foundation, "Conservative Conferences and Seminars," accessed July 15, 2013, http://www.yaf.org/Conservative-Conferences.aspx.

[58] Foundation for Economic Education, accessed July 15, 2013, http://www.fee.org/.

[59] "Tea Party Patriots on Education" accessed January 25, 2012, http://www.teapartypatriots.org/wp-content/uploads/2011/10/66571276-Education.pdf.

[60] A Conservative Teacher Blog, accessed January 25, 2012, http://aconservativeteacher.blogspot.com/2011/06/lessons-from-economic-recessions.html.

[61] Houston Independent School District, "America's Heritage: An Adventure in Liberty," accessed July 15, 2013, http://www.cdsar.org/AmericanHeritage/NHSL.pdf, 81–100.

CHAPTER 3

[1] Fred Anderson and Andrew R. L. Cayton, *The Dominion of War: Empire and Liberty in North America, 1500–2000* (New York, NY: Viking, 2005), x.

[2] Ibid., xi.

[3] Ibid., xii.

[4] Richard Lowry and Ramesh Ponnuru, "An Exceptional Debate: The Obama Administration's Assault on American Identity," *National Review On-Line*, March 8, 2010, http://www.freerepublic.com/focus/f-news/2457827/posts.

[5] Charles Krauthammer, "American Exceptionalism in the Age of Obama," from the "Teaching Freedom" series of speeches, The Fund for American Studies, http://issuu.com/tfas/docs/krauthammer, 1.

[6] William Widenor, *Henry Cabot Lodge and the Search for an American Foreign Policy*, (ACLS Humanities e-book), 113.

[7] Walter A. McDougall, *Promised Land, Crusader State: The American Encounter with the World since 1776* (Boston, MA: Houghton Mifflin, 1997), 104.

[8] Godfrey Hodgson, *The Myth of American Exceptionalism* (New Haven, CT: Yale University Press, 2009), 66.

[9] Ibid., 86.

[10] Ian Tyrell Blog, "Empire of Denial: American Empire, Past, Present and Future," accessed July 15, 1013, http://iantyrrell.wordpress.com/empire-of-denial-american-empire-past-present-and-future/.

[11] Richard H. Immerman, *Empire for Liberty: A History of American Imperialism from Benjamin Franklin to Paul Wolfowitz* (Princeton, NJ: Princeton University Press, 2010), 1.

[12] Dennis Prager, "Who Believes in American Exceptionalism?" Townhall.com, November 11, 2005, http://www.freerepublic.com/focus/f-news/1513113/posts.

[13] Lowry and Ponnuru, "An Exceptional Debate."

[14] Mike Marqusee Blog, "The Iron Click: American Exceptionalism and US Empire," August 1, 2009, http://www.mikemarqusee.com/?p=865.

[15] Michael Soto, "Plagiarized Work," *History News Network*, May 10, 2011, http://hnn.us/articles/126367.html.

[16] Greg Grandin, "The Death of American Exceptionalism," *The Nation On-Line*, February 2, 2011, http://www.thenation.com/blog/158186/death-american-exceptionalism.

[17] Mark Finkelstein, "David Stockman: American Exceptionalism is 'Neo-Con Code' for Aggressive Foreign Policy," NewsBusters, January 22, 2012, http://newsbusters.org/blogs/mark-finkelstein/2012/01/22/david-stockman-american-exceptionalism-neo-con-code-aggressive-for.

[18] Hodgson, *The Myth of American Exceptionalism*, 175.

[19] Kevin M. Levin, "If I Should Teach American Exceptionalism…," Civil War Memory (blog), March 17, 2010, http://cwmemory.com/2010/03/17/if-i-should-teach-american-exceptionalism/.

[20] Glenn Greenwald, "Obama and American Exceptionalism," *Salon On-Line*, March 29, 2011, http://www.salon.com/2011/03/29/exceptionalism_4/.

[21] Newt Gingrich and Vince Haley, *A Nation Like No Other: Why American Exceptionalism Matters* (Washington, DC: Regnery Pub., 2011), 13.

[22] Liberty University course syllabus for GOVT 329: American Exceptionalism, http://www.luonline.com/media/3415/courseguides/GOVT329_Syllabus.pdf.

[23] Karen Tumulty, "Conservatives' New Focus: America the Exceptional," *Washington Post*, November 10, 2010, http://www.washingtonpost.com/wp-dyn/content/article/2010/11/28/AR2010112804139.html?sid=ST2010112901818.

[24] Ibid.

[25] Bill Ames, "Insertion of Liberal's Texas History Warrants SBOE Action," September 9, 2009, http://www.educationnews.org/articles/do-you-want-your-children-to-be-patriotic.html.

[26] Bill Ames, "Insertion of Liberal's Texas History Warrants SBOE Action (Part II)," September 10, 2009, http://www.educationnews.org/articles/do-you-want-your-children-to-be-patriotic.html.

[27] Ibid.

[28] Peggy Venable, "Richardson ISD, others the public is concerned," The Red Apple Project, March 4, 2013, http://redappleproject.com/2013/03/richardson-isd-others-the-public-is-concerned/.

[29] Kyle Olson, Ben Velderman, and Steve Gunn, *Indoctrination: How "Useful Idiots" Are Using Our Schools to Subvert American Exceptionalism* (Bloomington, IN: Authorhouse, 2011), xiii.

[30] Ibid., 131.

[31] Richard Locker, "Tea Parties Issue Demands to Tennessee Legislators," *The Commercial Appeal*, January 13, 2011, http://www.commercialappeal.com/news/2011/jan/13/tea-parties-cite-legislative-demands/.

[32] Todd Starnes, "Nebraska Educators Debate American Exceptionalism," Fox News and Commentary, July 11, 2012, http://radio.foxnews.com/toddstarnes/top-stories/nebraska-educators-debate-american-exceptionalism.html.

[33] Mark Tooley, "Exceptional America?," *The American Spectator*, April 8, 2011, http://spectator.org/archives/2011/04/08/exceptional-america.

[34] Mike Huckabee, "Rethink 'Blame America First' as the Way to Teach History," *Investors.com*, September 8, 2011, http://news.investors.com/Article/584219/201109081840/Rethink-Blame-America-First-As-The-Way-To-Teach-History.htm.

[35] Learn Our History, accessed July 15, 2013, http://www.learnourhistory.com/LearnOurHistory.com//Frequently_Asked_Questions_files/widget0_markup.html.

[36] R. B. Bernstein, *HNet On-line* post, May 20, 2011, http://h-net.msu.edu/cgi-bin/logbrowse.pl?trx=vx&list=h-oieahc&month=1105&week=d&msg=s96f3eazITSxOT7BpCrM5A&user=&pw= 2/14/12.

[37] Sean Hannity, "Callista Gingrich on Mission to Educate Kids about American History," Gingrich Productions, September 26, 2011, http://www.gingrichproductions.com/reagan/callista-gingrich-on-mission-to-educate-kids-about-american-history.html.

[38] Janice Rogers Brown, "The Fortress Stone of American Exceptionalism: Clarity and Destiny or Confusion and Despair?," from the "Teaching Freedom" series of speeches, The Fund for American Studies, accessed July 15, 2013, http://www.tfas.org/page.aspx?pid=2174, 2.

[39] Valerie Strauss, "Protestors Call IB Program Un-American. Is it?," *Washington Post*, May 18, 2010, http://voices.washingtonpost.com/answer-sheet/apibhonors/protesters-call-ib-program-un-.html.

[40] Albrecht Powell, "International Baccalaureate is Anti-American & Anti-Christian?," *About.com* Guide, February 22, 2006, http://pittsburgh.about.com/b/2006/02/22/international-baccalaureate-is-anti-american-anti-christian.htm.

[41] Ibid.

[42] Strauss, "Protestors Call IB Program Un-American."

[43] Allen Quist, "The International Baccalaureate Curriculum," *EdWatch*, March 17, 2007, http://www.edwatch.org/updates07/031707-IB.htm.

[44] "IB in Monticello, NY, " Truth About IB, accessed July 15, 2013, http://truthaboutib.com/usschooldisputes/ibinmonticellony.html.

[45] "IB in Stow-Munroe Falls, Ohio," Truth About IB, accessed July 15, 2013, http://truthaboutib.com/usschooldisputes/stowmunroefallsohio.html.

[46] Ted Siefer, "Senate Kills Anti-International Baccalaureate Bill," *New Hampshire Union Leader*, May 16, 2012, http://www.unionleader.com/article/20120516/NEWS06/705169912.

[47] "Plus, Ridiculous Paranoia about the UN Infiltrating Bountiful and Provo," Utah Education Issues (blog), February 22, 2008, http://utahedu.blogspot.com/2008/02/plus-ridiculous-paranoia-about-un.html.

[48] Daniel Greenfield, "Teaching Your Child to Be a Dictator's Lackey," *Frontpage Mag*, October 31, 2011, http://frontpagemag.com/2011/dgreenfield/teaching-your-child-to-be-a-dictators-lackey/.

[49] Allen Quist, "The International Baccalaureate Curriculum," *EdWatch*, http://www.edwatch.org/updates07/031707-IB.htm, Accessed 6/18/2013

[50] Todd Starnes, "Texas Lawmakers Blast Anti-American, Anti-Christian Curriculum," Fox News Radio, February 5, 2013, http://radio.foxnews.com/toddstarnes/top-stories/texas-lawmakers.html.

CHAPTER 4

[1] Susan Jacoby, *Alger Hiss and the Battle for History* (New Haven, CT: Yale University Press, 2009), 12.

[2] This lesson can be found on Teachinghistory.org, one of the leading national websites for history education, http://teachinghistory.org/system/files/McCarthy_docB.pdf.

[3] Jacoby, *Alger Hiss and the Battle for History*, 114.

[4] Ann Coulter, *Treason: Liberal Treachery from the Cold War to the War on Terrorism* (New York, NY: Three Rivers Press, 2004), 10.

[5] Ann Coulter, "McCarthyism: The Rosetta Stone of Liberal Lies," *Human Events*, November 7, 2007, http://www.humanevents.com/2007/11/07/mccarthyism-the-rosetta-stone-of-liberal-lies/.

[6] See, for example, "Glenn Beck—McCarthy and the Venona Papers," YouTube, accessed July 15, 2013, http://www.youtube.com/watch?v=Zfq6URia1Zw.

[7] Sam Stein, "Michele Bachmann Channels McCarthy: Obama 'Very Anti-American,' Congressional Witch Hunt Needed," *Huffington Post*, November 17, 2008, http://www.huffingtonpost.com/2008/10/17/gop-rep-channels-mccarthy_n_135735.html.

[8] Douglas Burns, "Has King Left No Sense of Decency?," *Daily Times Herald*, October 5, 2005, http://www.carrollspaper.com/main.asp?Search=1&ArticleID=336&SectionID=4&SubSectionID=4&S=41.

[9] Much of the following discussion of the Venona Papers has been previously discussed by the author in Fritz Fischer, "The Texas History Standards: The Case of the 'Venona Standard' and Effective History Teaching," *History Matters* 23 (2010): 4–7.

[10] Harvey Klehr, "Was Joe McCarthy Right?," Raleigh Spy Conference Report, November 7, 2005, http://www.raleighspyconference.com/news/news_11-07-05.aspx.

[11] Jacoby, *Alger Hiss and the Battle for History*, 12.

[12] Ellen Schrecker, "History in Red—and White and Blue," *Radical History Review*, September 1, 2005.

[13] Jacoby, *Alger Hiss and the Battle for History*, 192.

[14] Phyllis Schlafly, "History Shows Joe McCarthy's Reputation Is Undeserved," *Free Republic.com*, January 28, 2008, http://www.freerepublic.com/focus/f-news/1960923/posts.

[15] TFN Insider, "More McLeroy Malarkey, Part 1," Blog post, October 21, 2009, http://tfninsider.org/2009/10/21/more-mcleroy-malarkey-part-1/.

[16] Don McLeroy, "Teaching Our children What It Means to Be an American in 2011," speech at the Educational Policy Conference, St. Louis, MO, January 28, 2011.

[17] "Schlafly and Noebel: McCarthy Was a 'Hero,' Communism Nearly Upon Us," *Right Wing Watch*, accessed July 15, 2013, http://www.rightwingwatch.org/category/people/joseph-mccarthy.

[18] Oak Norton, "Utah's Republic: Aren't We a Democracy?," Utah's Republic, accessed July 15, 2013, http://www.utahsrepublic.org.

[19] Although, as it turns out, the actual decoded message documents are disappointing in their lack of detail about the world of spies. To find the documents, go

to http://www.nsa.gov/public_info/declass/venona/dated.shtml. See also the translated KGB documents on the Cold War International History Project at http://www.wilsoncenter.org/topics/docs/Yellow_Notebook_No.1_Translated.pdf.

[20] Michael R. Lowman, George Thompson, and Kurt Grussendorf, *United States History in Christian Perspective: Heritage of Freedom*, 2nd ed. (Pensacola, FL: A Beka Book, 1982), 593–594.

[21] Larry Schweikart and Michael Allen, *A Patriot's History of the United States: From Columbus's Great Discovery to the War on Terror* (New York, NY: Sentinel, 2004), 644–646.

[22] Larry Schweikart, "Why It's Time for 'A Patriot's History of the United States,'" *A Patriot's History* (blog), accessed July 15, 2013, http://www.patriotshistoryusa.com/reviews-interviews/why-its-time/.

[23] NEW Staff, "Our Activist Roots: Conservatism in the 1950–1960s," NEW: Network of Enlightened Women, April 27, 2010, http://enlightenedwomen.org/our-activist-roots-conservatism-in-the-1950s-1960s/.

[24] Jennifer Buckett, "Values and Morals in American Society: The 1950s versus Today," September 23, 2007, http://www.stevenjthompson.com/varioustopics/culturaldecline/values_morals_in_american_society_1950s_vs_today.html.

[25] "It Takes a Family," transcript of a live Q&A with Rick Santorum, *Washington Post On-line*, July 25, 2005, http://www.washingtonpost.com/wpdyn/content/discussion/2005/07/20/DI2005072001515.html.

[26] NEW Staff, *"Our Activist Roots."*

[27] Phyllis Schlafly, "The High Costs of Marriage Abstinence," Eagle Forum, November 2011, http://www.eagleforum.org/psr/2011/nov11/psrnov11.html.

[28] "Conservatives' First Lady Sparked Pro-Family Effort," *The Washington Times*, October 7, 2005, http://www.washingtontimes.com/news/2005/oct/7/20051007-120157-1091r/?page=all.

[29] Schlafly, "The High Costs of Marriage Abstinence."

[30] Phyllis Schlafly, "America Is Becoming Non-White," *Eagle Forum* (blog), May 17, 2012, http://blog.eagleforum.org/2012/05/america-is-becoming-non-white.html.

[31] Stephanie Coontz, *The Way We Never Were: American Families and the Nostalgia Trap* (New York, NY: BasicBooks, 2000), 23.

[32] Ibid., 25, 28.

[33] Ibid., 30.

[34] Ibid., 32, 25.

[35] Jack Shafer, "Wasting Away in Dementiaville," Reuters Blog, January 24, 2012, http://blogs.reuters.com/jackshafer/2012/01/25/wasting-away-in-dementiaville/.

[36] David Kushner, *Levittown: Two Families, One Tycoon, and the Fight for Civil Rights in America's Legendary Suburb* (New York, NY: Walker and Co., 2009), 52.

[37] Ibid., 122.

[38] Michael Schaller, *Right Turn: American Life in the Reagan-Bush Era, 1980–1992* (New York, NY: Oxford University Press, 2007), 11.

[39] Phyllis Schlafly, "Good News and Bad News about Stay-at-Home Moms," *Eagle Forum*, April 21, 2004, http://www.eagleforum.org/column/2004/apr04/04-04-21. html.

[40] Nancy A. Walker, ed., *Women's Magazines, 1940–1960: Gender Roles and the Popular Press* (Boston, MA: Bedford/St Martin's, 1998), 5.

[41] Ibid., 8.

[42] Ibid., 19.

[43] Glynnis MacNicol, "Glenn Beck: During the Civil Rights Movement God Spoke through MLK, RFK,...and Roger Ailes," *Mediate*, July 14, 2010, http://www. mediaite.com/online/glenn-beck-during-the-civil-rights-movement-god-spoke-through-mlk-rfk-and-roger-ailes/.

[44] David Neiwert, "Beck Says Progressives Co-opted Civil Rights Movement: Seems He Forgot What Conservatives Did," *CrooksandLiars*, June 4, 2010, http://crooksandliars.com/david-neiwert/beck-says-progressives-co-opted-civi.

[45] Will Bunch, "Glenn Beck Rewrites Civil Rights History," CNN Opinion, August 26 2010, http://articles.cnn.com/2010-08-26/opinion/bunch.beck.history_1_beck-s-american-revival-glenn-beck-civil-rights?_s=PM:OPINION.

[46] Ibid.

[47] John Nichols, "No, Glenn Beck is Not a Civil Rights Icon," *The Nation Online*, August 28, 2010, http://www.thenation.com/blog/154200/no-glenn-beck-not-civil-rights-icon.

[48] Gabriel Winant, "Get Your Hands Off MLK, Glenn Beck," *Salon Online*, July 26, 2010, http://www.salon.com/2010/07/26/long_civil_rights_movement/.

[49] Jacqueline Dowd Hall, "The Long Civil Rights Movement and the Political Uses of the Past," *The Journal of American History* 91 (March 2005): 1237.

[50] Ibid., 1233–1263.

[51] Southern Poverty Law Center, "Teaching the Movement: The State of Civil Rights Education in the United States," Southern Poverty Law Center 2011, http://www. splcenter.org/sites/default/files/downloads/publication/Teaching_the_Movement.pdf, 11.

[52] Herbert Kohl, "The Politics of Children's Literature: What's Wrong with the Rosa Parks Myth," in *Rethinking Our Classrooms: Teaching for Equity and Justice*, vol. 1, Bill Bigelow, Ed. (Milwaukee, WI: Rethinking Our Schools, 1994), 137–138.

[53] Janet Shan, "Mike Savage Says, 'Thurgood Marshall Was an Outright Communist,'" *HinterlandGazette.com*, May 11, 2010, http://hinterlandgazette.com/2010/05/mike-savage-says-thurgood-marshall-was.html.

[54] Trevor Loudon, "Obama's Supreme Court Nominee, Elena Kagan's Socialist Associations (the Middle Years)," *Gulagbound.com*, July 6, 2010, http://gulagbound. com/429/obama-file-106-obamas-supreme-court-nominee-elena-kagans-socialist-associations-the-middle-years/.

[55] Lowell Ponte, "Unholy Trinity," *Frontpagemag.com*, July 16, 2004, http://archive. frontpagemag.com/readArticle.aspx?ARTID=12181.

[56] *Deseret News*, December 14, 1963, as quoted in Neiwert, "Glenn Beck Says Progressives Co-opted Civil Rights Movement."

[57] Loudon, "Obama's Supreme Court Nominee."

CHAPTER 5

[1] Bill Bigelow, "Occupy the Curriculum," *Rethinking Schools* Blog, November 7, 2011, http://rethinkingschoolsblog.wordpress.com/2011/11/07/occupy-the-curriculum/.

[2] Sam Wineburg, "Undue Certainty: Where Howard Zinn's *A People's History* Falls Short," *American Educator* 36 (Winter 2012–13): 27.

[3] Bill Bigelow, *A People's History for the Classroom* (Milwaukee, WI: Rethinking Schools, 2008), 2.

[4] Ibid., 14.

[5] Peter Stearns, "Social History and World History: Toward Greater Interaction," College Board AP Central, accessed July 15, 2013, http://apcentral.collegeboard.com/apc/members/courses/teachers_corner/180003.html.

[6] Luther Spoehr, *Saturday Review,* February 2, 1980, 37–39.

[7] Daniel J. Flynn, "Zinn's Biased History," *History News Network,* June 9, 2003, http://hnn.us/articles/1493.html.

[8] Ron Radosh, "The Zinning of America: How to Watch 'The People Speak' on The History Channel on Sunday Night," *PJ Media,* December, 12, 2009, http://pjmedia.com/ronradosh/2009/12/12/the-zinning-of-america-how-to-watch-the-people-speak-on-the-history-channel-on-sunday-night/.

[9] Larry DeWitt, "Howard Zinn: The Historian as Don Quixote," *History News Network,* January 25, 2009, http://hnn.us/articles/58544.html.

[10] Ibid.

[11] Michael Kazin, "Howard Zinn's Disappointing History of the United States," *History News Network,* February 9, 2010, http://hnn.us/articles/4370.html.

[12] Ibid.

[13] Wineburg, "Undue Certainty," 28.

[14] Ibid., 29.

[15] Ward Churchill, *On the Justice of Roosting Chickens: Reflections on the Consequences of U.S. Imperial Arrogance and Criminality* (Oakland, CA: AK Press, 2003), 18–19.

[16] Tara Mack and Bree Picower, eds., *Planning to Change the World: A Plan Book for Social Justice Teachers 2012-2013* (Milwaukee: Rethinking Schools, 2012), 3.

[17] Bill Bigelow and Bob Peterson, eds., *Rethinking Columbus: The Next 500 Years,* 2nd ed. (Milwaukee: Rethinking Schools, 1998), 11.

[18] Bill Bigelow, "Talking Back to Columbus: Teaching for Justice and Hope," in *Rethinking Columbus: The Next 500 Years,* 2nd ed. (Milwaukee, WI: Rethinking Schools, 1998), 115.

[19] Ibid., 117–118.

[20] Howard Zinn, *A People's History of the United States,* online version, Chapter 1, accessed July 15, 2013, http://www.historyisaweapon.com/zinnapeopleshistory.html.

[21] Ibid.

[22] Fred Anderson and Andrew R. L. Cayton, *The Dominion of War: Empire and Liberty in North America, 1500–2000* (New York, NY: Viking, 2005), 2.

[23] Ibid., 56.

[24] Bigelow and Peterson, *Rethinking Columbus,* 56–57.

[25] Wineburg, "Undue Certainty," 33.

[26] Howard Zinn, "Unsung Heroes," originally published in *Progressive Magazine,* June 2000, available at http://www.thirdworldtraveler.com/Zinn/Unsung_Heroes.html.

[27] Zinn, *A People's History,* Chapter 1.

[28] Carol Berkin, *A Brilliant Solution: Inventing the American Constitution* (New York, NY: Harcourt, 2002), 4.

[29] Bob Peterson, "Rethinking the U.S. Constitutional Convention: A Role Play," in *Rethinking our Classrooms: Teaching for Equity and Justice,* ed. Bill Bigelow, vol. 2 (Milwaukee, WI: Rethinking Schools, 1994), 64.

[30] Berkin, *A Brilliant Solution,* 5.

[31] Ibid., 66–69.

[32] Zinn, *A People's History,* Chapter 11.

[33] Kyle Olson, Ben Velderman, and Steve Gunn, *Indoctrination: How "Useful Idiots" Are Using Our Schools to Subvert American Exceptionalism* (Bloomington, IN: Authorhouse, 2011), 40.

[34] Norm Diamond, "One Hundred Years after the Singing Strike," Teaching *A People's History*: Zinn Education Project, January 11, 2011, http://zinnedproject.org/posts/15660.

[35] Bill Bigelow and Bob Peterson, "Lewis Hine's Photographs," Teaching *A People's History*: Zinn Education Project, accessed July 15, 2013, http://zinnedproject.org/posts/12005.

[36] "Wisconsin Law Requires Teaching of History of Organized Labor," *CNN On-line,* February 25, 2011, http://news.blogs.cnn.com/2011/02/25/wisconsin-law-requires-teaching-of-history-of-organized-labor/.

[37] "Labor Matters," Teaching *A People's History*: Zinn Education Project, accessed July 15, 2013, http://zinnedproject.org/posts/9899.

[38] Jody Sokolower, ed., *Teaching About the Wars* (Milwaukee, WI: Rethinking Schools, 2013), 3.

[39] Larry Miller, "A New US Bill of Rights," in *Rethinking our Classrooms: Teaching for Equity and Justice* vol. 2, ed. Bill Bigelow (Milwaukee, WI: Rethinking Schools, 1994).

[40] Bill Bigelow, "Christopher Columbus and the Iraq War," in Jody Sokolower, ed., *Teaching About the Wars,* 13.

[41] Bill Bigelow, "Repeat after Me: The United States Is Not an Imperialist Country–Oh, and Don't Get Emotional about War," Teaching *A People's History*: Zinn Education Project, January 12, 2012, http://zinnedproject.org/posts/15371.

[42] Kathleen Wootton and Christopher D. Stonebanks, "The Backlash on 'Roosting Chickens': The Continued Atmosphere of Suppressing Indigenous Perspectives," *Cultural Studies↔Critical Methodologies* 10 (2010): 112–113.

[43] Ibid.

[44] Kansas 7th grade standards , benchmark 3, indicator 1; South Dakota HS standard 2,1.

[45] Carol Berkin, "American Indians: From the Editor," *History Now* 28 (Summer 2011), http://www.gilderlehrman.org/history-now/2011-06/american-indians.

[46] Churchill, *On the Justice of Roosting Chickens,* 19.

[47] Ibid., 17.

[48] Ibid., 18.

[49] Ibid., 41.

[50] Ibid., 113, 101, 94.

[51] Ibid., 104.

[52] Zinn, *A People's History*, Chapter 12.

[53] Terrie Epstein, *Interpreting National History: Race, Identity, and Pedagogy in Classrooms and Communities* (New York, NY: Routledge, 2009), 5.

[54] Wayne Au, "'What We Want, What We Believe': Teaching with the Black Panthers' Ten Point Program," Teaching *A People's History*: Zinn Education Project, accessed July 15, 2013, http://zinnedproject.org/posts/170.

[55] Gilda L. Ochoa, "Pump Up the Blowouts: Reflections on the 40th Anniversary of the Chicano/a School Blowouts," Teaching *A People's History*: Zinn Education Project, accessed on July 15, 2013, http://zinnedproject.org/posts/1419.

[56] "The Most Dangerous Man in America Teaching Guide," Teaching *A People's History*: Zinn Education Project, accessed July 15, 2013, http://zinnedproject.org/posts/7325.

[57] Matt Taibbi, "The Hunters and the Hunted: book review of *Subversives: The FBI's War on Student Radicals and Reagan's Rise to Power*," *New York Times Book Review*, October 7, 2012, 11.

CHAPTER 6

[1] John McCaslin, "Reagan on Rushmore," *Townhall.com*, December 6, 2007, http://townhall.com/columnists/johnmccaslin/2007/12/06/reagan_on_rushmore/page/full/

[2] Christopher Hitchens, "Not even a Hedgehog: The Stupidity of Ronald Reagan," *Slate On-Line*, June 7, 2004, http://www.slate.com/articles/news_and_politics/fighting_words/2004/06/not_even_a_hedgehog.html.

[3] *Washington Times* commemorative issue on Reagan's passing, Feb 4, 2011, 3.

[4] Katherine Lackey, "In Reagan's Name, 'Teaching Moments'," *USA Today*, January 24, 2011, http://www.usatoday.com/news/washington/2011-01-24-ronald-reagan-names_N.htm.

[5] David Lightman, "The Reagan Name Game," *The Courant*, December 27, 1997, http://articles.courant.com/1997-12-27/news/9712270184_1_reagan-legacy-project-ronald-reagan-tax-bill.

[6] Real Clear Politics, "Gov. Chris Christie: Ronald Reagan & Real American Exceptionalism," September 27, 2011, http://www.realclearpolitics.com/video/2011/09/27/christie_addresses_reagan_library_obama_a_bystander_in_the_oval_office.html.

[7] Richard Herman, "A Time to Give Thanks to Ronald Reagan and American Exceptionalism," *HuffPost* Blog, November 24, 2010, http://www.huffingtonpost.com/richard-herman/a-time-to-give-thanks-to-_b_788108.html.

[8] Mike Laub Blog, accessed July 14, 2013, http://myclob.pbworks.com/w/page/21959547/Ronald%20Reagan#QuotesfromGovernorMittRomneyaboutPresidentRonaldReagan.

[9] Herman, "A Time to Give Thanks."

[10] Larry Schweikart and Michael Allen, *A Patriot's History of the United States* (New York, NY: Sentinel, 2007), 720–763.

[11] Timothy Keesee and Mark Sidwell, *United States History For Christian Schools, Teacher's Edition*, 2nd ed. (Pensacola, FL: A Beka, 1991), 606, 620.

[12] Lackey, "In Reagan's Name."

[13] The Heritage Foundation, "The American Founding," accessed July 4, 2013, http://www.heritage.org/initiatives/first-principles/basics#what-were-ronald-reagans-greatest-achievements.

[14] Ken Herman, "LASA Essayist Finds It Hard to 'Like' Perry, even Harder to Like Reagan, Commentary," *Statesman.com*, March 12, 2011, http://www.statesman.com/opinion/lasa-essayist-finds-it-hard-to-like-perry1317162.html.

[15] Lance Morrow, excerpt from "Why Is This Man So Popular?," *Time*, July 7, 1986, http://archive.mrc.org/specialreports/2004/pdf/Ronald_Reagan_PDF_version.pdf.

[16] Jonathan Alter, excerpt from *Newsweek*, December 31, 1991, http://archive.mrc.org/specialreports/2004/pdf/Ronald_Reagan_PDF_version.pdf.

[17] Bob Herbert in 1992, as quoted by Stephanie Gutmann, excerpt from *National Review*, June 21, 1993, http://archive.mrc.org/specialreports/2004/pdf/Ronald_Reagan_PDF_version.pdf.

[18] Michael Schaller, *Right Turn: American Life in the Reagan-Bush Era, 1980–1992* (New York, NY: Oxford University Press, 2007), 56.

[19] Ibid., 80.

[20] Ibid., 95, 91, 155.

[21] Will Bunch, *Tear Down this Myth: The Right-Wing Distortion of the Reagan Legacy* (New York, NY: Free Press, 2010), 59.

[22] Ibid., 61.

[23] Ibid., 224.

[24] Ibid., 17.

[25] Larry Schweikart, quoted at http://liveshots.blogs.foxnews.com/2010/03/11/president-reagan-gets-the-shaft-in-textbooks/.

[26] The Heritage Foundation, "The American Founding."

[27] Roman Joch, "To Eastern Eyes, Reagan a Liberator," *Washington Times*, February 3, 2011, 3.

[28] See the lesson plan, "He fought for freedom: Ronald Reagan," 2002, http://media.gatewaync.com/wsj/images/contactus/freedompdfs/reagan_lessonplan.pdf.

[29] Metropolitan Omaha Educational Consortium, "Ronald Reagan and the End of the Cold War (1947–1988)," accessed July 14, 2013, http://www.tahg.org/module_display.php?mod_id=44&review=yes.

[30] Learn Our History, accessed July 13, 2013, http://learnourhistory.com/go.cfm?do=Page.View&pid=9. See my note

[31] Bunch, *Tear Down this Myth*, 82.

[32] Tim Graham, "Rewriting Ronald Reagan: Reagan and National Defense," *NewsBusters*, February 3, 2011, http://newsbusters.org/blogs/tim-graham/2011/02/03/rewriting-ronald-reagan-reagan-and-national-defense. See my note

[33] Ibid.

[34] Robert G. Kaiser, "Gorbachev: 'We All Lost Cold War,'" *Washington Post*, June 11, 2004, A1.

[35] Matthew Dallek, "Not Ready for Mt. Rushmore: Reconciling the Myth of Ronald Reagan with the Reality," *The American Scholar*, Summer 2009, 6.

[36] Ibid.

[37] Graham, "Rewriting Ronald Reagan." See my note

[38] Ibid.

[39] Ibid.

[40] Exchange on CBS's "Face the Nation," March 5, 1995.

[41] Bunch, *Tear Down this Myth*, 91.

[42] Michael Kinsley, "Reagan's Record," *Slate On-Line*, February 9, 2011, accessed July 14, 2013, http://www.slate.com/articles/news_and_politics/readme/2001/02/reagans_record.html.

[43] Schweikart and Allen, *A Patriot's History* (New York, NY: Sentinel, 2007), 743–763.

[44] Bunch, *Tear Down this Myth*, 95.

[45] Ibid., 17.

[46] Gene Lyons, "The Real Reagan," *Salon On-Line*, Feburary 9, 2011, accessed July 14, 2013, http://www.salon.com/topic/the_real_reagan/.

[47] Larry Schweikart, *48 Liberal Lies About American History* (New York, NY: Sentinel, 2009), 748.

[48] Ibid., 749.

[49] Ibid., 750.

[50] Ibid., 233–239.

[51] Young America's Foundation, "Kate Obenshain," accessed July 14, 2013, http://www.yaf.org/kate-obenshain.aspx.

[52] "What Are My Kids Learning? Poll Shows Professors Fail Presidential History," *Townhall.com*, February 21, 2012, http://townhall.com/columnists/townhallcomstaff/2012/02/21/what_are_my_kids_learning_poll_shows_professors_fail_presidential_history/page/full/.

[53] Alex Seitz-Wald, "10 Things Conservatives Don't Want You to Know about Ronald Reagan," *Think Progress*, February 5, 2011, http://thinkprogress.org/politics/2011/02/05/142288/reagan-centennial/.

[54] Media Research Center, "Ronald Reagan, the 40th President and the Press: The Record," June 14, 2004, http://archive.mrc.org/specialreports/2004/pdf/Ronald_Reagan_PDF_version.pdf, 8.

[55] Ibid.

[56] Bunch, *Tear Down this Myth*, 50.

[57] Ibid.

[58] Mark A. Beliles and Stephen K. McDowell, *America's Providential History: Including Biblical Principles of Education, Government, Politics, Economics, and Family Life*, 3rd edition (Charlottesville, VA: Providence Foundation, 2010), 156.

[59] Newt Gingrich and Callista Gingrich, *Rediscovering God in America: Reflections on the Role of Faith in Our Nation's History and Future*, rev. ed. (Nashville, TN: Thomas Nelson, 2009), 90–91.

[60] T. Kenneth Cribb, "Ronald Reagan and the Moral Imagination," *The Intercollegiate Review*, February 4, 2011, http://www.firstprinciplesjournal.com/articles.aspx?article=1480.

61 Michael R. Lowman, George T. Thompson, and Kurt A. Grussendorf, *United States History in Christian Perspective: Heritage of Freedom*, 2nd ed. (Pensacola, FL: A Beka Book, 1996), 651–656.

62 William J. Bennett, *America: The Last Best Hope* (Nashville, TN: Thomas Nelson, 2012), 510.

63 "History: Chapter 23 and 24," Quizlet, accessed July 14, 2013, http://quizlet.com/12630951/historychapter-23-and-24-flash-cards/.

64 Bunch, *Tear Down this Myth*, 52.

65 Media Research Center, "Ronald Reagan."

66 Dallek, "Not Ready for Mt. Rushmore," 9.

67 Media Research Center, "Ronald Reagan," 11.

68 Allen White, "Reagan's AIDS Legacy: Silence Equals Death," *San Francisco Chronicle*, June 8, 2004, http://www.sfgate.com/opinion/openforum/article/Reagan-s-AIDS-Legacy-Silence-equals-death-2751030.php.

69 Bunch, *Tear Down this Myth*, 97.

70 Media Research Center, "Ronald Reagan."

71 Alex Pareene, "Ronald Reagan Cared more about UFOs than AIDS," *Salon Online*, February 4, 2011, http://www.salon.com/2011/02/04/reagan_aides_ufos/.

72 Zinn, *A People's History*, http://www.historyisaweapon.com/defcon1/zinncarebu21.html.

73 Ron Suskind "Without a Doubt," *New York Times*, October 17, 2004.

74 Bunch, *Tear Down this Myth*, 189.

75 Ibid., 157.

76 Dallek, "Not Ready for Mt. Rushmore," 3.

CONCLUSION

1 Gary B. Nash, Charlotte A. Crabtree, and Ross E. Dunn, *History on Trial: Culture Wars and the Teaching of the Past* (New York, NY: A. A. Knopf, 1998), 3–4.

2 Ibid., 6.

3 Edward Hallett Carr, *What is History?* (New York, NY: Vintage Books, 1961), 10.

4 Timothy D. Slekar, "Disciplinary History Versus Curricular Heritage: Epistemological Battle," *Journal of Thought* (Fall 2001), 65.

5 Samuel S. Wineburg, *Historical Thinking and Other Unnatural Acts: Charting the Future of Teaching the Past* (Philadelphia, PA: Temple University Press, 2001). For additional discussion of historical thinking in theory and practice see: Robert B. Bain, "'They Thought the World Was Flat?': Principles in Teaching High School History," in *How Students Learn: History, Math and Science in the Classroom*, ed. J. Bransford and M. S. Donovan (Washington, DC: National Academies Press, 2005); Susan Gillespie, ed., *Perspectives on Teaching Innovations: Teaching to Think Historically* (Washington, DC: American Historical Association, 1999); Thomas C. Holt and Dennie Wolf, *Thinking Historically: Narrative, Imagination, and Understanding* (New York, NY: College Entrance Examination Board, 1995); Linda S. Levstik and Keith C. Barton, *Doing History: Investigating with Children in Elementary and Middle Schools* (New York, NY: Routledge, 2010); Peter N. Stearns, Peter C. Seixas, and Samuel S. Wineburg, *Knowing, Teaching, and Learning History: National and International Perspectives* (New York, NY: New York University Press, 2000); Bruce A. VanSled-

right, *The Challenge of Rethinking History Education: On Practices, Theories, and Policy* (New York, NY: Routledge, 2011); Wilson J. Warren and D. Antonio Cantu, eds., *History Education 101: The Past, Present, and Future of Teacher Preparation* (Charlotte, NC: IAP, 2008); Ed Ayers, *The Next Generation of History Teachers,* AHA White Paper, http://www.historians.org/pubs/Free/historyteaching/situation.htm.

[6] Much of this section draws from the author's article on the subject. Fritz Fischer, "The Historian as Translator: Historical thinking, The Rosetta Stone of History Education," *Historically Speaking* 12, no. 3 (June 2011): 15–17.

[7] Bruce A. Lesh, *Why Won't You Just Tell Us the Answer?: Teaching Historical Thinking in Grades 7–12* (Portand, ME: Stenhouse, 2011), 186.

[8] Samuel S. Wineburg, Daisy Martin, and Chauncey Monte-Sano, *Reading Like a Historian: Teaching Literacy in Middle and High School History Classrooms* (New York, NY: Columbia University Press, 2011), v.

[9] David Gerwin and Jack Zevin, *Teaching U.S. History as Mystery* (Portsmouth, NH: Heinemann, 2003), 8.

[10] Nash, et al., *History on Trial,* 60.

[11] Flannery Burk and Thomas Andrews, "The Five C's of History: Putting the Elements of Historical Thinking into Practice in Teacher Education," in *History Education 101: The Past, Present, and Future of Teacher Preparation,* eds. Wilson J. Warren and D. Antonio Cantu (Charlotte, NC: IAP, 2008), 151–167.

[12] Lesh, *Why won't you just tell us the Answer?*

[13] Wineburg et. al., *Reading Like a Historian,* v.

ABOUT THE AUTHOR

Fritz Fischer has taught U.S. history at the college, middle, and high school levels for almost thirty years. Currently, he is professor of history and director of history education at the University of Northern Colorado, where he teaches American history and directs the teacher preparation program for secondary school history teachers. He received his BA and MA from Stanford University and earned his PhD in history at Northwestern University. He published *Making Them Like Us: Peace Corps Volunteers in the 1960s* in 1998 and has published more than a dozen articles and book chapters on history education and history education policy.

A national leader in the field of history education for the past decade, he served as chair of the Board of Trustees of the National Council for History Education from 2009 to 2012 and serves on the Board of Advisors of Mt. Vernon. He was co-chair of the 2009 Colorado Standards Writing Committee in Social Studies and History. Fritz has served as the project director or executive historian for six Teaching American History grants and has also presented papers and keynote addresses on the topic of history education policy at more than two dozen national and regional history conferences. He lives in Niwot, Colorado with his wife Lynn and four children.

THE MEMORY HOLE: INDEX

The Memory Hole: The U.S. History Curriculum Under Siege, pages 179–184.
Copyright © 2014 by Information Age Publishing

CPSIA information can be obtained at www.ICGtesting.com
Printed in the USA
BVOW04s0021280214

346242BV00004B/39/P